Prisoners of the North

Prisoners

You who this faint day the High North is luring
   Unto her vastness, taintlessly sweet;
You who are steel-braced, straight-lipped, enduring
   Dreadless in danger and dire in defeat;
Honor the High North ever and ever,
   Whether she crown you or whether she slay;
Suffer her fury, cherish and love her—
   He who would rule her must learn to obey.

— *Robert W. Service*

Pierre Berton

of the North

Anchor Canada

Library and Archives Canada Cataloguing in Publication
Berton, Pierre, 1920–2004.
        Prisoners of the North / Pierre Berton.

Includes index.
ISBN 0-385-66047-2

1. Canada, Northern—Biography. 2. Northwest, Canadian—Biography.
3. Canada, Northern—History. 4. Northwest, Canadian—History—1870–1905.
5. Adventure and adventurers—Canada, Northern—Biography. I. Title.

FC3957.B47 2005   971.9'009'9C   C2005-901094-0

Every effort has been made to contact copyright holders for the images in this book. In the event of an inadvertent omission or error, please notify the publisher.

Cover image: Vilhjalmur Stefansson, courtesy Dartmouth College Library
Cover design and maps: CS Richardson
Printed and bound in Canada

Published in Canada by
Anchor Canada, a division of
Random House of Canada Limited

Visit Random House of Canada Limited's website: www.randomhouse.ca

FRI   10   9   8   7   6   5   4   3   2   1

Books by Pierre Berton

The Royal Family
The Mysterious North
Klondike
Just Add Water and Stir
Adventures of a Columnist
Fast Fast Fast Relief
The Big Sell
The Comfortable Pew
The Cool, Crazy, Committed
  World of the Sixties
The Smug Minority
The National Dream
The Last Spike
Drifting Home
Hollywood's Canada
My Country
The Dionne Years
The Wild Frontier
The Invasion of Canada
Flames Across the Border
Why We Act Like Canadians
The Promised Land
Vimy
Starting Out
The Arctic Grail
The Great Depression
Niagara: A History of the
  Falls
My Times: Living With
  History
1967, The Last Good Year
Marching as to War
Cats I've Known and Loved
The Joy of Writing
Prisoners of the North

PICTURE BOOKS

The New City (with Henri
  Rossier)
Remember Yesterday
The Great Railway
The Klondike Quest
Pierre Berton's Picture Book
  of Niagara Falls
Winter
The Great Lakes
Seacoasts
Pierre Berton's Canada

ANTHOLOGIES

Pierre and Janet Berton's
  Canadian Food Guide
Historic Headlines
Farewell to the Twentieth
  Century
Worth Repeating
Welcome to the Twenty-first
  Century

FICTION

Masquerade
  (pseudonym Lisa Kroniuk)

BOOKS FOR YOUNG READERS

The Golden Trail
The Secret World of Og
Adventures in Canadian
  History (22 volumes)

Maps
Drawn by CS Richardson

Contents

Foreword

In the Yukon, where I spent my childhood and much of my teens, the old-timers had a phrase for those who had been held captive by the North. "He's missed too many boats," they'd say. When the sternwheeler *Casca* puffed out into the grey river on her last voyage of the season toward the world we called the Outside, the dock would be crammed with veterans waving goodbye—men and women who had given their hearts and their souls to the North and had no intention of leaving.

Dawson City in those days was a unique community, a cosmopolitan village where everybody knew everybody else, full of adventurous spirits who had come from every corner of the globe to profit from the great stampede of 1898. In my boyhood, the gold rush was history, but they were still here, this handful of survivors from the gaudy days.

They did not talk much about adventures that would seem prodigious to us today; it was old stuff to them. They had clawed their way up the passes, hammered together anything that would float, defied the rivers and the rapids, and notched the logs for their own cabins when at last they reached their goal. They had made it! When others flagged, or failed, or fled, they had hung on, secure in themselves, and isolated from the outside world—prisoners of their environment but free from the cacophony, and the glare, and the breathless bustle of the settled world. They had had their fill of all that. I once asked George Fraser, an old-timer who lived on Dominion Creek forty miles from Dawson, why he hadn't paid a visit to town in fifteen years. "Too many bright lights!" he told me. That says it all.

The North has its own sounds, but in my day when the temperature dropped and the roar of the river was stilled and the whine of the big gold dredges had ceased, the world of my youth was silent. Nothing seemed to move. Smoke rose from the chimneys in stately columns that did not waver. It was as if the entire community had been captured in a motion picture freeze frame. For many, I think, that was one of the attractions.

They came from everywhere, these old-timers we called sourdoughs. Men like Mr. Kawakami, a Dawson fixture who sold us fireworks and incense along with Japanese parasols and kimonos from his little shop on Third Avenue. A block away in her corner store, a distinguished, grey-haired Frenchwoman, Mme Émilie Tremblay, displayed the latest Paris fashions for the town's socialites as well as for the town's demimonde. No stranger just off the boat would have realized that in 1894, two years before gold was discovered on Bonanza and before Dawson existed, she and her husband had climbed the Chilkoot Pass and made their way into the empty Yukon.

One of her customers was the Chicago-born doyen of Dawson society, Martha Louise Black, who left her husband and climbed the Chilkoot pregnant, bore her baby in a one-room log cabin, and went on to become the second woman in Canada to win a seat in Parliament.

At St. Paul's Pro-cathedral on the Dawson waterfront I would watch the morning procession each Sunday, often led by the bishop, Isaac O. Stringer, who had been obliged to boil and consume his sealskin boots to ward off starvation on the Rat River trail, thus providing Charlie Chaplin with a memorable scene for his film *The Gold Rush*. At the other end of the social scale was a rough-hewn Slav, Jan Welzl, who had come to Dawson from Prague by way of the Arctic, so he claimed, with the help of the Inuit. He spent his time trying to develop a perpetual motion machine in an abandoned warehouse while bemoaning the fact that he had sold the rights to his memoirs, *Thirty Years in the Golden North*, for one hundred dollars before it became a Book-of-the-Month Club best-seller.

I went to school with the second and third generations of these captive Northerners. One classmate, Chester Henderson, was the grandson of the famous Robert Henderson, officially acknowledged as the co-discoverer of the Klondike's gold. Another was the son of Percy de Wolfe, known as the Iron Man of the North because of the hazards he encountered with his dog team on the mail run between Dawson and Eagle, Alaska. Helen Van Bibber, who beat me to stand first in our class, was the mixed-blood offspring of a marriage between a native Indian and a male descendant of Daniel Boone.

My father was one of these Northern hostages. He could have had a teaching job at Queen's but he chose the Yukon, refusing to quit even when the so-called Stikine Trail became a heaving swamp. He opted for the Chilkoot, built a raft, and made his way to the goldfields, intending to stay for two years. He found no gold but stayed for forty, and his only regret, I think, was when the Depression forced him to leave.

I was thinking of people like Mme Tremblay, Martha Black, Chester Henderson, and Helen Van Bibber when in a book for would-be authors I made a facetious suggestion: get yourself born in an interesting environment. It was my great good fortune, thanks to my father, the sourdough, and my mother, the journalist's daughter, that I was born in what was then the most interesting community in Canada. The North has been a rich literary source for me—far more valuable than the nuggets Chester's grandfather dug out of his Klondike claim.

In this work I have again gone back to my Northern heritage. It is my fiftieth book, and I have discovered, somewhat to my astonishment, that no fewer than twenty-seven have included some reference to the North or the Klondike—sometimes no more than a few paragraphs, sometimes a chapter or more, and on several occasions an entire book.

Time and again my heritage has intruded into my literary output, occasionally without my realizing its presence. Like my father before me and like the five remarkable characters that follow, I, too, in my own way am a prisoner of the North.

CHAPTER 1
The King of the Klondike

Joseph Whiteside Boyle in his trademark uniform with its Klondike gold lapel badges, wearing the Order of Regina Maria and the Star of Romania.

—ONE—

Joseph Whiteside Boyle was a force of nature, albeit a flawed one. In the early days of the twentieth century, he was famous, even notorious, on two continents. A man who craved action for its own sake, he had an uncanny instinct for finding where the action was. When the first news of the Klondike strike was making headlines in Seattle and San Francisco, Boyle was already in the vanguard of the ragtag army of gold seekers stampeding north. Old-time mining methods were not for him. Though he began with virtually nothing, he went on to build, under almost impossible conditions, the largest gold dredges in the world—monstrous floating machines that churned up the storied creek beds and helped revolutionize the placer mining industry in the Yukon. He made a fortune but squandered it all as a soldier of fortune in eastern Europe at the time of the Bolshevik revolution. Eulogized as the Saviour of Romania, he was named Duke of Jassy by her elegant queen, whose lover he was reputed to be.

Boyle was a loner all his life, an entrepreneur and an adventurer who had little time for intimacies. He kept his family—his two wives and his children—at a distance. One gets the impression that from time to time he considered them nuisances who got in the way of his ambitions. Boyle was a take-charge man, ever the leader, never a follower, contemptuous of generals, bureaucrats, and civil servants. He was beholden to no one; it was not in his makeup to settle for second place, an attitude that worked well enough in the Yukon, where he was totally in charge, but caused no end of problems to his superiors when he arrived in eastern Europe during the Great War.

The image that Joe Boyle projected to the world was one of bold confidence. With his square jaw, his heavy brows, and his strong Irish features, he looked the part. He was built like a boxer and in his younger days had been a good one. But there was a small boy quality to Boyle that clashed with his bluff exterior. In moments of high peril, as in courtship, he was impulsive to a fault. In his various adventures he seemed to be having the time of his life. "I like this sort of thing!" he exclaimed as he dashed about Odessa trying to bargain for the lives of a group of Romanian hostages. He was never happier than when he was at the centre of things, whether running a dredging company in the Klondike or influencing royalty in Romania. He disliked supervision and one can sympathize with the British and Canadian political and military authorities who tried to rein him in.

If Boyle had moments of introspection, he kept them to himself. Outwardly he gave no hint of any inner insecurity. Only Marie, the Romanian queen, knew his secrets and then not until the fading years of his life. He had long mastered the art of the public gesture, which made him famous in his own time. Journalists and biographers made much of him. Few of his fellow countrymen have had so much ink expended on them. Every generation of readers, it seems, has had its version of what Hollywood might call the Joe Boyle Story.

In 1938 his eldest daughter, Flora, devoted three long articles to him in *Maclean's* ("Who Was Joe Boyle?"). The magazine, in turn, published a fourth made up of letters from those who had known and venerated the legendary Canadian. Since that time three substantial biographies have been published: Kim Beattie's breathless *Brother, Here's a Man!* in 1949, William Rodney's scholarly *Joe Boyle: King of the Klondike* in 1974, and Leonard W. Taylor's revealing *The Sourdough and the Queen* in 1983.

Moreover, Boyle played a role in the published memoirs and reminiscences of a dozen or more contemporaries who crossed his path, from the Klondike to the Caucasus. These ranged from Herbert Hoover, who knew him in his gold-mining days, to Ethel Greening Pantazzi, whose husband Boyle saved from execution by the revolutionary Battalion of Death in Odessa. Boyle is a leading figure in two books of memoirs by Captain George A. Hill, a British spy, who found him "a man whose equal I have never encountered before or since." Every biography of Queen Marie of Romania, not to mention her own published memoirs, venerates Boyle, whom she called "one man in a million . . . a man it is a richness to know." Yet in Canada he is largely forgotten.

7

Had he been born American it is probable that he would have been claimed by Hollywood and turned into a popular icon, like Davy Crockett. But Boyle came from Woodstock, Ontario, and was a Canadian through and through. He named his mining enterprise the Canadian Klondyke Company, making it clear it was not an Alaskan venture, and when he built his enormous gold dredges he named them Canadian Number One, Canadian Number Two, Canadian Number Three, and Canadian Number Four. He made it a point to fly the Red Ensign from their masts—a sly dig at his American rivals.

Boyle, then, was a Canadian first and foremost and a *Northern* Canadian with all that that connoted: a man secure within himself and outwardly unflappable, having confronted and conquered the worst that nature had in store for him. Robert Service was his favourite poet, and he often transfixed his listeners, who included members of the Romanian royal family, by quoting aloud from the Yukon bard and telling stories of early days in the North. But he rarely talked about himself. His modesty, it was said, would have shamed a shrinking violet.

His career unfolded like a series of movies, but Joe Boyle, the Canadian puritan who neither smoked nor touched strong drink—who in fact chaired temperance rallies in rough-and-tumble Dawson City at the turn of the century—did not fit the Hollywood mould. In the early 1950s Hollywood did attempt a motion picture based on Kim Beattie's exclamatory biography, but his family put a stop to that, as they knew he would have. It was too, well, *American,* loaded with invented scenes and dialogue that didn't jibe with the Boyle character. There is no Joe Boyle story on film. Canada had no substantial movie industry and no television, either, for three decades after his death in 1923. Other countries had applauded him, but his own country had ignored him. The Russians decorated him with the Order of St. Anne and the Order of St. Vladimir; France awarded him the Croix de Guerre. Britain gave him the Distinguished Service Order, while Romania went all out with three decorations: Crown, Grand Cross, and Star. But Canada turned her back on him. The army tried to take away his uniform and his rank; the bureaucrats tried to order him back home, but

Boyle went his own way. It was not until the early 1980s that a popular campaign was finally mounted, thanks to Leonard Taylor, to move his body from Hampton Hill in Middlesex, England, to Woodstock, underlining the truth that this is not a land that indulges enthusiastically in hero worship except for hockey players.

From the acres of print devoted to his character and career, Boyle emerges as a romantic who found it difficult to sit still for long. This restlessness, a by-product, perhaps, of his Celtic blood (half Irish, half Scottish), is the key to his character. Some of it may have come from his father, a breeder of fine horses whose calling made it necessary to leave home in season and follow the racing schedule wherever it took him. Boyle's childhood seems to have been serene enough. He came from a middle-class family of four siblings, and there is no suggestion that his upbringing in the quiet ambience of Woodstock was anything but happy. There were signs of that serenity in his later years when on occasion he found himself at risk. He feared no man but held no grudges. He got along with his opponents, both legal and financial, and they got along with him.

And yet there are cracks in the Boyle legend. He was certainly not a family man. In 1884, at the age of seventeen, just out of Woodstock College, he visited his two elder brothers in New York City. Their relationship cannot have been close. One day the brothers returned to their quarters on lower Broadway to find a scribbled note on the table: "I've gone to sea. Don't worry about me. Joe." That was all: no explanation, no fond farewells, no hint of his plans or even the name of the ship, nothing. He was gone for the best part of three years, and in all that time they had no word of him—not a whisper, not a note, not a clipping, not a telegram, not even a message for his mother, "a sweet little woman from Dumfries, Scotland," in Flora Boyle's words. Toward the end of his absence they believed he had been lost at sea.

This callousness toward his blood relations—for that is what it was— was a blemish on Boyle's character that would manifest itself time and again during his career. With one exception he didn't seem to care greatly for those who were closest to him. Outwardly, he was always the life of the party—gregarious, hearty, an accomplished storyteller, so affable that even his critics and business rivals warmed to him and basked in his persona. Yet he was very much his own man with his own goals, to the exclusion of those who might have been near and dear to him. It is ironic that when at last he reached out for true love and companionship they were to prove unattainable.

He had haunted the Manhattan waterfront, tramping the docks and watching the three-masters come into port to unload or take on cargo, when adventure beckoned. With the impetuousness that was to mark his later years, the teenaged youth, hungry for action, climbed aboard the barque *Wallace* and was hired as a deckhand. He left as a callow youngster; when he returned, equally suddenly and unexpectedly, he was clearly mature beyond his twenty years. Where had he gone? What had he done? What had happened?

There are hints, but only hints. Boyle was not one to boast. At the end of his life at the Middlesex home of his oldest friend, Edward Bredenberg, he did indulge in a few moments of nostalgia: "We would sit back and dream of sailor days in the Pacific Islands and he would chaff me about the dusky-eyed belles." Bredenberg, an old Klondiker and a former sailor before the mast, wrote to the Romanian queen recalling how "we would sit and spin yarns of our younger days, or our fights on some of the hard Yankee ships." Apart from Bredenberg, she was the only one whom Boyle allowed to pierce that bluff exterior.

In one of his many letters to Marie there is a glimpse of an earlier Boyle, a lonely and romantic teenager, thrust into a hard, foreign world of adventure—a world of his own choosing, but one fraught with pitfalls. He was by far the youngest hand on the *Wallace,* and he was, in a sense, a kind of teacher's pet, hired on a whim by the ship's captain who had noticed him lazing about on the dock, taken an interest in him, and offered to sign him on. Those first days as a green deckhand took away much of the romance; but Boyle endured, and the memory of the early days endured, too. He wrote: "I have just been out looking at the stars who have so many times been my companions and comforters— as a boy sailor at sea on a ship on which every man was against me and was more alone than if I had been the only soul on her—I used to lie on my back on the hatch at night and pick out a bright star, which used to seem to send me a message and wink and get brighter and let me know that he would be there the next night."

How had he spent those three years aboard the *Wallace* and later the cargo steamer *Susan,* which brought him back to New York? The two brief glimpses we have of him through family tradition may be apocryphal, yet they ring true because they forecast events of his later career. When a fellow seaman tripped on the deck and tumbled into the water, Boyle was the first over the side to rescue his shipmate. That was the first time, but not the last, when he would risk his life to save another through quick thinking. Again, en route to the Indian Ocean the frail barque was crippled in a series of raging storms, and the exhausted crew working the pumps were about to give up the struggle when Boyle, the take-charge youth, rallied them, forced them back to work, and took command of the life-saving operation until the barque limped into port.

At twenty, having risen to ship's quartermaster, he turned up unannounced in New York. There he was reunited with his older brother Dave who introduced him to a fellow boarder, a lively and attractive divorcee, Mildred Josephine Raynor, whom Dave himself hoped to marry. Heedless of his brother's anguish, Joe plunged into a whirlwind courtship that swept Mildred off her feet. In just three days they were married. Dave Boyle, a shy, unassuming man, was deeply affected by the collapse of what had been a secret romance. Many years later Flora Boyle wrote, "No one will ever know how badly he was hurt. He never married and all through her tumultuous lifetime, he remained Mildred's closest, most faithful friend."

Joe Boyle certainly was not. He and Mildred were incompatible almost from the beginning. He was a skilled boxer and, like his father, a lover of horses. His natural homes now were the racetrack and the boxing ring; his cronies were bookmakers and pugilists. She had social pretensions. When their daughter Macushla died at the age of six months from scarlet fever, Boyle began to drink heavily. One night he and a playboy companion were arrested for being drunk and disorderly and

Macnabb

IVORETTE
PORTRAITS
·EXTRA FINISH·

813 BROADWAY
NEW YORK.

Mildred Raynor. She married young Joe Boyle after a whirlwind three-day courtship. She was nicknamed "Minky" bcause she loved costly furs.

12

also for trying to steal a cab and threatening the driver. A bookmaking friend eventually bailed them out, but the incident changed Boyle.

"It's obvious I can't drink like a gentleman," he told his companion as they waited in jail, "and since I can't hold my liquor I shall never drink again."

"You'll get so virtuous you'll be giving up smoking next," his cell-mate retorted. But in that moment Boyle had made up his mind.

"A good idea," he told his companion and handed him his expensive cigar holder. "Keep it," he said. "I'll have no further use for it." For the rest of his life he was a non-smoker as well as an active temperance advocate.

Mildred might have been a frivolous spendthrift (her detractors called her "Minky" because of her love for costly furs), but she went through six pregnancies for him (two of which were miscarriages) in the nine years of their marriage. Boyle, now engaged in a lucrative feed and grain shipping business in New York, had little time for her. He was far too busy trying to get backing for a grandiose scheme to establish a national chain of grain elevators. His plans collapsed and so did his marriage.

In the divorce that followed, the couple divided custody of their surviving children. Mildred's son Bill by her earlier marriage went with her along with the youngest of Boyle's progeny, Susan and another daughter yet unborn to be named Charlotte. The two older children, Flora and Joe, Jr., went with Boyle. Boyle's relationship with the younger girls, who remained with Mildred, was virtually non-existent after the divorce. It was as if he had erased them from his memory. With Flora and Joe it could best be described as distant. He shrugged them off and saw them sporadically during his various ventures, but it was never an intimate relationship. He had other concerns, other ambitions, and he put these first.

Flora Boyle remembered the first of many partings after the divorce when Boyle brought his two children home to their grandparents in Woodstock. "We were taken to the railroad station where, after kissing us goodbye and telling us he would be back soon, father stepped

Joe Boyle in 1900 with his daughter Flora, who worshipped him from afar.

on a train and was whisked away into the darkness. We must have made a forlorn picture, Joe and I, standing on that old station platform, waving our little handkerchiefs to our handsome young father, who was just thirty. Fortunately, we were too young to realize that he was off on another great adventure, without the faintest idea when we would meet again. I think we were too stunned to cry, our poor little minds could not grasp the situation entirely. . . . We were living in a new strange world and our greatest feeling was one of awe and loneliness."

Boyle was off on an exhibition tour with Frank Slavin, the "Sydney Cornstalk," who had ambitions to become a heavyweight-boxing champion. When the pair reached Victoria and heard whispers of a great gold strike in the Yukon, they lost no time in heading north, first to Juneau, Alaska, and then on to Skagway. By mid-July 1897, when the news of the great find burst upon the world, they had already reached the foot of the White Pass. A pack trail of sorts had just been opened to the summit. Boyle and Slavin hooked up to a party of fifteen men and a pack train of twenty-five horses, but the going was so tough that half the company turned back. The others elected Boyle captain to go on past the summit to blaze a trail through thirty miles of wilderness for the party to follow. At Bennett Lake , the headwaters of the Yukon, a growing number of tenderfeet were already sawing lumber for boats to take them downriver to Dawson. Here Boyle's foresight paid off. In the tons of goods he had packed over the trail was a twenty-four-foot collapsible boat he had purchased to take Slavin and himself through the headwater lakes and onto the great river, all the way to the city of gold.

Down the hissing Yukon they floated, propelled by a stiff current, drifting through a land of lonely prospectors panning for wages in the sandbars at the mouths of nameless creeks. This was the Cordilleran spine of the Americas, and everywhere, it seemed, were flickers of gold for those patient enough to seek it. Within that backbone of mountains, running north from the land of the Incas, lay the impressions of ancient watercourses plundered successively for their treasure by the Spanish conquistadors, the forty-niners, and the pioneers of the Cariboo. Now the line of hidden fortunes had veered off to the northwest.

This was a turning point in Boyle's career. He had started north on a hunch—to make a few dollars holding boxing exhibitions with Slavin. By the time they reached Juneau, he had caught a whiff of the gold fever that was raging along the Alaska Panhandle. He had no inkling then of what the future held, but as they drifted closer and closer to Dawson, the Yukon interior captured him. He could not imagine that he would spend nearly the next two decades, the most significant period of his life, tied to this unlikely corner of the North. That, one might say, was his destiny. He could not escape it.

The Yukon shaped Boyle. He was no longer the slender, callow youth who had gone off to sea on a whim. A big man, barrel-chested, he always thought big. The scale of the land with its mighty-mouthed valleys, its enormous rivers, and its endless, mist-shrouded vistas, fitted his personal style. In Dawson, soaking up the details of gold mining in the Yukon, Boyle and Slavin came to the conclusion that the present system was inefficient and wasteful. Surely there must be a better way of getting the treasure from the bedrock. Placer gold is known as Poor Man's Gold because one lone prospector can wrest it from the ground with little more than a spade and a sluice box. That wasn't good enough for Boyle and his partner. They would need a government concession to give them hydraulic and timber rights over a big chunk of the Klondike watershed.

All around them that fall of 1897 the carnival roared on. Men who had been paupers the year before were so fabulously rich they could fling their profits on the gaming tables and become paupers again. Others were buying champagne at thirty dollars a split for the dance-hall beauties who plied their trade in the upper boxes. None of this had any effect on the teetotalling puritan whose only ambition was to build a mining empire. He wanted to control a great swath of the goldfields instead of a single claim.

Leaving Slavin to work out the legal details, Boyle made his way to Eldorado, the richest of the gold creeks, to give himself a beginner's course in placer mining. Some were already planning to use small dredges, but Boyle was contemplating monstrous machines, the largest anywhere, to mine the Klondike's hoard more efficiently. While individual prospectors were utilizing wooden sluice boxes on separate claims, Boyle was negotiating for an eight-mile stretch of the Klondike Valley. He intended, in fact, to introduce the Industrial Revolution to this godforsaken corner of the globe, incurring the wrath of the latter-day Luddites who scrabbled and mucked with spade and mattock in the gravels of the gold creeks.

He chose to find work on Claim No. 13, which so many had avoided because of its unlucky number but turned out to be the richest claim of all. Here he encountered one of the several larger-than-life characters who people the Boyle saga, each worthy of a Hollywood movie of his own. This was Swiftwater Bill Gates, one of the most successful of the Klondike prospectors, with a moon face and a scraggly moustache, so eager to squander his sudden fortune that he offered to bet one hundred dollars on the turn of a card in Dawson's Monte Carlo saloon and dance hall, and to buy up every scarce egg in town, each at the price of a day's pay, allegedly to lay at the feet of Gussie Lamore, the toast of dance-hall row.

In Swiftwater, who owned a piece of No. 13 and who went on to lose more than one fortune, Boyle had a willing instructor. Each in his own way was a man of vision, but Boyle differed from the prospector. Gates, who owned the only starched shirt collar in town and went to bed rather than be seen without it, was a man who loved to watch himself lampooned on the stage of the Monte Carlo by Gussie Lamore's sister Nellie and revelled in his new sobriquet, the Knight of the Golden Omelette. Boyle had neither the time nor the inclination for that kind of frolic. He thought in terms of gigantic nozzles ripping up the over-burden from the verdant valleys, and of enormous floating machines clawing their way to bedrock.

One characteristic of the Boyle style was the speed with which he made up his mind and moved, often under appalling conditions. He threw himself into each new venture with all the enthusiasm of a small boy playing his first game of Parcheesi. Life to Boyle *was* a game. For him, it was always the race that counted, not the gold and certainly not the prestige. As a born leader, he needed to be first off the mark, ahead of the pack—determined to win.

He could not idle away the Yukon winter. He needed a hydraulic and timber concession eight miles long, from rim to rim of the Klondike Valley, before someone else could beat him to it. For that he had to go to Ottawa, so he signed the necessary documents and left Slavin to work out the application to the Gold Commissioner while he headed for the Outside before freeze-up. Less than two months after he landed in Dawson he was ready to make his move.

While thousands of men and women were struggling to reach the city of gold in the face of impossible natural obstacles, here was Boyle headed the other way. To live in Dawson in that first gold-rush winter was akin to living on the moon. For most there was no escape. Only the hardiest, the hungriest, or the craziest dared attempt the daunting journey to the Outside. But Boyle and Swiftwater Bill Gates were planning to do just that. As they set off in Boyle's collapsible boat, clinging to the eddies along the Yukon riverbank and inching their flimsy craft forward against a current that could reach seven miles an hour, winter was already setting in and pack ice was forming all about them. When Boyle's eccentric partner (who insisted on wearing a colourful four-in-hand tie beneath his furs) broke through the thin crust at one point, Boyle dragged him, soaking wet, to safety. The craft was just as vulnerable: the collapsible boat kept collapsing and had to be repaired three times before the pair abandoned it at Carmacks Post, 250 miles upriver from Dawson. There they came upon a huddle of men and horses about to give up and return to the Klondike, and it was then that Boyle's qualities of leadership were tested. At his suggestion, the group agreed to pool their resources and travel together under his command. They called him Captain, a title that certainly fitted.

They set off for Haines Mission on the coast, following a trail blazed through the mountains by Jack Dalton, an earlier pioneer. In good weather this was a four-day trip; at −25 degrees Fahrenheit it took them twenty-nine days. The horses gave up and had to be shot. Some humans also succumbed and were prepared to die on the spot, but Boyle would

18

Joe Boyle and the eccentric Swiftwater Bill Gates (in dress shirt and four-in-hand tie) on their way to the Outside in the autumn of 1897 while the rush was still on.

have none of that. In the words of one of his biographers, "he drove them like a chain gang," alternately making promises, cajoling, and insulting them as he spurred them on. They staggered into Haines on November 23 and managed to pick up a ship to Seattle. There, Boyle was presented with a gold watch by his followers who swore that without his leadership no one would have reached the coast alive.

It had soon become obvious to Boyle that the day of the individual placer miner was over. The thousands who rushed to the Klondike talked in terms of "digging for gold" as if the ground was knee-deep in nuggets. To their dismay, they were faced with a back-breaking procedure. Seeking out the hidden paystreak by thawing the ground with fire or steam and then drilling a shaft to bedrock was always a gamble. You might drill half a dozen shafts yet miss the serpentine paystreak, and even if you found the line of the old stream bed, it could turn out to be barren of gold. Those who did not give up and who were lucky enough to come upon the elusive evidence of a prehistoric watercourse then had the tedious task of hauling up the pay dirt, bucket by bucket, and sluicing it free of its treasure. Only about 25 percent of the available gold was recovered by this procedure.

Boyle was convinced that in order to separate the gold from the bedrock the leafy valleys would have to be torn apart, ripped up by huge nozzles. The gold would then be dug up by electrically powered dredges floating on ponds of their own creation, biting into the bedrock with an endless line of moving buckets and washing the gold free in monstrous revolving sieves.

The principle was not new; small gold dredges had operated well before Boyle devised his plan, but there was a difference. Boyle proposed to build huge dredges and to haul the necessary machinery— tons and tons of it—up the White Pass trail, over the mountains, down the fast-flowing Yukon to Dawson, and out by gravel road to the gold creeks—all in the shortest possible time.

The details would have daunted a lesser man. The entire dredge system would run on electricity, which meant building a hydroelectric power plant, digging vast ditches, and using the water of the north fork of the Klondike River to achieve his ends. And all this in a land when the first snow fell early in October and the country stayed frozen until April.

Speed was essential. Swiftwater Bill was off to San Francisco's Baldwin Hotel, where he tipped bellboys with gold dust to page him by name and continued to woo not only Gussie Lamore, who it developed was already married, but also her two sisters, Nellie and Grace. Joe Boyle headed for Ottawa.

In the capital while waiting for Parliament to sit, he encountered the diminutive Englishman who would become his rival in the Klondike. This was Arthur Christian Newton Treadgold, a direct descendant of Sir Isaac Newton, the renowned scientist. Himself an Oxford graduate and teacher, he was for the moment correspondent for the *Mining Journal* and the *Manchester Guardian.* That wasn't much more than a cover. Treadgold had ideas as big as Boyle's about controlling the Klondike goldfields. But Treadgold was wary of dredges. He thought instead of using giant scrapers and land-going digging machines, none of which ever worked.

This odd pair, around whose personalities so much of the Klondike's mining history revolves, were opposites in every way. Treadgold was short and stubby with a shaggy blond moustache and a face that was all teeth when he smiled, in contrast to the robust former boxer. Treadgold was conceited, secretive, and cunning, quite prepared to flirt with the truth if it suited his purposes, an incompetent manager, possessed of an uncontrollable temper and an inability to take advice— character flaws that would eventually doom him. Boyle, on the other hand, was a big man in every way, open-minded and open-hearted, who scorned personal publicity but could be a terrier when facing setbacks to his personal plans for corralling the Klondike gold. It was significant that Treadgold to his employees and friends was always "Mr. Treadgold." Boyle to all and sundry was simply "Joe."

Both men had one quality in common: they were adept at raising funds for their ventures. Each had the ability to charm financiers with deep pockets. There was a certain magic in the word Klondike that conjured up visions of unlimited profits. It did not seem to occur to normally hard-headed investors that the Klondike's main resource was a diminishing one. Gold was not grain. Two of the richest families in America—the Guggenheims and the Rothschilds—were included in dredging enterprises after the turn of the century, ventures that included both Boyle and Treadgold, each of whom was prepared, it seemed, to sell his soul in order to gain control of the Klondike's resources.

In Ottawa Boyle pressed his case for a hydraulic lease on Clifford Sifton, Wilfrid Laurier's Minister of the Interior. In June 1898 he got part of what he wanted: an undertaking in writing reserving eight miles of the Klondike Valley, rim to rim, exclusively for hydraulic operations. In November 1900 the government issued a lease in his favour. This was the famous Boyle Concession, which effectively barred all individual prospecting in the area and caused so much controversy in the Yukon. Boyle clung to it through a series of lawsuits and countersuits that would have dampened the ardour of a less persistent man. His daughter Flora has testified to the passion with which he flung himself into each new legal battle. "Lawsuit," she wrote, "was his middle name." He loved a fight. Each time he was sued he immediately countersued. Before he achieved his aim he had lawyers in Dawson City, Vancouver, London, New York, and Detroit.

To describe his reputation in Dawson during the early days as controversial would be an understatement. Meetings were held, petitions forwarded to Ottawa, and local politicians pressured in a series of attempts to cancel the Boyle Concession. The timber rights to that chunk of the Klondike Valley were as valuable as the ground that lay beneath. Because lumber was needed for sluice boxes and cabins on the creeks, Dawson was enjoying a building boom that saw the price of logs soar from $18 a cord in December 1898 to $48 a cord the following summer. Boyle saw this coming. He and Slavin (who later left the partnership) established a sawmill near the mouth of the Klondike River that turned out more than a million feet of dressed lumber in 1899. Much of the timber came from his own property, an asset so valuable that it is said he was forced to drive poachers off at rifle point.

Meanwhile, in New York City, Treadgold sweet-talked Daniel Guggenheim into a major investment to buy up as many claims as possible in the heart of the gold country in order to consolidate water and mineral rights on the richest creeks—Hunker, Bonanza, and Eldorado. By the summer of 1901, he too had wheedled a hydraulic concession out of Ottawa, one that was arranged to free him from any of the work commitments prescribed by mining law, thus tying up the gold country for six years. It was, in the heated words of the *Klondike Nugget*, "a malignant and unpardonable outrage . . . the blackest act of infamy that ever blotted the history of the country." After a storm of protest the government cancelled the Treadgold hydraulic concession. Boyle went on to form the Canadian Klondyke Company with backing from the Rothschild interests in Detroit; Treadgold would shortly become resident director of the rival Yukon Gold Corporation, a Guggenheim enterprise.

Joe Boyle (back row, right) at the Bear Creek office of his Canadian Klondyke Mining Company in the heart of the gold country.

23

When I was a small boy in Dawson the name Treadgold seemed to pop up in every conversation around our dinner table. Boyle was gone by then, but Treadgold was very much alive, the central figure in a tangle of court actions that occupied him for most of his days. He left the Guggenheims, formed his own mining company, and had his eye on the Boyle interests, hoping to consolidate all corporate mining into one big enterprise. He failed, went broke, and left the Klondike, apparently forever, only to return in the mid-twenties after Boyle's death to pursue his dream. Even then "Klondike" had a touch of magic for investors, and Treadgold, with his smooth tongue and a name that hinted at riches underfoot, was able to form the Yukon Consolidated Gold Corporation out of borrowed money and the remnants of earlier ventures. (I worked for it in the late thirties as a young mucker.) In the end Treadgold was eased out and lost everything. But in 1951, when he died at the age of eighty-seven, several of the original Boyle dredges were still churning up the pay dirt in the golden valleys of the Klondike.

—TWO—

Boyle spent almost two decades of his adult life in the Yukon. He liked to claim that he had arrived in Dawson with only nineteen dollars in his pocket. In his pocket, no doubt, but in the bank? In New York he had operated a lucrative feed and grain business, and though he was clearly hard-pressed for money—he depended on boxing exhibitions for his living after his New York stay—it stretches the imagination to suggest he was penniless. Clearly he was not without resources. It cost money to travel to Ottawa, and it cost more to live at the Russell House, the most luxurious hotel in the capital. Boyle certainly put whatever money he had to good use, as William Rodney has noted. He owned among other things several valuable pieces of Dawson real estate, a 20-foot-long wharf, a warehouse 100 feet long, a lumber dock, a half interest in a hydraulic grant, and 16 placer claims. His sawmill was certainly profitable, though Boyle and Slavin would have needed some sort of nest egg to launch it. But ten years after he arrived he would be a millionaire—self-made and proud of it, as his casual reference to the nineteen dollars suggests.

Boyle was out of Dawson sometimes for months, even years, but it is clear that he thought of himself first and foremost as a Klondiker. From the beginning he was a leading figure in Dawson City. There is no sign that he had political ambitions. He was too much of a maverick to follow any party line, nor was he the sort who could stand to be pinned down by a pre-arranged political program. The only active role that would have suited his personality was that of leader; his ego would not have settled for less.

In Dawson during the stampede summer of '98, anarchy reigned. The harried local government—a federal responsibility—could not cope with the myriad problems thrust upon it by the influx of thousands of men. Nothing worked. There were no street addresses. The town had been under water as a result of a sudden flood when the ice breakup dammed the Yukon. The whole of Front Street—dance-hall row—was an impassible swamp. The steamboats couldn't unload cargo and the horse-drawn wagons couldn't move in the mire. Then Boyle took over. He organized every teamster in town and built a slab road all the way from the docks to the Mounted Police barracks. Under his goading the job was done in one day.

Boyle made a point of buying his company supplies locally rather than from the Outside, as his rivals did, no doubt as a sop to his local critics but also because he was a community booster. He fought for a special tax to underwrite St. Mary's Hospital, and he arranged regularly for a steamboat to take all the school children on a picnic upriver (and even splashed about himself, with his trousers rolled up and a toddler on his shoulders). His glee on such occasions was infectious, his energy boundless, and his generosity prodigal.

He built a special church in Moosehide, the native village downriver from Dawson, with the stipulation that it must be open to worshippers of all faiths. On one occasion when he spotted the pregnant wife of a Yukon Gold Corporation executive staggering down a hill not far from his headquarters at Bear Creek (a tributary of the Klondike), he dashed to her aid and delivered her of a strapping baby on the spot.

His community spirit came easily as part of his natural ebullience. Some, no doubt, was purposeful and political. He needed the support of the community for his mining ventures, and he also needed the support of the press, which alternately praised him and damned him. His great political rival was George Black, the loyal Conservative who would later become Speaker of the House of Commons. In spite of their differences the two men liked and admired each other. Boyle had need of Black. He had gained his mining concession with the help of Clifford Sifton, the most prominent Liberal west of Ottawa, who dealt out political favours like sweetmeats. But when the government changed in 1911 after Boyle had launched the first of his big dredges, Dawson became a Conservative town, and Boyle was shrewd enough to cultivate a Tory ally. He became one of the founders of the Dawson Amateur Athletic Association and chairman of its gymnasium and sports committee. That led to a new enterprise when he became manager of the Dawson Nuggets, a local hockey team that had the temerity to challenge the Ottawa Silver Seven, holders of the Stanley Cup in 1904.

Boyle was already Outside when the Nuggets reached Ottawa, more than a little the worse for wear. They had set out for Whitehorse in mid-December, some on foot, others on bicycles. The bicycles didn't make it, but the team did in just nine days, hoping to catch the ss *Amur* out of Skagway for Vancouver. That would allow them four days' rest, according to Boyle's schedule, before they played the first game in a series.

A howling blizzard shut down the White Pass railway for three days after which they managed to struggle aboard the *Romano* for Seattle. Seven days aboard the tossing craft confined most to their beds. The trip back north to Vancouver and the transcontinental journey to the capital left them exhausted. They had been twenty-four days on the road without a chance to practise. The first game was scheduled for January 13, two days after their arrival, and Boyle was unable to secure a postponement. Not surprisingly, they lost that contest 9–2.

This dispiriting result did not in the least rattle Boyle. Indeed, his regular reports to the *Dawson News* reached new heights of optimism. "It was a great game," he wrote, noting that one of his charges had broken his stick over an Ottawa player, knocking him unconscious for ten minutes (retaliation for a cross-check), and drawn a fifteen-minute penalty. "We have a good chance to win the cup," Boyle enthused. "The beating is no disgrace."

When the Nuggets lost the second game by a devastating 23–2 (a Stanley Cup record that still stands), Boyle's exuberence continued. "Nevertheless it was a good game," he reported, admitting that his team "was broken up and in no condition to play." To give his players some rest he cancelled the coming exhibition games and sent the team on a tour of eastern Canada where, reinvigorated, they won six of eleven games, drawing enthusiastic crowds at every community.

The idea of a hockey team travelling four thousand miles from a godforsaken subarctic village to challenge the Stanley Cup champions caught the public's imagination. Six thousand people watched the final contest, played in Montreal. To George Kennedy, one of the Dawson forwards, "it was the roughest match ever played in Montreal" and "the most sensational ever witnessed here." It did not matter that the Nuggets were defeated by Ottawa (at a more acceptable 4–2); Boyle's Klondikers were heroes wherever they went, touring as far as Pittsburgh and Brandon and winning almost as many games as they lost. Then they set off individually for the Yukon leaving Boyle to grapple with problems, legal and financial, involving his concession.

"Straitlaced" is not an adjective that springs readily to mind when describing a man who spent three years at sea, who mingled with the fight crowd in New York, and who propelled himself into the gaudy whirlwind of a gold-rush town. Yet there are elements of self-restraint in Boyle's otherwise unorthodox personality. The abstemious, non-smoking temperance crusader did not ogle dance-hall girls from a box in the Monte Carlo or the Palace Grand as his erstwhile companion Swiftwater Bill did. Women played a minor role in Boyle's Klondike career.

Was he ever in love during these early days? Capable of infatuation, certainly, as his sudden courtship in New York makes clear, but too impetuous for the good of that unfortunate marriage. "Few people ever thoroughly understood my father," his daughter Flora was to write. "And it was unfortunate that my mother was not one of them." Flora's comments suggested the marriage was placid enough—too placid for Boyle. "There was no adventure, no fight, no difficulties to be vanquished. He became restless and unhappy. He was tired of this smooth, ordered existence, of bricks and mortar, smug houses and smug people." In his daughter's view, Boyle should never have married for "he could not endure to be bound."

During this period in the Klondike, Boyle's children in Woodstock had little contact with their father save during the brief visits he made during his business trips to the Outside. They heard stories about him and wrote to him regularly, but it was not until years later that they heard the details of his operations. "We were lonely for him," Flora remembered, "and he was lonely for us, too. By this time we were old enough to be with him. . . . He sent for us, and we went west thrilled, excited and eager."

In Flora Boyle's memoirs there is a good deal of admiration for her father, but one does not get much sense of affection. She hero-worshipped him, that is certain. But how could they have been close? As for Joe Boyle, Jr., observers noted a certain coolness between father and son. Boyle's nurse, Dorothy Wilkie, who spent some time with him during the last year of his life, told his biographer William Rodney that Colonel Boyle was "not on friendly terms with his son." His long-time Klondike friend Teddy Bredenberg recorded an indifference between the two. Young Joe rarely came to see his father during his last illness. Their estrangement sprang mainly from Boyle's own neglect; engrossed in his own affairs, he rarely bothered to write to his family.

Three years after his first marriage broke up, a mysterious woman briefly entered Boyle's life. Rodney (whose biography of Boyle is the most authoritative) discovered in the Personal Mentions column of the *Dawson News* of July 19, 1899, an item reporting that "Mrs. Joseph

Boyle has arrived from the Outside." Nothing more. Who was this unknown creature? Wife? Almost certainly not. Mistress or paramour would be a better guess. But who was she? That there was another woman in Boyle's life about this time is only hinted at by his daughter. It is an abiding mystery, rendered more baffling because, after that one brief notice, the elusive "Mrs. Boyle" vanishes from the record.

In 1907, a second, legitimate Mrs. Boyle entered the picture. Again the marriage was sudden enough to cause a shock to his family. She was a hotel manicurist, Elma Louise Humphries, whom Boyle had met in Detroit during his long and ultimately successful legal struggle with Sigmund Rothschild and other company directors who were attempting to take over his hydraulic concession.

Flora, now living in the Yukon, describes her stepmother as "a nice quiet little person who could have been happily wedded to a good substantial business or professional man"—but not to Boyle. He brought his new wife to Dawson and settled her in a little house at nearby Bear Creek, the centre of his mining activities. It is clear that Flora was uncomfortable with Elma Louise as her father's wife. He was so different from the glamorous parent she had admired from afar. "It was not in this big, hot-blooded adventurous man to settle down quietly with a wife and family," she wrote. The relationship between daughter and wife was clearly strained, but Boyle was too immersed in his mining ventures to make any real attempt to bring the two together. He solved the impasse in typical fashion by getting his daughter out of the way—shipping her off on a round-the-world cruise with a family friend: out of sight, out of mind.

With his life organized to his satisfaction, Boyle could pursue his dream. The Guggenheims, operating as the Yukon Gold Corporation, had several smaller dredges on properties that Treadgold had assembled and consolidated before he sold out his shares and quit. Boyle's company already had one large machine in operation, but the three new monsters he was planning would be twice its size and built on Canadian soil by a Canadian company in a corner of the North that many Americans and Englishmen confused with Alaska.

Boyle had reason to be optimistic. Canadian Number One, gouging out the pay dirt at Bear Creek, had cost $200,000 to construct and had paid for itself in just sixty days. Now Boyle determined to build much bigger boats. His company was responsible for the superstructure; the Marion Steam Shovel Company of Ohio would design and build the machinery. Boyle signed the Marion contract in January 1910 and, with a work crew of one hundred, had Canadian Number Two operating before freeze-up in December, a remarkable feat considering the problems involved. His rivals were scoffing at the prospect of these gigantic new machines, but they proved highly efficient. Though the construction costs were doubled, their seventy-one manganese steel buckets, each weighing more than two tons, could process in one day three times as much gravel as their smaller counterparts.

The statistics recorded in the Dawson press were enough to send shivers down the spines of the individual pick-and-shovel placer miners. Boyle was importing 1,700 tons of steel parts over the White Pass and down the river by barge at a freight cost of $110,000. Twenty-four horses were needed to drag the two 27-ton steel "spuds," or anchors, each 65 feet long, on which the great dredge would pivot. The bucket lines, which could dig as deep as 45 feet, moved up a 97-foot digging ladder to dump the contents into a 63-ton inclined revolving screen that separated the pay dirt and hurled the dross gravel into another inclined travelling belt.

This "stacker," as it was called, disgorged its contents to become part of the mountainous gravel tailings that the dredge left in its wake and that would soon choke the Klondike River valley and its tributary gold creeks. The screaming sound of the dredge at work—its cables whining and groaning as it pivoted from side to side—could be heard for miles. Each time it lurched forward as the spud was hauled up, this sound, together with the guttural growling of the bucket line and the clamour of the inner drum, resonated through the hills. It is part of my boyhood memories, this eerie sound, wafting down the valley twenty-four hours a day, ten months a year. As a child I thought it was some kind of strange animal lurking just behind the hills, and I feared it. But to Boyle it was welcome music.

30

Although dredges cannot work in permafrost, Boyle was both lucky and prescient. The Guggenheims were thawing their ground with steam under pressure, an expensive process. Boyle merely diverted the main channel of the Klondike River and let the water flow over the ground where the dredge would operate. It wasn't until 1918 that new research established that cold water thaws more effectively than steam, but Boyle had divined that ten years earlier and made an enormous saving.

To provide power for his dredges, Boyle built a hydroelectric power plant at the north fork of the Klondike some seven miles upriver from his concession. To divert water for the plant he dug a conversion canal six miles long and twenty-eight feet wide, a remarkable piece of wilderness engineering that also had its quota of scoffers. He knew that to be profitable his big dredges would have to operate for much of the winter. But how could that be achieved if his great canal froze over? Boyle installed electric heaters at intervals along the route. With these and other techniques he was able to extend the working season by more than a month.

By 1912, Boyle was King of the Klondike, a title originally bestowed upon Alex McDonald, "the Big Moose from Antigonish," who dealt in gold claims as if they were playing cards but died broke, chopping his own wood on Cleary Creek. Boyle not only ran Dawson's telephone company, electric system, and running water but also owned the town's laundry and was supplying power to his rivals. He ordered two more big dredges with Marion equipment, Canadian Number Three and Number Four. The mammoth floating machines, working day in and day out, lasted until mid-century. Canadian Number Four was still in working order when the successor to Boyle's company shut it down in 1961.

The industrial revolution in the gold country sparked by Boyle had changed the face of the Klondike, and there was no environmentalist movement to protest or prevent it. The low, rolling hills had long since been denuded in the growing hunger for lumber. The broad and verdant valleys were reduced to black scars by the big nozzles that tore at the topsoil and overburden to send the muck and silt coursing down to the big river. As the years rolled by, the dredges themselves, gouging

Boyle's monstrous dredge Canadian Number Four floating on its own pond and dipping into the bedrock for gold. The stacker is dumping gravel tailings at the stern.

33

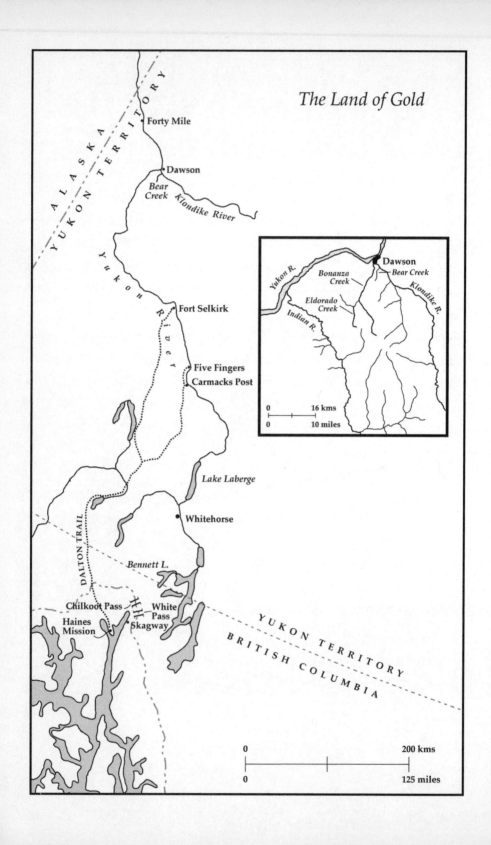

The Land of Gold

Forty Mile

Dawson

Bear
Creek

Klondike River

Yukon River

ALASKA

YUKON TERRITORY

Fort Selkirk

Five Fingers
Carmacks Post

Lake Laberge

Whitehorse

DALTON TRAIL

Bennett L.

Chilkoot Pass

White
Pass
Skagway

Haines
Mission

YUKON TERRITORY

BRITISH COLUMBIA

Dawson

Bear Creek

Bonanza
Creek

Yukon R.

Eldorado
Creek

Indian R.

Klondike R.

0   16 kms

0   10 miles

0   200 kms

0   125 miles

out their own ponds, would reshape the rivers and creeks, leaving their own dung behind in the huge tailings piles of washed gravel that would choke the goldfields for more than forty miles.

The irony is that, with the gold gone, the rape of the Klondike has become an asset. The tailings are now a tourist attraction; when some were bulldozed flat for a new housing development there was an outcry from those who saw them as part of the country's history. Driving past this moonscape, goggle-eyed tourists are treated to another spectacle from the old days: Canadian Number Four, raised from the silt of the creek by the army, restored by Parks Canada, and officially designated an historic site, towers over its visitors on Bonanza Creek as a reminder of a romantic era and its Klondike King. There is no other monument to Joe Boyle in the land of gold.

But the king was growing restless. He had achieved everything he set out to do in the Yukon. His four great dredges were breaking all previous records; he had become a leading figure in Dawson, admired now as a local booster and praised for his philanthropy. On September 3, 1914, shortly after war was declared in Europe, he plunged into the fray in his characteristic Boyle fashion, offering to raise at his own expense a fifty-man machine-gun battery made up entirely of Yukoners. He also provided morning jobs for the new recruits in his company so that they could drill every afternoon. There were precedents for such grand gestures: the Princess Patricia's Canadian Light Infantry and the Lord Strathcona Horse had similar histories.

Speed was essential if Boyle was to get his men Outside before the ice made river traffic impossible. But even as they prepared to leave, Boyle had to acknowledge clouds gathering on his horizon. Hostilities had scarcely begun in Europe when Canadian Number Two, working the Klondike River, sank in some twenty feet of water. That meant the dredge would be out of operation for the best part of a year, eating up the profits as several score men tried to salvage the boat. As a result, gold production was cut by 20 percent or more. The dredge was raised at last the following July and placed on piles for inspection. Alas, it toppled from its makeshift perch, killing one man and injuring three others. Worse, three months later, on October 29, 1915, Boyle's big steam generating and heating plant at Bear Creek, which serviced Dawson, burned to the ground.

War was another factor Boyle had not envisaged when building his big dredges. Operating costs had risen by $20,000 since 1913 while gold production values had fallen by the same amount. Dredging has some of the uncertainties of a Las Vegas roulette wheel. As the early stampeders had discovered, some claims were fabulously rich, others worthless. By this time Boyle's dredges were working poorer ground—so poor that wages had to be postponed until better prospects showed up.

Until this point Boyle's active life had been crowned with a series of successes, and he had reason to feel content. But now his career had begun to unravel, or so it must have seemed to him. In his pride he could not have foreseen that one of his mammoth machines might fail or a world war force up his costs and bring down his profits.

October 10, 1914, was a bittersweet benchmark in Boyle's peripatetic career. That was the day when the recruits for his machine-gun battery would leave the Yukon for active service. And that was the very day on which Canadian Number Two sank in the Klondike. Boyle worked all day at Bear Creek to help save it. That evening he hurried to Dawson to bid his detachment farewell. In its spirited account of the unit's departure, the *Dawson News* noted a silent man who stood at the edge of the barge with bared head as the steamer plowed past the shouting crowd and "watched the ship and her brave boys until she was out of hailing distance." It was Boyle, who seemed "transfixed, gazing until only the dancing lights were visible on the water." Then he quietly turned from his place and marched up the street with the crowd.

Boyle, ever the man of action, desperately wanted to be where the action was—not in Dawson, declining into a ghost town, but with his brave boys, far from the growing frustrations (financial, mechanical, and legal) that would continue to bedevil him. His brave boys, however, were not in Europe but languishing in Vancouver's Hastings Park, transformed

36

into a military camp, "a forlorn outfit," in the words of Leonard Taylor, "with no spiritual home, condemned to hours of square bashing and route marching, dulling to the soul of Yukon individualists."

Boyle put on the pressure, went over the heads of the army, and straight to the Minister of Militia, the choleric Sam Hughes. Finally he got his way: the unit was posted overseas in the summer of 1915. In England, Boyle's frustrations increased when he attempted to have a Canadian put in charge of the battery and was told peremptorily that the machine-gun section was under the control of Imperial authorities. In the end the battery was broken up and its identity destroyed, shattering Boyle's hopes for a close-knit band of Northern brothers, side by side, attacking the hated Hun.

The zest was going out of Boyle's life. His ardour was dampened by the news that his old rival George Black, the Tory lawyer who had opposed him in his court battles, had been given leave to organize a Yukon infantry company to fight in France. Not only that, but Black was studying for a commission to lead his men in action. This must have galled Boyle, who was itching to get into service but at the age of forty-nine was not eligible. Black was forty-three.

In the Yukon, Boyle would remain a controversial (if engaging) figure long after his death. Andrew Baird, a friend of my family and a regular guest at our dinner table during my Dawson days, wrote in his memoirs that the story of Boyle's activities in the Klondike was more like a fairy tale than a factual record. "He wrecked his company with ill-conceived policies and left it in a hopeless muddle," he wrote. Baird of course was not unbiased, being associated with A. C. N. Treadgold and the rival Yukon Gold Corporation.

When Flora Boyle told her *Maclean's* readers that her father "could not endure to be bound," one suspects that she was referring to more than his unfortunate marriage. Boyle was tied to his faltering company and confined to the far-off Yukon at a time when others were flocking to their king's aid in the poppy-dotted fields of Flanders.

It was too much. The man who had solved his daughter's problems with her stepmother by pushing her off to distant climes now chose

The Boyle contingent of Yukon machine-gunners at their barracks in Dawson City.

Boyle
Contingent
At Barracks
Dawson
Oct 5 1914

Yukon Archives

39

another form of escape. Like a small boy who picks up his marbles sobbing "I don't want to play any more," Joe Boyle slipped quietly out of town in mid-July 1916, leaving the Klondike behind forever.

This was a surprising decision and, given Boyle's long history of success in the Klondike, a remarkable one. He was not a man to let sudden setbacks deter him. Or was he? There is an adolescent quality to Boyle's unexpected flight from reality, for that is what it was. Certainly, wartime conditions had made his business affairs more difficult. It was hard to get the supplies, the equipment, and the men he needed to keep the company alive. Dawson was slowly dwindling, and so was the supply of gold. But surely this was not the time to abandon the mining empire that had been his pride. What was needed was a firm hand on the tiller. For Boyle at this juncture to turn the whole enterprise over to his son Joe was akin to a dereliction of duty. If the senior Boyle had stayed on the job, could he have saved his ailing business? The answer is that fifty years later, after others reorganized and consolidated the company, the great Boyle dredges were still working the famous creeks and still producing gold.

For Boyle, the fun had gone out of the mining business. The real "fun" lay elsewhere, in the battlefields of France. Boyle wanted to escape the burdens of the Klondike. He wanted to be known as Klondike Boyle, and for the rest of his life he was, but he wanted the glamour without the responsibilities. The outside world, of course, from Ottawa to Odessa, did not know that in the Klondike he was a failure.

Now, in the twenty-first century, it is hard for us to comprehend the mindset of the Great War generation, when the soldiers and the generals, too, were idolized as lily-white heroes and a man out of uniform, even a middle-aged man, was seen as a slacker. The propaganda that sold the war as Great Adventure was designed to recruit young men— the flower of the nation—and send them willingly, even joyously, into the trenches of Flanders: to make them feel themselves noble crusaders for their country doing battle with the Antichrist. No one in Boyle's generation would ever censure him for abandoning his business enterprise in order to save civilization.

When Boyle left Canada for London, he took a piece of the Yukon with him. That was a purposeful decision. He could run away from all the frustrations and unexpected financial problems that had been visited upon him, but he could not escape the aura of the golden North that attended him—nor did he want to. In London, his circle of acquaintances, carefully cultivated during his earlier trips, grew wider. "Klondike" had become a word in the language that connoted glamour, adventure, heroism, and sudden wealth. Now he was Klondike Boyle, a title worth more, in some circles, than a knighthood because it was unique. At the level in which he moved he was not seen as a lone prospector who had stumbled upon a paystreak; he was the King of the Klondike. It was for Boyle a kind of brand name providing a conversational gambit that gave him easier access to military, business, and social circles that might otherwise have been closed to him. He had left the North but the North had not left him. In that sense, he would always be its captive.

Now Boyle's contribution to the war effort in the form of a machine-gun battery, costly as it was, began to pay off. On September 16, 1916, he was gazetted an honorary lieutenant colonel in the Canadian militia. It gave him a title and a touch of authority. But it also burdened him with a reputation. He spent the rest of his life subconsciously living up to it—the bold sourdough and entrepreneur who feared nothing and dared everything. Fortunately, he had the stamina, the will, and the zest to press forward against all odds.

He did his best to wipe out the intimacies of his past. Save for one letter, Elma Louise never heard from him again although she made repeated attempts to seek him out. Nor was his son, Joe, who took over active management of the company, able to reach him once he had plunged into new adventures. Again it was out of sight, out of mind, which helps explain the indifference that young Joe, burdened now by the responsibilities his father had saddled him with, exhibited in Boyle's last days.

The rank had no military significance. The army doled out many honorary commissions to prominent citizens who had helped the war effort. Boyle was little more than a civilian in costume, but he made much of it. He lost little time in switching to a well-tailored uniform of officer's serge complete with Sam Browne belt. Now he was "Colonel Boyle" also, and he revelled in the title, which was to become useful to him in eastern Europe. Few would realize that he was not a regular officer. He was never seen in mufti but made a point of wearing his uniform at all times, complete with the word YUKON in large black letters stitched on his shoulder straps. He went further: on each lapel, a Canadian maple leaf gleamed with unaccustomed brilliance. These caused considerable comment because they needed no polishing, being fashioned of genuine Klondike gold—a regimental quiff for a man without a regiment.

It is tempting to think of Joe Boyle in cinematic terms. We can almost see the word FINIS on the screen as he boards the steamboat and fades into the distance. He has dispensed with his own past and we can only wait for the movie sequel: KING OF THE KLONDIKE Part 2, subtitled *The Saviour of Romania,* which, unlike most sequels, manages to surpass the original.

In London, the man of action wanted, once again, to be where the action was—if not in the front lines, at least serving his country as part of the war effort. Boyle's own pride was involved. How could he, a powerful man of forty-nine, be cast aside like a used topcoat? Other men of his age were being shamed as slackers by aggressive young women who taunted them with white feathers. Boyle's uniform protected him from that, but there is little doubt he himself felt he was not pulling his weight. He lobbied intensely, using his social connections (Herbert Hoover was one), to try to get into the fight. That didn't happen until the United States entered the war and the Russian czar, Nicholas II, abdicated. The American Society of Engineers was formed that spring to help support wartime Washington, and Boyle knew the honorary chairman, who had shown an interest in his dredging operations. One connection led to another, and on June 17, 1917, Boyle, who spoke no word of Russian, went off to Russia on the recommendation of another American friend, Walter Hines Page, U.S. ambassador to Great Britain, ostensibly to help reorganize the Russian railway system. He knew very little about railways, but he certainly knew a good deal about organization, and that turned out to be exactly what was needed.

—THREE—

When Boyle arrived in Petrograd (St. Petersburg, then capital of Russia) in July 1917, eastern Europe was in chaos. The provisional Lvov–Kerensky government, which had replaced the old czarist regime, was clinging to power, shored up by the Allies who needed to keep Russia active in the war in the face of Bolshevik insurgents. Boyle made contact with the Russian military authorities who accepted his services, though with some hesitation, while the British War Office was trying not very successfully to find out what he was doing and under what authority.

Boyle soon moved southwest to Romania to try to assess the stalemate caused by the tangle in the Russian and Romanian transportation systems. Romania had declared war on the German-led Central Powers in August 1916, but her railways were in such a state of disorder—half-finished in some cases, ending abruptly in others—that it was impossible to ensure a steady stream of supplies to the troops of either country.

Boyle got the system working by making use of Lake Yalpukh (now in Ukraine). This was a long finger of water running north from the Danube River near its delta. He saw that one end of an existing rail line could be extended to the southern tip of the lake where ships could be used to replace the gap in the rails. The link to the railhead at the northern shore thus formed unravelled the transportation snarl.

Here the new movie begins, with a montage of overlapping shots showing Boyle in action in the no man's land of the post-revolutionary Eastern Front. There is a fictional quality to these tales of Boyle's adventures in eastern Europe—the kind of stories that English schoolboys thrived on through the pages of the *Boy's Own Paper*. They come to us not through Boyle, who tended to shrug off his own exploits, but from a reputable eyewitness, Captain G. A. "Podge" Hill, the British intelligence officer who was from time to time Boyle's comrade-in-arms. Indeed, Hill himself later confessed that he had played down Boyle's role in some dauntless deeds in his memoirs to build up his own part in them. If Boyle's new adventures seem to have the earmarks of a Saturday matinee movie serial—and they do—they are not the less impressive because they are true.

The southeastern sector of Europe at this point was in turmoil. Romania had been torn in half by the advance of the Central Powers. The provincial town of Jassy (Iasi) had replaced Bucharest as its temporary capital. The Russian army was disintegrating and the provisional government was tottering.

Boyle was in the thick of it, as Hill's memoirs, *Go Spy the Land*, make clear. He records one incident where Boyle prevented a near riot in the provincial town of Mogilev on the Dnieper (now in Belarus). Feeling was running high at the presence of the Allied Military Missions to Russia, which were doing their best to counter German-Austrian propaganda among members of the newly formed Soldiers', Sailors', and Peasants' Council. A meeting of the council was agitating to have the missions expelled or their members murdered. In the midst of this hullabaloo, Boyle strode onto the stage of the assembly and started to speak, with Hill translating. There was a movement to rush the stage, but Boyle's voice, "clear and musical," to quote Hill, held the audience. In a short speech, full of references to Russian history, Boyle reminded his listeners that Russians had never surrendered. "You are men, not sheep!" he told them. "I order you to act as men!" Thunderous applause followed as one young Russian leaped on the stage and cried, "Down with the Germans!" That ended the anti-Allies uproar.

A stranger who didn't speak a word of the language walking onto the platform and subduing an angry mob! It strains credulity. But Hill was there, on the stage with Boyle, translating his words sentence by sentence as he uttered them. As so often in the Boyle story, fact again outdid fiction.

At the request of the Romanian government through its consul general in Moscow, Boyle undertook a special mission. Some twenty tons

44

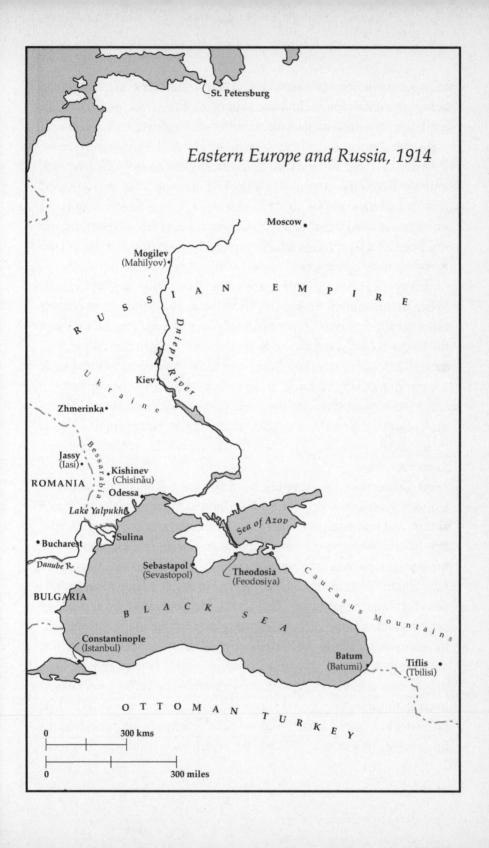

Eastern Europe and Russia, 1914

of paper, including diplomatic documents and all the currency that the beleaguered Romanians had had printed on Moscow presses, were in peril. Because the Russians were impressed by Boyle's work on organizing the Romanian railway system, he and Hill were able to secure a private carriage and the rolling stock they needed to pack four cars with the Romanian papers. They hooked these up to an overcrowded southbound train and set off for the harassed country nearly a thousand miles to the southwest. The journey was fraught with danger, for the route lay directly through territory over which the Bolsheviks and the Russians were contesting.

Boyle and Hill were running the gauntlet through a land in ferment. When undisciplined Bolsheviks tried to uncouple the cars at a small railway station, Boyle crept out under cover of darkness and knocked the leader cold. On the way to Kiev, the train stopped dead for lack of fuel, and Boyle organized a human chain of passengers to bring back logs from a nearby clearing in the forest. With some men up to their armpits in the soft snow, the logs were passed back to the stranded locomotive until the tender was piled high. The engineer finally got up steam and they reached Kiev, where they were able to attach their cars to another train.

At Zhmerinka, forty miles from the then Romanian border, a Bolshevik officer stopped the train, shunted the rescuers' cars onto a siding, and trained a gun battery on the station to prevent any escape. Boyle's response was to throw a party and an impromptu concert for the Bolshevik soldiers to show his lack of concern and to conceal his next scheme. Fortunately, in the yard an engine stood in constant readiness for shunting purposes. Hill and Boyle boarded it and forced the engineer and stoker at gunpoint to pick up the cars carrying the Romanian treasures. After Boyle cut both the telephone and the telegraph wires, the train with the pair aboard set off at top speed. Twenty minutes later they reached a level crossing barred by a gate. When the engineer refused to crash through, they kneed him to the floor. Seizing the throttle, Hill opened it to full speed and "the good old shunting engine carried everything before it in its stride." When they finally reached Jassy, they were met by an escort of 250 Romanian railway gendarmes and a body of Romanian army cavalry to secure the country's vital papers. It was Christmas Eve, 1917—a bright moment in an otherwise dark year.

Boyle was in Petrograd when the Kerensky government fell and the Bolsheviks took over. Six days of street fighting prevented any trains from leaving the capital, and Moscow was starving. The untried Bolshevik regime was forced by circumstances to release the former minister of war, General Alexei Manikovskii, from prison with orders to feed the army. Manikovskii sent for Boyle, who had just been made chairman of the All-Russia Food Board, and asked him to go to Moscow to untie the railways knot and get supplies moving.

Boyle's methods were unorthodox, but they worked. By pitching entire trains over embankments and pushing empty cars into the fields, he eliminated the bottleneck in three days, and the Russian armies on the Eastern Front were saved from starvation.

Both Russia and Romania had signed armistices with the Central Powers that December, and the Germans were moving in to occupy the country. Boyle now turned his attention to averting a war between the Russian Bolsheviks and Romanian forces. After weeks of hard negotiations with the Germans at the very gates of the capital, Boyle, shuttling by light plane between Jassy and Odessa (and once nearly brought down by a Romanian anti-aircraft battery), finally got his way. An agreement between the Russians and Romanians brought an end to hostilities in late February 1918 and was followed in May by a peace treaty between Romania and the Central Powers signed at Bucharest.

In effect, Boyle was acting as an unofficial and unaccredited agent, as William Rodney has noted and as Hill well knew. Boyle had contacts among high-ranking Soviet officials as well as some senior Allied representatives; moreover, he could move freely about the country, unlike the Allied ambassadors and ministers who were cooped up in Petrograd and cut off from what was going on in Russia because their governments had not yet recognized the new regime.

Early in January 1918, for example, an important and dangerous plan was worked out by the commander of the French mission to

Romania in which Boyle would use the authority he had been given by the Bolsheviks "to drift locomotives from the North to South Russia and create as much disorder and confusion in the Railways Systems in the North as possible": in short, an act of sabotage. In that same period the Romanian prime minister, Ion Brătianu, asked Boyle to go to Petrograd on his behalf on a delicate mission to assure Leon Trotsky, then Bolshevik commissar for foreign affairs, that the Jassy government wanted to avoid friction between Romania and the new Soviet regime.

Motion pictures, like stage plays, tend to be divided into three acts. The first act of *The Saviour of Romania* was now complete. Since every good movie requires a love interest, the second begins in March 1918, when Boyle meets Marie, the alluring Queen of Romania.

She was Queen Victoria's granddaughter, tall, elegant, spirited, intelligent, and still beautiful at forty-three—everything, in short, that a queen should be. It was she who had stiffened the spine of her Hohenzollern husband, the weak and vacillating King Ferdinand, persuading him to put his natural inclinations aside and join the Allies in their war against the Germans and the Central Powers.

She was a romantic in the grand sense. At the moment of her greatest despair, the arrival of a bold and unconventional Yukoner gave her courage. At their first brief meeting on March 2, she had only the vaguest idea of who he was, but he was certainly impressive. "A very curious, fascinating sort of man, who is frightened of nothing, and who, by his extraordinary force of will, gets through everywhere. The real type English adventurer books are written around."

The second meeting lasted two hours, with the Queen at her lowest ebb. The Allied missions were vacating Jassy, fearing the German advance would cut them off, and the Queen stayed up to make her farewells. It was a black night, the rain pouring down as if to accentuate her anguish. Then, into the reception hall, uniform dripping from the deluge, walked Joe Boyle. "Have you come to see me?" she asked as he advanced to meet her. "No, Ma'am," Boyle replied, "I have come to help you."

48

Queen Marie of Romania, Boyle's friend, confidante, and reputed mistress who enjoyed striking poses like this for the camera. She was a granddaughter of Queen Victoria.

Marie's fervent recollections of those midnight hours vibrate with the kind of passion one associates with cheap nineteenth-century novels or early twentieth-century movies. "I tried to let myself be steeled by the man's relentless energy, tried to absorb some of the quiet force which emanates from him. I poured out my heart to him in those hours. . . . I do not know all that I told him, the memory is a blur, but I made a clean breast of all my grief and when he left me and I said that everyone was forsaking me, he answered very quietly, 'But I don't,' and the grip of his hand was as strong as iron."

Boyle left almost immediately for Odessa to implement the peace treaty with Russia that the Romanian cabinet had finally signed. Before he went, Marie reminded him that more than two dozen of her country's most notable citizens—ex-ministers, politicians, industrialists, members of the aristocracy—were being held hostage in Odessa by the Bolsheviks, awaiting a prisoner exchange for Russians held in Romania. The situation was precarious. The prisoners were locked up in Turma, a heavily guarded prison fortress. Around them, something close to civil war was breaking out between leaders of the inexperienced Bolshevik regime and so-called White Russians. Under the new treaty, which Boyle himself had pressed for, the hostages were to be dispatched by rail from Odessa to Jassy while the four hundred Russians hived in Romania would get safe transport back to their own country. It was not to work out that way.

Now another remarkable woman enters the picture—a doughty Canadian, Madame Ethel Greening Pantazzi, whose husband, a high-ranking Romanian naval officer, was one of the hostages. A friendly source within the prison had bad news for her. The Bolsheviks in charge, she told Boyle, had decamped with all the prisoners' money, valuables, and personal papers, leaving them guarded by the much-feared pro-Bolshevik Battalion of Death. Instead of being taken to the railway station for the journey home, they were being pushed onto the waterfront where the steamship *Imperator Trajan* waited to take them away, perhaps to their deaths.

Odessa was in a state of chaos. With Madame Pantazzi as his interpreter, Boyle hurried here and there vainly seeking a Romanian official who might be empowered to assist in an exchange of prisoners that he himself had negotiated. "I've been up in the Yukon and know how to deal with men like these," he told her. "They have never gotten the best of me yet!"

Boyle was in his element at such moments. At the dockside they found that active preparations were being made to spirit the hostages away. As they rushed off again in search of aid, Boyle turned to her with a smile. "Quite a day for a lady!" he remarked. "I like this sort of thing—do you?" And Madame Pantazzi had to admit to herself that "in spite of the anguish tearing at my heart about B. [her husband], I was surprised to find I rather did."

Unable to find help, they returned to the dockside. Here a series of tussles took place, with some hostages who were forced onto the ship trying to shoulder their way back down the gangplank and into the crowd while others were being driven back by guards. Members of the death battalion were firing indiscriminately into the throng, and Boyle realized that the safest place for the prisoners was aboard the ship. Pinned down momentarily by the press of people, he spotted Madame Pantazzi and shouted, "I can't stand this. I'm going with them!" To which she replied, "Go! Or they are all dead men!" (The dialogue may seem overheated, but the story of this venture, as recorded in Madame Pantazzi's book *Romania in Light and Shadow*, was confirmed subsequently by the hostages themselves.)

Unarmed and with only the uniform he stood in, Boyle forced his way up the steep gangplank to reach members of the death battalion who were beating an old man. He seized two of the tormentors, banged their heads together, and threw them back on the dock. The ship finally pushed off with a thousand Bolsheviks on board and all the hostages lined up on deck to be counted by the meticulous Boyle, who found that nine were missing or dead.

Where were they headed? Clearly not to Romania. After three days poking about the Black Sea and being turned away at several ports, the *Imperator Trajan* with its hungry and dispirited human cargo, was finally allowed to dock at Theodosia. The Battalion of Death refused

Boyle and the high-class Romanian hostages he rescued from the death battalion.

to give up its prisoners—an alarming state of affairs, especially when Boyle received a whispered warning from a sympathizer aboard the ship. The prisoners, he said, were to be marched to an ammunitions shed and "accidentally" blown up.

Boyle moved quickly. Borrowing money from the British consul in town, he bribed the captain of a small freighter, the *Chernomor,* to take the group to Romania. He had already engaged twenty Chinese soldiers from the Bolshevik International Brigade ostensibly to guard the hostages but actually to keep an eye on the unreliable members of the death battalion. At the last moment as the freighter made ready to sail off, the Chinese escorted their charges on board, catching the death battalion watchmen aboard the *Trajan* off guard. When two rushed over to find out what was happening, Boyle suggested they board the freighter and he would explain. When they did so, he locked the pair in a cabin and the *Chernomor* steamed away.

It took days of negotiation at the Black Sea ports of Sebastapol and

Sulina, marked by threats, bribery, and bluff on Boyle's part, to get his charges back to Jassy. There he found himself a national figure, cheered by thousands and decorated with the country's finest honour for what Marie, in her diary, called "a prodigious feat of unselfish energy." Suddenly the man from the Yukon was the Saviour of Romania, providing that country with a hero when it most needed one.

None of this was lost on the British army hierarchy or the bureaucrats and politicians in Canada who had struggled to put a damper on Boyle's activities and vainly tried to keep him under close control. The elusive Boyle was hard to pin down. Every time the War Office tried to reach him, he had slipped away on a new adventure. The British ambassador in Petrograd considered Boyle a meddling freelancer with no military authority and at the end of December 1917 had wired his Foreign Office urging that he be recalled. The British in turn put pressure on Canada, and as a result the Duke of Devonshire, as governor general, issued an order unique in Canadian military history requiring him to come home. But where was Boyle? Somewhere in eastern Europe where the British couldn't reach him. By the time he reappeared in Jassy to a tumultuous welcome, the authorities were forced to backtrack. The British ambassador in Jassy was told to retain Boyle "so long as his services were considered useful."

This was the climax of Boyle's career. He had helped negotiate the Russian–Romanian peace treaty, had risked his life to save some of the country's notable citizens, and had brought back the nation's archives and currency. The Bolshevik leaders of Russia held him in greater esteem than did the Canadians. As Bruce Lockhart, the unofficial British agent in Moscow, reported to the Foreign Office in April, "Trotsky has frequently asked about him and would be glad to make use of his services."

To the snobbish military establishment he was nothing more than a civilian and a nuisance. He continued to wear his uniform long after hostilities had ceased, a stubborn insistence that galled one highly placed Canadian staff officer who described him as "a bluffing adventurer . . . who should not receive official encouragement." Every effort was made to force him out of this trademark costume, but he had an answer to that. He had switched to civilian clothes just once, he said, but that act had nettled George V, who admired him, often inviting him to breakfast at Buckingham Palace. The King told him that as his sovereign he was ordering him to get back into the uniform that he had earned by his work for the Allied cause. At least that is the story Boyle told, and no one had the temerity to check it with the crusty monarch.

Boyle went on wearing the uniform for two more years in spite of further attempts to stop him. When much of Romania was under German occupation he had made a point of going everywhere in khaki. "Tell him to take off that uniform or I shall have him shot," Mackensen, the commanding German field marshal, told the Romanian war minister. Boyle's response was forthright. "Tell him that no German living will compel me to take off my uniform. I carry a single action Colt, and I am a man of my word. I promise to drill holes in the first German be he general or private who lays violent hands on me." They left him alone from that moment.

Why this insistence on wearing the uniform? Other field officers sometimes wore mufti on informal or private occasions. Not Boyle. For him, the pleated serge with the lapel buttons of gleaming Klondike gold and the YUKON shoulder flashes identified him not just as a Canadian but as a special kind of Canadian—a Northerner from the most glamorous corner of the Dominion, known the world over. It made him unique. No other officer bore that form of identification. It gave him status, and in eastern Europe it gave him authority.

There was more to it than that. Here, in the company of strangers, these magical symbols, combined with his field officer's crown and pip, served to give reassurance to a man whose financial edifice was tottering. They reminded him, as they reminded others, that on the face of it he was Colonel Boyle, King of the Klondike—commander of men, mining magnate, soldier of fortune, confidant of a queen. He wore his uniform like a second skin and he had no intention of peeling it off.

There is little doubt that in the final months of 1918 the Saviour of Romania had fallen deeply in love with its queen. He saw her period-

54

ically as he moved in and out of Jassy. They managed to spend hours together after rides through the countryside. He told her about the Yukon, which she had long confused with Alaska, and the great gold dredges of the Klondike (but not about the wife he had left behind with whom he did not bother to correspond—a later revelation that shook Marie). He spoke of returning to the North and read to her from the works of Service, long passages of which he knew by heart. One of the Queen's biographers has called her "the Last Romantic." That she admired him and felt sustained by him there is no doubt. But was their relationship physical?

Boyle's two leading biographers differ. Certainly there were whispers about "Colonel Lawrence of Romania," as the catty court ladies dubbed him behind his back. The Romanian court was a hotbed of sexual intrigue, the by-product of a network of arranged marriages consummated in the interests of the state. Affairs, both grand and fleeting, were common and expected. The Queen herself enjoyed a long-standing relationship with Prince Barbu Stirbey, a courtier with a lengthy pedigree, but she did not distribute her favours widely, if at all. In Boyle she discovered "an unexpected touch of early Victorian Puritanism that added much to his quaintness."

It is possible, as William Rodney has suggested, that in his relations with Marie, Boyle saw himself as a white knight, too chivalrous to sully this, the most important relationship of his life, with mere carnal appetite. Leonard Taylor, who had access to a newly discovered cache of Boyle papers after Rodney's book was published, disagrees. "That they became lovers seems certain," he wrote, pointing out that "both were full-blooded passionate individuals who made their own rules. . . . They were living at a pace only those who have survived a war can understand. When you may be dead tomorrow there is every reason to live today."

Given the situation, it is hard to dispute Taylor's assessment. Though the sentimental and elegant queen might have seemed unapproachable to a Romanian courtier, Boyle was not a man to let such class restraints deter him. To her, the Yukoner appeared the epitome of

Queen Marie (left) in peasant costume with Joe Boyle and Princess Ileana.

rugged masculinity. To him, she was almost the direct opposite of his previous partners—a highly intelligent woman of the world who before her death would publish no fewer than sixteen books and innumerable articles in magazines ranging from *Ladies Home Journal* to the *Paris Review*. The fact that they came from totally different worlds only increased their mutual attraction.

In June 1918, the two were thrown together by an unexpected circumstance. Boyle, who hadn't had a real holiday since he left Great Britain, was felled by a near fatal stroke that left him partially paralyzed. For a fortnight his life hung in the balance. Marie was devastated. "I felt my heart die within me," she wrote; "Boyle, my great strong invincible friend."

He had been stricken in Kishinev (now Chisinău, the capital of Moldova), but as soon as he could move she had him installed in a small cottage on the grounds of the summer palace in the Romanian hill country. There he fought back against his condition, exercising his stricken arm and leg and smoothing out the paralyzed side of his face in front of mirrors—a minor spectacle made to order for Act Three of *The Saviour of Romania*. Finally he managed to shave himself with an old-fashioned razor and it was clear that he was recovering. Marie had breakfast with him daily and took him on drives in the country. Her ten-year-old daughter, Ileanna, became his constant companion, and Boyle delighted the little princess by reciting for her Service's "The Shooting of Dan McGrew." At last the King of the Klondike had found a warm and fulfilling family.

Marie had never met a man like Boyle. He did not fit the palace stereotype. To the stuffy salons of the Romanian court he brought a whiff of the clean, northern Canadian air. There, he was "Klondike Boyle," a soubriquet bestowed in admiration but one that also stamped him as an alien, albeit a glamorous one.

For all of his career he had been beholden to no one, but now, day by day, he was becoming a slave to a new kind of passion. Marie had only to crook her finger and he stood ready to do her bidding. Back in Canada his demure little wife tried vainly to get an answer to her official inquiries about him. In the Yukon, Joe Boyle, Jr., was trying to reach his father to discuss his concerns about the state of the Canadian Klondyke Company. From the maelstrom of eastern Europe there was no response. His company was now in receivership, yet Boyle appeared indifferent to the collapse of his empire. Though he yearned for the Klondike, as Marie's writing makes clear, he didn't try to launch a rescue attempt.

Why? Was it that he had done what he set out to do and moved on? To quote his favourite poet: "It wasn't the gold that I wanted, so much as just *finding* the gold." But these excuses for his inaction are not very plausible. Something else was holding him back, keeping him tied to the exotic kingdom, and that something, surely, was Marie. He could not bear to slip away with scarcely a goodbye, as he had slipped away from Elma Louise, still waiting for him wistfully on the other side. The great dredges had been his toys, but now he had put away childish things and flung himself into a romance that some might consider adolescent but that turned out to be the first abiding love affair of his life.

As he recovered from his devastating illness, new challenges presented themselves, all revolving around the needs and desires of his royal confidante. In the late fall of 1918 he masterminded a successful campaign to spirit the Grand Duchess Marie of Russia, the Queen's cousin, out of Odessa. In Paris in December he persuaded his old Klondike acquaintance Herbert Hoover of the Allied Food Council to dispatch three shipments of food to starving Romania. Next, in London he negotiated a twenty-five-million-dollar loan for that beleaguered country, lobbied (unsuccessfully) for a massive Allied intervention in Russia, and arranged for young Prince Nicholas, Marie's son, to attend Eton.

In the midst of this whirlwind of activity he was "knocked clean out" by an attack of influenza that weakened him further. The Saviour of Romania was also, thanks to Marie, now the Duke of Jassy. That did not deter the War Office, which was back with annoying questions about his right to wear the King's uniform. Boyle continued to resist all attempts to put him into mufti. Grudgingly, the War Office agreed to allow him to continue the masquerade until September 1920, a deadline later extended to the following January.

Joe Boyle recovering from his near fatal illness, Kishinev, Bessarabia, 1918.

59

By this time, political opposition to Boyle in Romanian court circles was building. His attempts, at Marie's behest, to separate Crown Prince Carol from his commoner mistress were seen as an intrusion into internal affairs that was much resented. The government had changed, and there was continuing uneasiness about the supposed influence of an outsider on the royal family. The intrigue began to tell upon the Queen herself. "They one and all torture me about faithful old Boyle and my unshakeable belief in him," she wrote. Yet the crisis only deepened their affection for each other. "You and I are man and woman and we have come together at a late period of our lives and come together in a way but few could understand," he wrote to Marie. In the end, however, it became obvious that Boyle was no longer welcome at court, and it fell to Marie herself to break the news as gently as she could.

In later years, Marie briefly drew aside the veil of circumspection that had masked her own inner passion for the soldier of fortune whom she had admitted into her personal life. She had been, she said, "torn between two loyalties and two affections." (She did not name anyone, but she may well have meant Prince Stirbey or even her husband.) "It was unbearable to me to hurt anyone and yet I was hurting them and myself even more." Boyle was devastated by this unexpected blow. In the correspondence that followed, it is possible to discern another side of Boyle, one that he had concealed perhaps even from himself. He had always been the loner, the leader who faced every setback with aplomb. Women had been secondary in his career. Now, in middle age, he found himself consumed by the kind of ardour usually associated with lovesick youths. From the moment of their first meeting he was the rock to which Marie clung, the haven to which she retreated. Now the tables were turned, but there was no way in which he could reach out to her. In one remarkable and revealing letter that has all the resonance of a wail in the night, he laid himself bare. "I do not think in my whole manhood I actually knew what fear was until . . . you told me I must go." The bold adventurer was now the prisoner of a hopeless passion. "I found myself paralyzed with fear, preventing myself from screaming . . . by cramming my hand in my mouth and nearly biting my fingers off."

Boyle's life had been marked by a series of stunning successes. Now, at last, he had a family on which he doted; the young crown prince and his siblings called him Uncle Joe. He had found a woman who could easily have been his life's companion—a contrast to his dizzy first wife and her uninspiring successor. He was in love with Marie, and on more than one occasion she demonstrated her affection and respect. But the ultimate consummation of that unlikely affair was denied them by circumstances over which they had no control. Indeed, much of the fire in his heart may have been fuelled by the lure of the unattainable. For the first time in his life, Boyle, the take-charge man, found himself powerless to act.

Boyle's career at this critical time was winding down, but he refused to admit it. Settling down . . . taking it easy . . . resting on his laurels—such senior-citizen goals were foreign to his makeup. He had one last service to perform for his queen. He had finally managed to separate the future king, Carol, from the arms of his unsuitable morganatic wife, Zizi Lambrino, and nudge him in the direction of an acceptable (if unlovable) princess, Helene of Greece.

He needed a new adventure, a new career goal, and he found it in the petroleum-rich Caucasus between the Black and Caspian seas. In May 1921, Royal Dutch/Shell, the international oil conglomerate, made him its representative in dealing with the Soviets, and he was off again for Constantinople (Istanbul), pausing for a bittersweet two-week idyll in the Romanian countryside with Marie. His treatment at the hands of the Romanian court had left him depressed. "In spite of his mighty spirit and energy he does mind being so unfairly attacked," Marie noted as he reluctantly took his leave. He felt the Canadian cold shoulder no less keenly. He had undertaken his several adventures on behalf of the Romanians and the western Allies at his own expense, and all he had received from the military (apart from the grudging gift of a DSO) was a long haggle about his right to wear his uniform.

By the end of August, Boyle was back in London, outwardly the man of action but inwardly at odds with himself. Only Marie understood the extent of his despair. "I am gone," he wrote to her in a melodramatic letter at the end of October. "Do not let me be a shadow on your life—you never owed me anything—always you gave and I am grateful and love you—remember only that." He had written her many letters but tore them up because they were "just lonesome wails," and Boyle was not a man to wail. She was, he told her, the "one human being that fills every spare moment of his mind" and one who also haunted his sleep. "There are nights when I am so completely worn out that I am almost dazed and the only way I can settle it is to conclude with 'I love her and I don't know anything more nor do I want to.'"

The following spring, having set up a network of trusted followers in the Caucasus, he was off again to Constantinople and then across the Black Sea to Batum to meet Podge Hill, who was again his associate. Hill was disturbed by Boyle's appearance. This was a sick man, "aged almost beyond recognition," whose clothes hung in folds over what had been a robust body. The pair set off for the Georgian capital of Tiflis (modern Tbilisi) on an inspection tour, but not for long. An international economic conference was slated for Genoa, and Boyle was determined to attend it.

The train journey to Tiflis had exhausted him. Hill noticed that he was increasingly short of breath and looked worn out. Nonetheless, he insisted on heading back on a dangerous and jolting journey through the mountains on a dilapidated train that at one point plunged headlong into a gorge. Its brakes had been tampered with by dissident anti-Bolshevik saboteurs, and the crash that followed killed the crew and many passengers. The Boyle party escaped, but Boyle's condition worsened. His breathing was laboured and his legs were swollen so alarmingly that he had to walk with two canes. The subsequent voyage to Constantinople aboard a pitching vessel battered by a Black Sea squall only increased his suffering. Taken on a stretcher to his hotel, he was told by the examining physician that if he tried to continue on to Genoa he would be risking his life. But risk it he did by way of the Orient

Express, eager to make an oil deal with the Russians who were attending the conference. When not confined to his bed in Genoa he moved about by wheelchair.

Back in London in May, having lost sixty pounds, Boyle was examined by one of the city's leading heart specialists who told him to put his affairs in order and abstain from worry and from any thought of travel, under which conditions he might live for two or three more years. Go straight to a nursing home, the doctor told him—don't even bother to go back to the hotel.

Boyle followed instructions but proved a difficult patient, holding board meetings with Shell officials and his own staff in his bedroom, to the consternation of the nurse who was now attending him. In June he stubbornly insisted on going to an international conference at The Hague, hoping to continue to negotiate with the Russians on behalf of Shell in its increasing rivalry with Standard Oil. The conference accomplished nothing, and when Shell, in effect, abandoned him, Boyle, ever litigious, turned to the courts for compensation, an action that was settled quietly by the company with Joe Boyle, Jr., after his father's death.

Ill or not, he could not resist embarking on one more piece of derring-do. In September, when he found out that one of his associates, Charles Solly, was locked up in a Tiflis prison, he set off again for the Black Sea, shooting off telegrams of protest en route. There he learned that Solly had been released as a result of diplomatic pressure and also, perhaps, because of Boyle's stream of protests. He made his way from Constantinople back to London by way of Greece, where he visited with Marie's eldest daughter, now queen of that country, albeit temporarily (she fled to Romania in mid-December). But his pride kept him from Romania. He did not want Marie to see the shadow of the big man she had known and loved. They had corresponded regularly, but now, in one last letter, he rejected her invitation to come to her. "I want you to remember me as the man I was," he wrote back. "I am no more Joe Boyle."

He spent his last days in the spring of 1923 at the home of his old Klondike friend Ted Bredenberg in Hampton Hill, Middlesex, reminiscing about the old Yukon days, rereading Service's verse, and, in Marie's words, "longing to get back to his mountains, his river rapids, his great forests and silent snows." He did not speak of his illness and fought it to the end, as his last words make clear. The date was April 14, 1923. He had spent a peaceful but sleepless night and now he seemed ready for action. "I want to get up," he said, and struggled to raise himself, only to fall back upon the pillow. At the age of fifty-six, the King of the Klondike was dead.

Though he did not die intestate as some writers have suggested, most of his great fortune had been dissipated as a result of his many philanthropies, the expense of his failing dredging company, and his costly and varied exploits in Europe. Marie learned the full details of his passing in a letter from his former Russian interpreter, a trusted employee, Dimitri Tzegintzov, who planned Boyle's funeral service. She responded in an emotional and affecting twelve-page letter in which she described the special understanding between the two as "something deep, real, strong, I may say holy, based upon a perfect belief, faith, and respect." Fate, she wrote, had brought them together. "We had clasped hands at the hour of deepest distress and humiliation and nothing could part us in understanding. No one knew his heart better than I. Women played but little part in his life and he had a wealth of love unspent . . . when he had his stroke I was the haven in which he anchored for awhile."

When she visited his grave at Hampton Hill—and she returned to visit it almost yearly on her visits to England—she was not impressed. She immediately arranged for a more appropriate memorial in the shape of an ancient six-foot stone slab to be placed atop the grave, engraved with the insignia of the Order of Maria Regina together with Boyle's name and relevant dates. There was something more. At the foot of the slab appeared a line from "The Spell of the Yukon" that she had often heard from his own lips and that would serve as his special epitaph:

Man with the heart of a Viking and the simple faith of a child.

CHAPTER 2
The Blond Eskimo

Vilhjalmur Stefansson, the last of the old-time explorers, on a hunt with the Canadian Arctic Expedition in 1914.

—ONE—

In the tangled history of Arctic exploration, it is safe to say that no man had so much calumny visited upon him nor enjoyed such public admiration as did the Canadian-born Icelander who called himself Vilhjalmur Stefansson.

In the early decades of the twentieth century he was the best known and also the most controversial of that singular breed of venturers who set out to unlock the secrets of the frozen world. His supporters ranged from Sir Robert Borden, the Prime Minister of Canada, to Gilbert Grosvenor, president of the National Geographic Society. His critics included two fellow explorers, Roald Amundsen, the first to sail a ship through the Northwest Passage, and Fridtjof Nansen, the first to cross the formidable Greenland ice cap.

Richard J. Diubaldo, who has written the most critical study of Stefansson's Arctic career, admits that his explorations between 1906 and 1918 were monumental by any standard. In his third and best-known expedition, sponsored in its entirety by the Canadian government, Stefansson discovered some of the world's last major unknown land masses—Brock, Borden, Meighen, and Lougheed islands—thus identifying one hundred thousand square miles of territory in Canada. In addition, he outlined the continental shelf from Alaska to Prince Patrick Island and revealed the presence of mountains and valleys beneath the frozen surface of the Beaufort Sea.

In spite of this record, Canada declined to make further use of his abilities after he returned from the Arctic. He was not an easy man to deal with and had a cavalier attitude toward budgetary restrictions. Egotistical, iconoclastic, and dogmatic, he was always convinced that his way was the right way. He was impetuous to the point of rashness and heedless of peril in a perilous environment, gambling his life aboard the drifting ice islands north of the Arctic coast and testing himself against the snow-choked crevasses of the great pack.

He was built for the challenges that faced him, always in superb physical shape, able to lope hour after hour and day after day behind a dog team without tiring while others became exhausted. It is estimated that he covered twenty thousand miles in this fashion, rarely sitting on a sledge but trotting behind it. He was also a crack shot with a rifle and could bring down a caribou at several hundred yards. And he had one more quality that every Arctic explorer needed: he had incredible luck. He survived and thrived as much by happenstance as by design. The caribou turned up at the last moment; the ice cracked beneath his feet, but he endured. Given up for dead time and time again, he emerged from the unknown glowing with health to the astonishment of his "rescuers."

The last of the old-time Arctic explorers, he was prescient enough to foresee the changes that the airplane and submarine would bring to the land of the dogsled and mukluk. Unlike his nineteenth-century British predecessors—Franklin, Parry, Ross, and the others—who insisted on bringing their environment and their way of life with them, Stefansson was not repelled by the idea of "going native." Indeed, he revelled in it. For most of his dozen years in the Arctic he lived with the Inuit, adopted their diet, spoke their language (including several dialects), and adopted their dress, their customs, and their lifestyle.

No previous explorer had gone quite so far as Stefansson. To him, the Inuit were not an inferior people, as the elite of the white world—the police, missionaries, and whalers—then believed. In the Arctic he saw them as superior. They were his teachers, and from the moment of his arrival in their land he set out doggedly to learn from them.

The Inuit trained him in the difficult technique of building a snow house (or iglu)—how to chop out the building blocks of ice, each a different shape from its neighbours, and fit them neatly into the frozen spiral that formed the structure. They taught him to wear loose clothing with few or no buttons that could be donned quickly after sleep to allow the body's heat to circulate under the fur (as opposed to the tight naval serge of the British). They told him how to keep his face from frostbite, not by rubbing snow on it—a superstition that Stefansson called idiotic—but by always keeping the hands warm and pressing them to the cheeks every few minutes.

"When a man is properly dressed for winter," Stefansson learned, "his coat is a loose fitting one with the sleeves cut so that any time he likes he can pull his arm out of the sleeve and carry his hand on his naked breast inside his coat. The neck of the coat is made loose, and whenever any part of his face refuses to wrinkle up he pushes his hand up through the loose-fitting neck of the coat and presses it for a moment on the stiffened portions of the face. As soon as the frozen spot is thawed out he pulls his hand in upon his breast again. In this way he can walk all day facing a stiff steady breeze at −35°or −40° Fahrenheit, which is the worst kind of weather one ever gets in the Arctic, for when the temperature falls below −50° Fahrenheit there is always a dead calm."

Stefansson learned from the Inuit to keep his face shaven; if he wore a beard, the moisture of his breath would congeal in it, creating a frozen mask that would prevent him from getting at the cheek or chin to thaw it out with the warmth of his hand. His Inuit instructors exploded another of the white man's misconceptions: that one must never fall asleep during a blizzard for fear of not waking up. The real problem, the explorer was to write, was that too many white men became so exhausted from the effort of trying to stay awake they placed themselves in danger. The secret was to wait until the blizzard ended, conserve energy, and try not to perspire and freeze their clothing.

Stefansson also learned to do without salt or sugar and to thrive on the Inuit diet of 60 percent fat and 40 percent raw or rare meat. He existed year after year on this all-meat regime and remained in the best of health. With his shock of white hair, his high cheekbones, and his full lips, he was himself a kind of "blond Eskimo," an unfortunate newspaper term that his critics would later use to his detriment.

His most important and effective native teacher was a remarkable Inuit widow, Pannigabluk, who appears in passing throughout his accounts, but only as a name. He refers to her fleetingly as "Pan"—the only hint of familiarity he ever allowed himself. She was, in fact, his sexual partner through most of his Canadian-sponsored expedition— his "wife" in the true native sense though he never acknowledged her

68

even to his closest friends. She was clearly the key figure in his retinue—strong, capable, independent, and a skilled seamstress who "made the finest boots I have ever seen." On more than one occasion she helped Stefansson in his ethnographical studies since she could comment on the people he met and discuss such topics as Inuit shamanism, seances, and hunting methods. Her position as his wife and the presence of their son, Alex, was no secret in the Arctic, where many an explorer or trader took a sexual companion. Stefansson's Yukon friend, Richard S. Finnie, author of *Canada Moves North,* often tried to draw him out on the matter, but when it came up, Stefansson changed the subject or pretended not to hear. Once, when leafing through an album of photographs with the explorer, Finnie remarked on one. "There's Alex!" he exclaimed, but Stefansson turned to the next page without a word. Finnie eventually met Alex (who proudly bore the name Stefansson) during his travels in the Arctic and told Vilhjalmur about the encounter. The explorer replied vaguely that he didn't remember many people whom he had met in the Mackenzie delta. But Finnie noted that Alex, with his Nordic features, bore a striking resemblance to the youthful Stefansson. "He was the only half-breed Eskimo I ever saw with a cleft chin."

Finnie recounted one story he had heard in the North when Stefansson seemed to take responsibility for Alex, though not in words. In the midst of a conversation, Pannigabluk approached the explorer, saying, "Missionary going to baptize Alex; give me five dollars." Stefansson silently fished a bill from his pocket and Pannigabluk marched off with it.

In his private life Stefansson was remarkably, even painfully, discreet. During his last expedition, he suffered from hemorrhoids so acute they sometimes confined him to camp; but he could not bring himself to discuss the ailment with his companions and so suffered in silence to the point where some believed he was malingering. One of Stefansson's biographers, D. M. Le Bourdais, wrote a long manuscript about him but withdrew it after a disagreement that centred on the explorer's health. "Such things are never mentioned in biographies,"

Pannigabluk with her son, Alex Stefansson. The explorer never admitted that she was his wife though it was common knowledge in the Arctic.

70

he told Le Bourdais. Finnie has commented that his friend's reticence was understandable. "It was unromantic and out of harmony with the picture of a hardy explorer and hunter on the march." But why the refusal to acknowledge a relationship that was public knowledge and acceptable throughout the Arctic? In the North, Robert Peary, for one, had made no secret of his Inuit wife; Stefansson acted as if his did not exist. That was out of keeping with his general view that the Inuit were the equal of the whites and, in the Arctic, even superior.

Much of Stefansson's silence on these matters can be attributed to his North Dakota upbringing, especially the influence of his mother, whose deepest desire was that he should become a clergyman. He was born William Stephenson in 1879. Both his parents were Icelanders of Norwegian descent who had immigrated to Manitoba two years before. In the devastating flood of 1880 they lost two of their children and most of their possessions and fled Canada for North Dakota, where young Willy Stephenson attended school with his surviving brother and sister.

They were Lutherans and, in that conservative stronghold, committed liberals, which suggests a certain independence of mind. Willy's father was a modernist who wanted his church to temper its teachings to meet every advance in knowledge. "No amount of ridicule or social pressure could have induced him to modify his beliefs or his expression," Stefansson remembered.

The family were all great readers, in the Icelandic tradition. Young Willy had devoured the Old Testament by the age of six. He read avidly and would collect books—thousands of them—all his life. By the time he arrived at the University of North Dakota, he was familiar with the works of Robert Ingersoll, the leading American freethinker, and was a follower of Charles Darwin—enthusiasms that prompted the straitlaced family with whom he stayed to dismiss him from their boarding house.

He was popular with his fellow students but not the professors, who found him far too cocky. When he entered university he had already learned to speak Norwegian, Danish, Swedish, Icelandic, and German and was not above showing off his superior knowledge by challenging his professors. At the end of a term, it is said, one of the faculty checking on attendance found to his dismay that his pupil wasn't turning up at classes. "How is it," he asked, "that you got a grade of ninety in my own class and only attended two lectures?" To which the brash student responded, "If I hadn't attended those two, I would doubtless have got a hundred." Or so the story goes.

The story is typical of the future explorer, who all his life was at war with traditional authority. In his junior year the university expelled him on the grounds that he cut classes. The true reason was that the faculty considered him the ringleader of a group of undergraduates who were getting out of hand. As one professor saw it, Stefansson "had settled the problem of life a little too decidedly and dogmatically." Unfazed, he moved to the University of Iowa, which allowed him to study and take classes on his own time. His reputation as a prize-winning debater—a hint at his future platform style—gained him an invitation to be a delegate to a conference of Unitarian ministers in Winnipeg, which later led to a scholarship at the Harvard Divinity School. He accepted but made it clear that he considered religion to be mere folklore—in short, a legitimate branch of anthropology. The ministry was not for him. After a year at Harvard he was offered a fellowship in anthropology.

Those college years marked several significant changes in Stefansson's outlook. In 1899, after some soul-searching, he had decided to change his name from plain William Stephenson to the more exotic Vilhjalmur Stefansson, a jawbreaker of a moniker but one that would establish him as an unconventional figure with a romantic background. The new name set Stefansson apart from the John Smiths and Bob Browns. Unpronounceable it might be, but it would be remembered— the perfect brand name for an Arctic explorer. (His critics would often cattily refer to him as "Windjammer.")

Stefansson's total rejection of religion included Unitarianism, a liberal faith that had itself rejected the concept of the Holy Trinity. As his friend A. E. Morrison declared, "Any assembly of theologians is the best example we have of insanity reduced to a science, a systematic fraud . . . that . . . wastes the life of man and shrivels up his soul." Disillusioned by his experience as a delegate to a Unitarian convention, Stefansson could only argue that, though everything in nature denied the existence of a personal God, "this does not break on clouded minds chained like slaves to tread the mills of toil, to make brick without straw." To Stefansson, the world was full of sheep who believed what they were told and refused to explore the dogmas that bound them.

The romantic young student had originally intended to be a poet, and for a time poetry was his life and his passion. He read quantities of it and in his own words, "had written verse by the yard," committing Kipling's *Barrack-Room Ballads* and other works to memory and exulting when his own poetry was published in the university monthly. He mused vaguely on becoming Kipling's successor, but the dream collapsed when he read a poem in *Scribner's* by William Vaughan Moody, a young man of his own age of whom he had never before heard. He saw that it was superior in every way to his own work and, dejected, never wrote another line. As he put it later, "I began to see that there is not only a poetry of words but the poetry of deeds."

The poetry of deeds! The phrase would define Stefansson's view of Arctic exploration over the next twelve years. In the autumn of 1905, after a summer spent as a physical anthropologist in Iceland, he secured a teaching fellowship at Harvard. He was looked upon, he said, as "the Anthropology Department's authority on the polar regions, particularly the Arctic, I suppose, because my parents were Icelandic and I had been born 'way up North in Canada.'"

Having written several articles for academic publications, he was offered in the spring of 1906 the position of anthropologist with the Anglo-American Arctic Expedition sponsored jointly by Harvard and the University of Toronto. Its chief task would be to determine whether an undiscovered continent lay somewhere in the Arctic and, if so, to study its native population. Nothing came of this hare-brained scheme. Stefansson was dispatched by way of the Mackenzie Valley and

Herschel Island, a tiny speck on the Arctic map just east of the Yukon–Alaska border, but by the time he joined the leaders, the expedition was disbanded. Nevertheless, it had a considerable effect on Stefansson's career, for it provided him with his first experience of the Inuit, with whom he spent some time. It also helped launch him on a wild goose chase that brought him worldwide publicity but at the same time touched off a storm of criticism from which he would never be free.

On Herschel Island he encountered a Danish whaling captain, Christian Klengenberg, a Jack London character, "unscrupulous . . . and two-faced," who admitted to at least one murder as well as the theft of an entire ship. Stefansson believed a story this dubious rascal told—perhaps because he wanted to. He claimed to know of a mysterious race of native people who dressed and acted like Inuit but did not look like them; some, indeed, appeared to have light hair and blue eyes. The young anthropologist was entranced: an unknown race who had never seen a white man! Klengenberg's tale continued to obsess him after he returned to civilization. Did these strange people actually exist or was the story he had heard too romantic to be true? The whalers who visited Herschel Island had dismissed the tale, but some Inuit seemed to confirm it when they told him that several of their race on Victoria Island looked as if they were white men in native clothing. If he could actually discover and report on a new race of people living in the Arctic untouched by civilization, it would be the discovery of a lifetime! Discovery rather than mere exploration was Stefansson's stock-in-trade, and when he came at last to write his memoirs, *Discovery* would be the title he gave them. "Discovery," he wrote, "has been my life."

Back in New York in the fall of 1907, he had one goal in sight: he must return to the Arctic, make his way through unexplored country to Victoria Island, and seek out its strange inhabitants. To do that he would have to mount an expedition of his own. That was a tall order for a twenty-eight-year-old anthropologist, but Stefansson managed to get backing from the American Museum of Natural History in New

York as well as some assistance from both the Meteorological Service and the Geological Survey of Canada to add prestige to the venture. With his enthusiasm and charm he had no difficulty raising money. His costs, he told the museum, would run no more than a measly two or three thousand dollars since he intended to live off the land, like the Inuit, for most of the time. The museum shipped two thousand dollars' worth of goods to Stefansson on the Arctic coast, none of which he ever received because of the vagueness of his itinerary. Convinced that he was either lost or starving, the museum ended up spending fourteen thousand dollars trying to find him. All the while Stefansson was flourishing on a diet of seal meat and blubber. It was the first but by no means the last time that he would be given up for dead in the Arctic, only to confound both his admirers and his detractors by turning up unexpectedly, having stayed healthy on a food regimen entirely of meat, with neither a vegetable nor a slice of fruit.

He delighted in such surprises. His original plan had been to go north alone to live with the Inuit and travel as they did. But when he received an offer from an old college friend, Dr. Rudolph Anderson, to go with him, he quickly accepted. Anderson, an ornithologist, was an exceptional scholar, a top athlete, and a one-time soldier in the Spanish-American war with several learned articles and books to his credit. The museum was enthusiastic; Anderson's involvement would add to the institution's prestige.

How could Stefansson guess that in the controversial years to come Anderson would turn on him and become his bitterest critic and enemy? They were opposites in almost every way except for their mutual desire for fame within their respective disciplines. As Richard Diubaldo has written, "Anderson's diffidence was the perfect foil for Stefansson's ego." One bone of contention was Stefansson's view of the Inuit as the "chosen people." Like most whites at that time, Anderson considered them inferior, an attitude that Stefansson himself would help change.

Anderson held his tongue publicly but admitted in a letter to his sister, written just after their arrival in the Arctic, that "one point of disagreement is that he considers any attention to cleanliness, hygiene, and camp sanitation as a 'military fad.' If you have read his articles in *Harper's* you may have noticed that there is really only one great Arctic and Eskimo authority—who has learned more in one year than all previous explorers combined. But I understand the situation and don't worry much about it." Fortunately, for long periods during this four-year exploration, each man went his separate way and there was no open breach between them.

The two met in Toronto in April 1908 and reached Herschel Island in late summer. It was Stefansson's intention to leave Herschel, head east toward the Mackenzie delta, and then move on to Victoria Island. But now he faced an unexpected and frustrating delay. Francis Fitzgerald, a Royal North West Mounted Police inspector on Herschel Island, was convinced that Stefansson would perish during his proposed journey. It was the task of the Mounties to protect all travellers who entered the Yukon, as they had been doing since the gold rush days. Now, when Stefansson asked to borrow a winter's supply of matches for Anderson and his party of pipe-smoking Inuit, Fitzgerald refused. He offered them lodgings near the barracks; but he would not be party to their suicide, for that was how he envisaged Stefansson's search for the blond Eskimos.

Fitzgerald couldn't conceive of an explorer living off the land. He believed that a white man needed twelve months' provisions to exist in the Arctic. To him both men were destitute, and since they had no visible means of support, he had the right to ship them out of the country. Stefansson was infuriated. His time with the Inuit had convinced him that anyone who adopted their methods and lifestyle could easily live off the land. For him that would become a public crusade. Now there was this whipper-snapper of a policeman suggesting that he and Anderson couldn't look after themselves!

They could go west to Point Barrow, Alaska, four hundred miles along the coast, for matches, the Mountie told them; the whaling station there was well provisioned and there was no chance they would starve. *Starve?* In the midst of plenty, where seals and caribou abounded? Stefansson was frustrated at the prospect of this delay. He never touched tobacco himself; now, instead of heading east toward his goal, he would have to trek along the coast in the opposite direction for the sake of his companions' nicotine craving. (By a bitter irony, a Mounted Police patrol led by Fitzgerald himself starved to death two years later in attempting to reach Dawson by way of Fort McPherson. They travelled light—too light, as it turned out. Had they adopted Stefansson's credo of living off the land, it is more than possible they would have survived.)

By the spring of 1910, two years after the expedition left New York, the impetuous explorer was still at Cape Parry, three hundred miles west of Victoria Island. The party had spent two winters on the Arctic coast, plagued by the vagaries of weather, by sickness, by the reluctance of their Inuit companions to move into unknown country, and also by the need to spend much of their time in the ceaseless hunt for game to stave off starvation. They had just come through what Stefansson called "a winter of misfortunes." They had lost more than half of their dogs, including some of the best ones, during a period of such scarcity that the very wolves had starved to death. Now Stefansson was ready to travel east into unknown territory. He still had faith that a white man could live off the land when an Inuk could, but he was not certain that any natives existed where they were going. None had been seen on this stretch of coastline.

The party split up, with Anderson heading back west to the Mackenzie country, told by Stefansson "to take action and to answer questions in case we failed to return." These instructions included the date after which he would need to worry about Stefansson's safety and the effort he must make to rescue them.

On the afternoon of April 21, with Pannigabluk and two male Inuit, Stefansson set off for Coronation Gulf, a body of water that hugs the southwest corner of Victoria Island. As Stefansson admitted, "No one but myself was very enthusiastic about the enterprise." The Inuit feared that this unknown country would be empty of game; even more they dreaded the legendary "people of the caribou antler," a barbarous and bloodthirsty tribe who were said to kill all strangers.

None of these warnings deterred the super-optimistic explorer, who was keeping his eyes focused for clues that would lead him to the mysterious race. Nineteen days into the search he found a hint that made his heart beat faster. On a driftwood-strewn beach he came upon a piece of wood that was marked by crude choppings apparently made by a dull adze. More of these chopped pieces of wood were scattered along the beach for over a mile. Apparently they had been tested to see if they were sound enough to use for making sledges.

He could not sleep that night, nor could his companions, who were even more excited than he, not to mention apprehensive. They talked far into the night, their curiosity about dreaded strangers growing stronger than their fears. Their search took on some of the aspects of a detective story. The next day they found more shavings, more chips, more evidence of the hewing and shaping of wood. Then—a footprint in the crusted snow and after that a sledge track no more than three months old. A little later they came upon the ruins of a deserted village whose size—more than fifty snow houses—took their breath away.

The trail followed the ice of Dolphin and Union Strait, which separates Victoria Island from the mainland. Stefansson and two of the Inuit followed it with the dogs and soon came upon another village at Point Wise near the mouth of the strait. From the top of one of the snow houses he could see a group of men squatting around seal holes. Soon he was surrounded by the seal hunters, not in the least menacing but excited by the spectacle of mysterious beings from another world. They were brimming over with hospitality, insisted on building a snow house for the travellers, and urged them to stay until the last scrap of food was eaten.

These almost Stone-Age people, who had never before set eyes on a white man, had knives made of copper, just as Klengenberg had told him. Stefansson could not contain his excitement. It was an encounter that the would-be poet would never forget. "It marked my introduction to men and women of a bygone age," he recalled years later when he likened the experience to that of Mark Twain's Connecticut Yankee, who went to sleep and woke up in the court of King Arthur. "I, without going to sleep at all," he wrote, "had walked out of the twentieth century into the intellectual and cultural world of men and women of an age far earlier than Arthur's. . . . Their existence in 1910 on the same continent with our populous cities was an anachronism representing a time lapse of more than ten thousand years."

The marvel was that he was able to converse with them in their own tongue—a dialect that differed from that of the Mackenzie River natives but was easily understandable. His months of living in the houses and camps of the western Inuit had paid off. What a triumph! "It cannot have happened often in the history of the world that the first explorer to visit a primitive people was one who spoke their language."

This was in itself a remarkable achievement. It would certainly ensure his reputation as a true Arctic explorer and a practical anthropologist. But for the ambitious explorer that was not enough. He had discovered a primitive Inuit band—"Copper Eskimos" they would come to be called—who were astonished when he lit a sulphur match and demonstrated the marvels of his rifle. But were these Klengenberg's pale-skinned natives? The following day he made it clear that he was a white man, the kind they called *kablunat,* whom they had heard about from other tribes. "Couldn't you tell by my blue eyes and the color of my beard?" he asked. Their reply must have brought another thrill. "We didn't know," they told him, "what sort of complexion the *kablunat* have. Besides, our next neighbors north have eyes and beards like yours."

Those words were enough to convince Stefansson that Klengenberg's tale, which had occupied his imagination for four years, was not fictional. He had already half-persuaded himself that the mysterious race of "blond Eskimos" existed. Now he set off across Victoria Island with Natkusiak, the most faithful of his Inuit companions, to prove it. What a prize it would be!

On May 15, he found what he thought he was looking for. "We were not prepared for what we saw," he wrote. Standing in front of their house of snow and skin were nine men and boys who seemed to him

A member of the band of "blond Eskimos" who Stefansson thought were descended from Leif Ericsson's Norse expedition, some thousand years before.

similar to the Inuit that Klengenberg had described. Their faces seemed paler and one or two had brownish hair. Buoyed up by his companion's remark that "these are not Eskimos, they merely dress and talk and act like Eskimos," Stefansson again could not contain himself. "I knew I had come upon either the last chapter and solution to one of the historical tragedies of the past, or else that I had added a new mystery for the future to solve: the mystery of why these men were like Europeans if they were not of European descent."

Where had they come from? The romantic explorer considered the possibilities. Were these descendants of the lost Franklin expedition, whose ships had foundered off King William Island across the water from Victoria Island? Or did they trace their ancestry back to Leif Ericsson, or to the Scandinavian colony of Greenland, which had disappeared into the Arctic mists?

All these suppositions have since been discredited. It has long been recognized that not all Inuit are alike, that occasionally a blue-eyed native does turn up, and that skin and hair pigments come in different shades. These isolated people were simply a branch of the Copper Eskimos, whom Stefansson could rightly claim to have discovered. But Stefansson couldn't settle for that. In the years to follow, his insistence that within that tribe was to be found another fair-skinned tribe with a different historical and, perhaps, ethnic background would only cause confusion and cast a cloud over his reputation.

One might have expected Stefansson to dash back to civilization to break the news of his discovery. He did nothing of the sort. In fact, almost two years elapsed before he finally boarded a ship from Nome, Alaska, to Seattle. His reasons were sensible. First, he wanted to study the Copper Eskimos, and he was one of the few scientists with the experience and the language to do so. Secondly, he wanted to explore the unknown territory that lay for three hundred miles between Cape Parry and Coronation Gulf. A host of matters, both archaeological and ethnological, needed inquiry. There was, for example, the controversy over whether or not the Inuit used pottery. Stefansson solved that by collecting specimens of pottery utensils discovered on the ground—a slap in the face for Dr. Franz Boas, a leading authority, who had insisted there was no evidence that Inuit pottery existed. Stefansson delighted in this piece of archaeological one-upmanship. Boas was in his view a mere theorist; he, Stefansson, was a practical scientist. It was another triumph for his burning desire to be the best-known and best-informed Arctic specialist in the world.

There was also the need to impress the natural history museum with the work that he and Anderson, working separately, had done. During the first two years he had produced very little. If he were to get funds for the future expeditions he was planning, he would now have to show results. But had he accomplished enough, he wondered. He was not a man normally afflicted with self-doubt, yet there were moments when he questioned his own achievements. Was he satisfied with his own work, he asked himself. And would the professional world be satisfied—"the small circle of scientific men who are not always sympathetic or generous"? Such men, he told his diary glumly, were "not even always scientific."

Therein lay the paradox. Stefansson expected to spend another twenty years in the Arctic and to become the greatest living expert on the Inuit; but at the same time he relied for funds on those who had what he considered old-fashioned and obsolete beliefs about the country and its people. He had little use for the British naval explorers, portrayed as the heroes of polar exploration, because they declined to "go native" as he had. In his view they were tragic failures. He admired Dr. John Rae, the Hudson's Bay trader, and Charles Francis Hall, the eccentric American publisher-explorer, who had learned from the Inuit. But since old prejudices die hard, old attitudes prevailed, as he discovered some years later when he lectured to the Royal Geographical Society in London. The response of his audience to his lavish praise of Rae's adaptation to Inuit methods of travel was chilly. Rae was a mere trader who had gone native, the only explorer of consequence who had not received a knighthood or a peerage like the gentleman officers of His Majesty's Royal Navy.

Stefansson was well aware that his theories would meet with criticism and disbelief—his view that the Inuit were just as intelligent as white men, his argument that winters were colder in North Dakota than in the Arctic, or his insistence that winter was the best time to travel and that there was no need to hole up in a cabin for the duration. To support himself and also to raise funds for another expedition with Anderson, he planned to lecture and write articles as well as a book, which would include a spirited account of his discovery of the "blond" Eskimos of Victoria Island.

The conventional scientific approach would have been to prepare a scholarly article for a recognized academic journal outlining his theories about the "Copper" Eskimos, and follow up with more popular publications and press interviews. But Stefansson could not keep the story of the strange Inuit to himself. He talked about them on board ship, and when he reached Seattle, a former Alaska newspaperman, John J. Underwood, was on hand at the dock to interview him. The next day, September 9, 1912, the *Seattle Times* headlined Underwood's interview "AMERICAN EXPLORER DISCOVERS LOST TRIBE OF WHITES, DESCENDANTS OF LEIF ERIKSSON."

> Ranking next in importance . . . to the discovery of the lost tribes of Israel is the discovery made by Prof. Vilhjalmur Stefansson of the American Museum of Natural History of a lost tribe of 1,000 white people, who are believed to be direct descendants from the followers of Leif Eriksson who came to Greenland from Iceland about the year 1,000 and a few years later discovered the north coast of America.

The story went on to say that all the members of the tribe had rusty-red hair, blue eyes, and fair skins. Underwood later admitted he had used his "ingenuity and imagination" to enhance his story, but there is little doubt that Stefansson, in his excitement, had perhaps unwittingly contributed to what was certainly a sensational tale. Since he had been for a time a newspaper reporter before going north, he should have understood the consequences of blurting out the details of his exploit to a seasoned journalist as he had done to his fellow passengers on the boat out of Alaska.

83

The wire services seized upon the story, and the following day, the *New York Times* had its own version:

STEFANSSON TELLS OF WHITE ESKIMOS
The American Museum Explorer
Thinks Alaskan Tribes Descendants of Scandinavians
TALLER THAN OTHER NATIVES
Many of the Strange Tribes Had Never Seen
A White Man Before Meeting Stefansson

The story would not go away and overshadowed Stefansson's and Anderson's real contribution to the American Museum of Natural History. The next day the *Times* ran a story (headlined "NEW RACE SOLVES MYSTERY OF AGES") in which it stated: "Stefansson's Discovery of Tribe of White Eskimos Stirs Scientists." The paper quoted Henry Rood, editor of *Harper's*—for whom Stefansson wrote—who declared: "If Stefansson says he has proofs of this remarkable find I would believe him absolutely and so would anyone else who knows him."

Perhaps. But other scientists were skeptical. The *Times* reported in a cable dispatch from London that "Professor Stefansson has not hitherto been regarded here as an authority." The London *Morning Post* interviewed several authorities who disputed Stefansson's report, which they described as "improbable."

Stefansson now found himself at the centre of a full-fledged controversy. What hurt most were the attacks by two of the Arctic explorers he most admired, Fridtjof Nansen and Roald Amundsen. Nansen tempered his criticism when he read Stefansson's side of the story in a special article commissioned by the *New York Sun*. It occurred to him that no Icelander could be as ignorant of the North as the Seattle stories suggested. Amundsen never changed his view that Stefansson's discovery was "the most palpable nonsense that ever came from the north." His tale of a separate race of blond Eskimos, Amundsen declared, "merits no more serious consideration than a sensational news item in the boulevard press."

It was the term "blond Eskimo" that caused the trouble. If Stefansson had announced the existence of a Stone-Age people who had never seen a white man but used tools fashioned of native copper, he would have been on solid ground. But he could not free himself from the original tales of mystery that had sparked his long quest. "Blond Eskimo" (or "White Eskimo," to use the *New York Times*'s eye-catching phrase) fitted neatly into the headlines at a time when other strange tribes in distant corners of the globe were exciting the public's imagination.

The controversy dogged Stefansson all his life. Few major articles were written about him that did not refer to it. His detractors put it all down to a lust for publicity and press coverage. Certainly, he had been a master of public relations before that phrase came into popular use. But to be fair, he needed the public's attention in order to raise funds for his next expedition. If the blond Eskimo dispute made him famous it also helped turn the eyes of the continent—indeed, the world—to a forsaken land that even the government of Canada had neglected and to a large race of aborigines who had too long been the objects of the white man's mythology.

A group of Copper Eskimos whom Stefansson discovered on Victoria Island.

A page from Stefansson's diary, March 1912.

86

In his book *My Life with the Eskimo,* Stefansson devoted a whole chapter—5,100 words—to the subject, using literary, scientific, and historical references to support his conviction that this *might* be a unique band descended from survivors of the long-gone Greenland colony. "There is no reason," he wrote, employing a lame bit of reverse logic, "for insisting now or ever that the 'Blond Eskimos' of Victoria Island are descended from the Scandinavian colonists of Greenland, but looking at it historically or geographically, there is no reason why they might not be."

—TWO—

Stefansson's new expedition, which again included Rudolph Anderson, was to search for new land in the Beaufort Sea, notably "Crocker Land," which Robert Peary claimed to have seen in the misty distance during his quest for the Pole. It would be a three-winter, six-man expedition, and it would also attempt to measure the extent of the continental shelf in Arctic waters. For this Stefansson again secured the co-operation of the American Museum of Natural History but also that of the National Geographic Society, each of which was prepared to contribute $2,500 to the enterprise. Through his friendship with Professor James Mavor of the University of Toronto, another Arctic enthusiast, he also lobbied the prime minister, Robert Borden, for official support.

The whole question of Canadian sovereignty over the Arctic had become a major issue, and Borden was eager to ensure that any newly discovered lands would be Canadian. Stefansson, who knew exactly how to handle the prime minister, pointed out that as an American citizen and leader of the expedition, he would have to claim any new land for the United States—unless, of course, Canada became a partner in the venture. Borden turned the matter over to cabinet, whose members could not stomach any Yankee-led expedition claiming territory for the Land of the Free. They decided, in Stefansson's words, "that it would be beneath Canada's dignity to go into partnership with others in such an expedition." Instead, the Canadian government would take over the entire venture, placing it under the Department of the Naval Service. With that the two American institutions bowed out, and the Canadian Arctic Expedition of 1913 was born.

Herein lay a recipe for trouble. When Stefansson reported his new deal to the National Geographic Society in February 1913, that organization made one condition: unless he got the Canadian expedition underway by June, the society would revert to its own investigation of Crocker Land. At the same time, the Canadian government decided it wanted to expand the venture beyond mere exploration. There would now be *two* parties, both acting for Canada and both under Stefansson's leadership.

The Northern Party would follow an expanded version of the original plan. Its task would be "to discover new land, if any exists, in the million or so square miles of unknown area north of the continent of North America and west of the Parry Islands." The vast frozen expanse of the Beaufort Sea stretched from the continental coastline north to the Pole. You could hide the province of Newfoundland in its waters and still have plenty of room left. Who was to say that another continent might not lie hidden under the ice? Peary had surely seen *something* when he glimpsed "Crocker Land" in the distance.

The Southern Party would be formed under Anderson, acting as Stefansson's deputy, to engage in anthropological, archaeological, and zoological research on the Arctic coast. That would require fifteen trained scientists, most of whom had no Arctic experience, together with a support group to travel with them. Thus Stefansson's tight little party of six was expanded to more than seventy, including Inuit.

That was a tall order, given the early deadline set by the National Geographic Society. It would have been sensible to forget about Crocker Land, which didn't exist anyway, as later explorations would reveal. But Canadian nationalism together with Stefansson's own impetuosity forced the issue. Now, on short notice, he had to comb North America and Europe for an appropriate scientific staff, complete some contracted articles for *Harper's* magazine, take passage to England to enlist the aid of the Canadian High Commissioner, Donald A. Smith (Lord Strathcona, who gave him a personal cheque for a thousand dollars), and try to complete his book, an early chapter of which he managed to dictate during the Atlantic crossing.

Before Canada became involved, Stefansson had taken it upon himself to buy a ship to navigate the Beaufort Sea and the Arctic coast. He had several in mind but settled on a 247-ton brigantine, the *Karluk,* which had done duty as a whaler but was now laid up in San Francisco. Although it was not ideal for the purpose, the impulsive explorer insisted it was the only ship available, and besides, it was a bargain—a mere $10,000. He closed the deal with a down payment of $500, expecting that whatever sponsor took on the venture would underwrite the cost. The *Karluk* was sent to the government's naval dockyard at Esquimalt, B.C., where it underwent repairs at a cost of $6,000, a hefty sum since it had already undergone repairs before being sold.

Bob Bartlett, the *Karluk*'s designated captain, a seasoned Arctic hand who had been with Peary in 1909, was more than dubious. The ship, in his opinion, was absolutely unsuitable for spending a winter in the ice. Should it take the expedition north, it would have to return south before the freeze-up; it didn't have sufficient beams or sheathing to withstand the pressure of the ice pack.

Stefansson's response was that the ship had wintered in the Arctic a dozen times and was as good as any whaler in the western Arctic. "Besides," he said, "we have to use [the] only ship we have." As usual, he was eager to get moving, and in this he was abetted by the government, which was as anxious as he was to get Canada's name on any unknown islands in Arctic waters.

As an explorer, Stefansson preferred to plunge ahead, heedless of detailed planning, confident that everything would work out. His friend Richard Finnie described him as "really a lone wolf explorer . . . at best when travelling by himself or with a few congenial followers." Later, at a ceremony in New York, Robert Peary would describe him as "the last of the old school" of Arctic explorers, "the worker with the dog

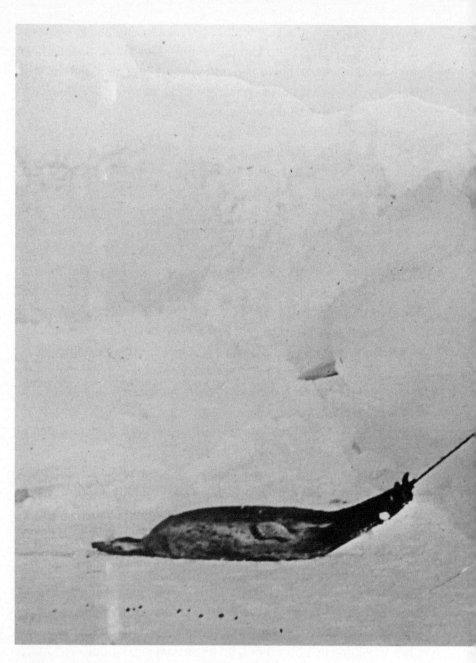

Stefansson dragging a seal across the ice, an image that was reproduced on the cover of The Friendly Arctic, *perhaps his most controversial book.*

91

and the sledge." But now he was "leading an expedition that would eventually entail the use of half a dozen vessels."

As a one-man operator Stefansson had always been an improviser, roaming the frozen wilderness, acting instinctively on his own, free of authority, always sure that something would turn up. Now he was in charge of a major enterprise that his sponsors had expected him to plan perfectly—but he had left too little time for organization. In fact, there was no organization. During the time the venture was being mounted in Victoria, B.C., he was absent because of his other commitments. There was no supervisor because he could not delegate, and he did not turn up to take charge until late in the enterprise.

There were further complications. Not only did the fifteen scientists lack Arctic experience but nobody, apparently, had figured out a system of packing and stowing the goods of the two parties. To carry the scientists and the extra equipment, two gasoline schooners had to be bought, the *Alaska* and the *Mary Sachs,* both with auxiliary engines. The supplies purchased for both parties were put aboard without any thought or planning. Boxes intended for the Northern Party were mixed up with others intended for the Southern. The *Karluk*'s decks were piled with fifty tons of bagged coal and sacks of fresh meat, vegetables, snowshoes and skis, canoes, alcohol, drums, and assorted wooden boxes. The same disorder existed below deck.

Kenneth Chipman, the expedition's topographer, was angered and disillusioned by the disorganized arrangements. As he told his diary, "The responsibility for systemizing things has never been given to any one man." Boxes repacked in Esquimalt, when the division between the two parties was made, were either poorly packed or even half empty. As Stefansson himself wrote, "we have had a good deal of trouble and difficulty in finding certain articles that got shoved underneath other cargo."

By the time he reached Victoria, the full complement of the two parties and the ship's crew had already been selected. It was not a happy group. William Laird McKinlay, a diminutive twenty-four-year-old meteorologist who had been hired by telegram for the Southern Party, was skeptical of the crew that had been picked up from Pacific Coast ports before Bob Bartlett took over the captaincy of the *Karluk*. McKinlay, who was to become a lifelong critic of Stefansson, thought they were good enough seamen but lacked "the other qualities which would be necessary for harmonious living in the kind of circumstances which might face us in the north." One crew member, he noted, was a drug addict; another suffered from venereal disease; two more had managed to smuggle liquor aboard ship.

Most of the scientists, of course, had no idea what they were facing and were given no training in polar conditions before the ship left Victoria. Chipman tried to stir up enthusiasm for the venture among other members of the party but failed. There was "practically no confidence in the leader [Stefansson] and little assurance of getting good work done."

Much of this pessimism sprang from the cumbersome mix of the two-party expedition insisted upon by the Canadian government. Stefansson was to report to the Naval Service; the scientists were to report to the Geological Survey, an arrangement marked by interservice rivalry. The scientific staff was alarmed to find that Stefansson would be in overall charge while Anderson of the Southern Party would be his deputy.

Stefansson had made it clear to the government that he didn't want a salary of any kind. He would work for free because he expected to pay for his efforts by writing magazine articles and a book and by giving lectures about the Arctic. As an unpaid leader he would be, in his own mind at least, answerable to no one. He would make his own decisions as he always had, without bureaucratic interference, and he alone would profit financially from the expedition. He would retain exclusive publication rights in Canada, the United States, and Europe for a full year after the end of the adventure. In Victoria he directed that all expedition members must turn over all their personal diaries to the government office after the expedition ended. That did not sit well with the scientists, who insisted on confronting their leader. Several members of the Southern Party, including Anderson, tried to resign, but as Chipman recalled, "the thing had gone so far that we could simply make the best of it." Stefansson calmed down, giving Anderson the rights to reports on the activities of the Southern Party for two New York newspapers with which he, Stefansson, had a contract, but no others.

The problems did not go away. The scientists had little faith in Stefansson's personal ambitions. His determination to live by his wits and push aside all obstacles clashed with the cautious, conservative attitude of the Southern Party members, whom he tended to patronize, as his published reference to the poor physical condition of one of them suggests. "Such softness," he wrote, "is the inevitable result of the time-honoured polar explorer custom of spending the winter in camp. . . . Such idleness makes muscles flabby and (what is worse) breeds discontent, personal animosities, and bickering. . . ."

The discontent continued after the *Karluk* reached Nome. Stefansson, who was used to a lean, mean operation, was dealing with a group of

National Archives of Canada PA-74063

The Southern Party of experts, who often clashed with Stefansson over scientific matters (Stefansson in foreground in bowler hat).

Stefansson and the scientists on the cluttered deck of Karluk, *just before it set off from Esquimalt, B.C. They had no idea what they were in for.*

scientific experts, many of whom had not comprehended that life in the Arctic differed from a cozy existence in Ottawa. He grew irascible at the questions flung at him about the expedition's plans. When some-body wanted to know if the twenty tons of provisions purchased in Seattle would be suitable for sledge travel, he declared that the questioner had no right to ask. When James Murray, the oceanographer, acting as a spokesman for the party, asked what arrangements had been made for fur clothing, Stefansson retorted that the question was impertinent. Murray feared that the *Karluk* might get crushed in the ice and tried to suggest that the Northern Party establish a base on shore as well as on the ship. But Stefansson insisted on dealing with all the problems in his own way. When he bluntly told the scientific members that lives were secondary to the success of the expedition, they were shocked at what to them was inexcusable callousness. Irritated by their flood of queries, Stefansson told them that he was in command of the expedition and they must have confidence in him. According to Chipman, he made the remarkable statement that the expedition was not essentially scientific, and that scientists were inclined to be narrow-minded and engrossed in their own lives.

The gap between the two parties—created by the scientists' ignorance of the Arctic on one side and Stefansson's long polar experience on the other—is illustrated by the continual concern about drinking water. The scientists were worried because the tanks aboard the *Karluk* were much too small to handle enough fresh water for an expedition of this size. But Stefansson had long ago learned from the Inuit that fresh water always forms in pools on old ice and is easily available to Arctic travellers. He could not get that across to them, even when he appealed to Bartlett, who explained that in Newfoundland there was always plenty of fresh water available on the icecaps.

At Nome there was much sorting, repacking, and reorganizing, but with the Arctic summer ending (it was now August) there was no time to tarry. Stefansson reassured the party with the words "we'll sort it all out when we get to Herschel." But the *Karluk* would never reach that island, and its struggles with the ice pack would touch off one of the great Arctic tragedies of that time.

The *Karluk* rounded Point Barrow and moved eastward along the Arctic coast, leaving the Southern Party's *Alaska* behind as well as the *Mary Sachs,* a forty-one-ton ship carrying much of the equipment. Besides the three larger vessels, the Canadian Arctic Expedition eventually consisted of five whaleboats, two motorboats, three canoes, two dories, a dinghy, and several skin boats—a small but costly navy.

Stefansson advised Bartlett to hug the shore in order to stay in sight of land and safe from drifting ice. As Stefansson was to point out, there were two main theories of ice navigation: the bold Atlantic policy of keeping away from the land to face the ice and take one's chances, and the cautious western Arctic policy of playing it safe, hugging the coast, and "if you don't get there this year you may have another chance next."

OPPOSITE: *The overloaded* Karluk *forcing a path through the ice pack.*

Bartlett, who belonged to the Atlantic school and had never navigated in the western Arctic, followed Stefansson's advice but became frustrated when the ship went aground several times in the shallow coastal waters. He was as bold as he was stubborn, and what had been good enough for Robert Peary, whom he worshipped, was good enough for him. Stefansson himself had been urging him forward, emphasizing the need for haste before the winter set in.

Finally on August 12, while Stefansson was asleep, Captain Bartlett turned the *Karluk*'s prow north, hoping to find a lane of open water in the ice. That was a foolhardy decision. Soon the ship was out of sight of land and having followed one open lead north now found itself entering another that led south again. She was moving east, pushed by the shifting ice that imprisoned her. Those on board felt trapped. The white world stretched out bleakly in every direction, hazy with falling snow, and with no sign of land. By the end of August, the inactivity began to tell as it became clear to the old Arctic hands on board that there was no escape. They could now expect to be cooped up here for the winter. Even the Inuit on board were frightened.

As the moving ice continued to force the ship eastward, it became obvious that there was no chance of finding an open lead of water and nothing could be done about it. "How long will this continue?" McKinlay, the meteorologist, asked in his diary. "This . . . inactivity is becoming unbearable," he wrote. "In the minds of all is the unuttered question: When will things change?" Things did not change: the snow continued; the temperature plunged.

The frustration and inactivity began to grate on Stefansson, whose desire to press forward at any cost was thwarted by the vagaries of the ice pack. The ship, which had been carried east of Point Barrow, was still some distance from Herschel Island, where presumably it would meet *Alaska* and *Mary Sachs*.

Now Stefansson realized that his hope of exploring the Beaufort Sea would have to be postponed for another year. And what if somebody else beat him to what would be his greatest discovery—Crocker Land?

He was also concerned about the need for more fresh meat, without which scurvy would incapacitate all on board, as it had on the ill-fated Franklin expedition. He felt himself helpless, unable to sleep. Day by day his restlessness increased until, on September 19, he told his crew that he intended to leave for a week or ten days to hunt in the Colville River area. The following morning he left, taking with him several dogs, two Inuit hunters, Asatsiak ("Jim") and Pauyurak ("Jerry"), together with his secretary, Burt McConnell, the anthropologist Diamond Jenness, and the expedition's photographer, George Wilkins, who as Sir Hubert Wilkins later explored the Antarctic by air.

This decision was to haunt Stefansson for most of his life. His detractors would attack him as a leader who left his post when he was most needed. Some, indeed, would suggest that he did it on purpose, believing that the *Karluk* was doomed. That was nonsense; there is no doubt that for the rest of his years, Stefansson bitterly regretted the move and underwent a great deal of soul-searching because of it.

To be fair, he had no reason to believe that the *Karluk* could escape the iron grip of the ice pack, and he was right to be concerned about the need for fresh meat. Despite the several rivalries that existed on board, a week or so of absence would not make much difference. Or so he thought.

But when the hunting party returned some days later, the ship had vanished, carried away to the westward by the ice after a dreadful two-day gale that tore at the pack and opened leads down which the *Karluk* was driven by the storm. Of the ship and her passengers there was no trace except a vague report that her masts had been seen in the distance twenty miles east of Fort Smyth, Alaska. Missing were twenty-two men, one Inuit woman and her children, sixteen dogs, and the ship's cat. Of that beleaguered company, eleven would not survive the horrifying aftermath. The story of the *Karluk* is one of the bitterest of all the Arctic tales of struggle and survival. No fewer than four published books have dealt with the question of Stefansson's judgment and the fate of those he left behind.

Stefansson leaving the Karluk, *September 20, 1913, with a hunting party. The ship was never seen again, and the explorer was criticized for his actions.*

100

The loss of the ship dealt a staggering blow to the projected work of the Northern Party. All their essential equipment including the oceanographical tools designed to test the depth of the Beaufort Sea was gone. And there was only one Inuit woman aboard the ill-fated vessel to make and repair clothing for the entire company, "an impossible task" in McKinlay's words. Here was further evidence of the unseemly haste and lack of organization that had marked the expedition's planning. Surely Stefansson with his long experience of the Inuit should have known that the expedition required more than one seamstress.

Now the key persons and equipment of the Northern Party were missing, along with the ship. Nobody knew where it was in that limitless ocean, and Stefansson realized that any search would be futile. He would have to shoulder full responsibility for any mishap it suffered. He had chosen the vessel. He had been in charge when Bartlett made his fateful decision. He had left it, albeit temporarily. All that would return to haunt him. McKinlay would never forget or forgive Stefansson's declaration, in one of his early dispatches, that the "attainment of the purposes of the expedition is more important than the bringing-back safe of the ship in which it sails." Understandably, that attitude nettled the scientists, who could not comprehend their leader's single-minded credo that an explorer must be prepared to risk his life for the sake of discovery. Stefansson had already flirted with disaster more than once and was prepared to flirt with it again. For the time being he remained, as usual, optimistic. He did not consider that the *Karluk* was in any great danger. If it were crushed in the ice, the people aboard could reach shore by using the skin boats that were available for that purpose. That may have been wishful thinking, but Stefansson, obsessed by the need to find new land somewhere beneath the ice of the Beaufort Sea, put aside such concerns and determined to press on.

By late November he had reached Collinson Point on the Alaskan coast, after a six-hundred-mile sledge journey from Barrow to hook up with the Southern Party and the schooners *Mary Sachs* and *Alaska*. He informed Ottawa that he would leave Jenness to study the Inuit in

The Southern Party of the Canadian Arctic Expedition.

the Colville River area while others explored the Mackenzie Delta. Anderson demurred, pointing out that the government had ordered a study of Coronation Gulf. Stefansson was irked and highly critical of what he considered the scientists' sloth. The Southern Party had intended to sit idle for the winter and had made "a picnic-like attempt at hunting with no success." The gap between the lean, rugged explorer and the "soft" scientists was widening.

In Anderson's opinion, Stefansson had become a leader without followers. Since there was, in effect, no longer a Northern Party, he opposed Stefansson's plans to take over the equipment and supplies it had left behind. For Reginald Brock, director of the Geological Survey of Canada, the scientific work had become the paramount objective. He sent a blunt message to Stefansson via Herschel Island that "the disappearance of the *Karluk* puts an end to the northern expedition, except what you may be able to accomplish yourself." Anderson threatened to resign as second-in-command, but Stefansson refused to accept his resignation. The explorer set off for Herschel to arrange for stores to replace those lost on the missing ship and to make his own arrangements for his survey of the Beaufort Sea.

For most of the winter he was absent from Collinson Point, but a few miles out of Herschel Island he received a letter from Anderson, by way of several members of the Southern Party, announcing that he had received Stefansson's instructions but was refusing to obey them. Since the Canadian expedition reported directly to the Naval Service, this was mutiny. Anderson told Stefansson that in the opinion of his colleagues, the leader's proposed journey over the frozen Beaufort Sea was merely a ploy to get him newspaper notoriety.

Returning to Collinson Point, Stefansson had quietly secured the support of several in Anderson's party. Now he asked each man whether or not he would volunteer to join him on the ice. The first he polled was Captain Joseph Bernard, a seasoned Arctic skipper, because he hoped Bernard would support him. Bernard's prompt agreement came as a surprise. "I fear that some of the men had in a measure deceived Anderson," Stefansson wrote later, "misleading him into thinking he would have the wholehearted support of the entire staff. Answering when their names were called, more than half were firmly on my side and a number of the rest wavering." Anderson, who was "sometimes shallow," at last consented to a face-saving agreement: Stefansson was to sign a statement promising that he would let all the scientists go on with their work. Since that had been his position since the beginning, Stefansson cheerfully accepted, and with that the mutiny dwindled.

On March 22, 1914, Stefansson set off at last on his ice journey across the inhospitable Beaufort Sea. The starting lineup consisted of twenty-five dogs, seven men, and thirty-five hundred pounds of equipment. Once the party worked its way through the expanse of jagged shore ice, it would be reduced to six dogs, one sled, and three men, while the others would act as a support party. No wonder the scientists left behind at Collinson Point were convinced that Stefansson was going to his doom. This was a new departure in polar exploration. As Stefansson recalled, "We were traveling over ice floating over an unknown ocean, far from any known lands, and without any immediate intention of turning back."

Stefansson's objective was to get farther north travelling on the ice than any ship had been able to navigate. By the time the support party left, he had achieved that objective. "No human beings of any race had set foot on the ice in this longitude so far from the coast of Alaska. Our position was dramatic and we knew it. We were about to settle the great question: Is the Arctic a barren waste incapable of supporting life, or is it hostile only to those who persist in thinking and living like southerners?"

Stefansson proved his answer, at least to his own satisfaction. He tried to make it sound easy, but of course it wasn't. At the outset, a raging eighty-six-mile-an-hour gale drove them forty miles east, and when they struggled north, skirting lead after lead of open water, seals seemed to be non-existent, as some of the explorers' colleagues had warned.

By mid-May they were down to three-quarters of a pound of meat a day while the dogs subsisted on old skin boots and grizzly bear hides, the hair of which had been clipped for bedding and later, when the kerosene ran out, for fuel in the absence of blubber. Only at the last moment, with about a day's rations left, did they finally shoot a seal—so tasty they overindulged and were too ill to travel the following day.

On May 24 they found themselves marooned on an ice island four or five miles square. A fortnight passed before they were able to make their escape. The going was maddeningly slow. "Sometimes we waded through water nearly up to our waists while the dogs had to swim with the sled floating behind like a log being towed across a river." On June 25, ninety-six days from the Alaskan coast, they made land on Norway Island. On July 31, they managed to cross over to Banks Island and establish a base camp. It was a daring enterprise and a remarkable physical achievement, but no wonder the other members of the Canadian Arctic Expedition thought they were long since dead. They had walked and trotted for seven hundred miles behind their dog team and had made a series of soundings through four degrees of latitude and nineteen of longitude that established the line of the continental shelf north of Alaska and west of Banks Island. And Crocker Land? It clearly didn't exist, except as a figment of Peary's wishful thinking.

Meanwhile, the battered and leaky *Mary Sachs* had made a memorable voyage under George Wilkins. By the time it finally reached Banks Island in late August, news of Stefansson's death had been flashed around the world. Wilkins later described the general opinion of the enterprise among natives and whalers as "one crazy and two deluded men going north over the sea ice to commit suicide." On arriving at Stefansson's camp, Wilkins must have thought he was seeing a ghost, and a remarkably robust one, for Stefansson had thrived on his all-seal diet. When he realized that Stefansson had not perished, he "went wild with joy." As he remembered, "never before or since, have I been stirred with such emotion. To this day I do not know what capers I cut . . . any observer might have thought I was mad."

Now at last Stefansson had word of the fate of the *Karluk*. It had drifted west with the ice pack at the rate of nine miles a day until, when some three hundred miles north of the Siberian coast, it had, predictably, been crushed by the ice. Before it sank, the survivors were able to leave the doomed ship and move with as much equipment as they could carry over the ice to a point eighty miles north of Wrangel Island. They set up a base—Shipwreck Camp, they called it—from which to reach the rocky, ice-sheathed island.

They were a disgruntled company. Relationships were rent by quarrels over food, and as William McKinlay noted, "there was a feeling of every man for himself in the air." They reached Wrangel Island at last on March 12, 1914. Here Bartlett decided to cross the ice to the Siberian mainland in search of help. He took with him a single Inuit hunter, Katakovik, realizing the need to move quickly before the ice broke. They set off at once, travelling across the sea ice for two hundred miles. That was only the beginning of a memorable and heroic race with time. On reaching land, they headed southwest along the coastline, guided by natives, on a gruelling seven-hundred-mile trek to the nearest settlement.

From that point Bartlett was able, after a long wait, to take a ship to St. Michael's, Alaska, and telegraph for help. A rescue ship eventually reached Wrangel Island with considerable difficulty in October to discover that the seven-month travail on that rocky and desolate shore had cost eleven lives through scurvy, illness, starvation, and, in one instance, apparently suicide. Stefansson continued to take responsibility for Bartlett's impetuous and, as it turned out, disastrous decision to move the *Karluk* into the ice, though in private he was highly critical. He realized that Bartlett's remarkable rescue journey had eclipsed his tragic mistake.

Stefansson was preoccupied, too, with plans to discover new lands. This had always been his priority and it was the basis of his disagreement with Anderson. His exploration over the Beaufort had convinced him that there was no possibility of a new land hidden somewhere in that vast body of water, but he thought there was every chance that undiscovered islands could be found to the northeast of Prince Patrick Island.

Accordingly, in mid-June 1915, he led three men to the shores of Prince Patrick Island. One of the party, Storker Storkerson, who was five miles in the lead, climbed up on an ice hummock and surveyed the horizon with his binoculars. As Stefansson watched from a distance, Storkerson slowly swung his glasses toward the northeast. Without removing them from his eyes, he raised one arm as a signal, and his companions sensed something spectacular. As he turned to dash toward them, Stefansson rushed forward to meet him and climbed the ice hummock himself, trying to keep his excitement in check as his eyes swept the northeastern horizon. There was no mistaking what he saw: new, uncharted land "stretching blue and white and tawny gray from northeast to east by north."

He could not contain himself. This was the prize that he had been seeking for the best part of a decade—the last great triumph left for an Arctic explorer, now that the Pole and the Passage had been achieved. "I have always thought," he was to write, "that the discovery of land which human eyes have never seen, is about the most dramatic of possible experiences. I don't pretend to be used to it or past the thrills that go with it." It was this promise, now fulfilled, that had caught the imagination and brought the support of the stolid prime minister, Robert Borden.

Having planted a flag and taken possession of the new island for Canada, Stefansson named it Brock Island after the head of the Geological Survey, a generous gesture considering the survey's earlier objection to him as leader of the Canadian Arctic Expedition. It turned out that Brock Island was actually two islands, the second larger than the first. Stefansson named this one Borden Island after his sponsor. Many years later it was found that Borden Island also was two islands. The second was named for Mackenzie King.

The world applauded his triumph, especially in Canada, whose prime minister exulted that many thousands of square miles of territory had been added to the country. But for what? Borden and Stefansson were both held captive by a nineteenth-century conceit: that the acquisition of real estate, in peace or in war, is conducive to success or victory. It was a principle familiar to every schoolchild who sang "Land of Hope and Glory," with its wistful hope that "wider still and wider shall thy bounds be set." As Stefansson caught his first tantalizing glimpse of Brock Island, a savage war in Europe was making that concept obsolete. Thousands of young lives were being snuffed out in a futile attempt to gain a few yards of No Man's Land or a few acres of mud and wire. If Stefansson was a hero, it was not because he found a few chunks of barren rock for a country that had too much already; it was because, like a long-distance champion, he set out against all odds, and in the face of bitter criticism, to do the impossible, and he succeeded.

The party headed south again and reached Stefansson's base at Cape Kellett. Once again the outside world had given up the explorer for dead. Stefansson must have enjoyed the weird little scene that took place on the shore when the schooner *Polar Bear* arrived. As he strolled along the beach to meet the dinghy from the ship, he could overhear

108

the men in the boat discussing his identity. "He's not an Eskimo," said one. "He's got field glasses." Then he heard Constable Parsons of the Mounted Police, one of the party, exclaim, "That's Stefansson." Louis Lane, captain of the *Polar Bear,* shook his head. "Don't you ever think it. The fish ate him long ago." Stefansson's identity was established only when the dinghy was a few yards from the shore. Lane immediately shouted to an orderly, "Don't a damn one of you move till I shake hands with him!"

Stefansson chartered the *Polar Bear* from Lane and took it to Herschel Island, where he was "rescued" again, having been presumed dead. There he learned that Ottawa had issued orders to the Southern Party to pack up, but to try to learn the exact nature of his fate before returning to civilization in 1916. But Stefansson was determined to stay in the North. "In spite of the lack of renewed authority, I decided that, since I was not dead, Ottawa would, if the facts were known, approve of my course." Stefansson ignored the order, bought the *Polar Bear* outright, and headed back north again. The government had other, more serious problems to contend with than the fate of one recalcitrant explorer. With the war in Europe siphoning off the country's richest resources, who could be overly concerned with the fate of one man in the chilly waters of the Beaufort Sea?

The breach with Anderson was not healed, nor would it ever be. In Anderson's view Stefansson's explorations were mere grandstanding; what he really wanted and needed was notoriety. "I've wasted three years of my life on your fool errands," he snapped when, at Collinson Point, Stefansson had tried to get some support for his first ice journey. The explorer's championing of the Inuit and the Inuit way of life irritated Anderson. To him, the white northerners—missionaries, police, trappers—were far superior to the natives. They hadn't even bothered to learn the Inuit tongue. How could Stefansson berate him for failing to appreciate the verities of the Inuit's communal life? His leader's insistence that he and the others turn in their personal diaries and refrain from writing for any publication convinced him that the expedition was no more than "a newspaper and magazine exploiting scheme."

Anderson, a shy and conservative scientist, was clearly envious of Stefansson's genius for turning accounts of his adventures into hard cash. He himself had no such talent, realized it, even mourned it. "Whenever I think of 'exploring' I get disgusted with it," he wrote to his wife, ". . . because I haven't any talent for making it pay. There are a good many things I like to do for the work's sake, but I get sort of panic stricken when I think of having to tell about it afterward. . . ." Nor could he stomach Stefansson's devil-may-care attitude to possible disaster.

Anderson's antipathy toward his leader was fuelled by his wife, Bella, whom he had married in 1913 after the earlier expedition. She had followed him to Nome where she gave birth to a baby who died within three days. After that, she wanted no more of the Arctic. She was convinced that her husband was being badly underpaid for the work he was doing and the fact that his name was not on the title page of *My Life with the Eskimo*—for which he had done considerable work and writing—added to her antagonism. In one of her letters to Stefansson she made it clear that she "expected more from the expedition than a tiny salary and a baby's grave."

Stefansson, meanwhile, had discovered two more new islands farther to the east of Borden Island—Meighen Island, which he named for Borden's successor as party leader, Arthur Meighen—and Lougheed Island, named for Sir James Lougheed, leader of the Conservative Party in the Senate.

It was not easy for the Canadian government to pry him out of his beloved Arctic. Ottawa wanted the expedition to wind up in 1916, but in April, the Minister of the Naval Services admitted to the Commons that it would not be over for another year. In June 1917, Ottawa ordered Stefansson, who was at Herschel Island, to return home, and that August, the minister gave another assurance to the Commons that it would all soon be over. But the stubborn explorer continued to linger, using a variety of excuses.

He was planning another ice expedition in the spring of 1918 at the age of thirty-nine when he was felled by a series of illnesses—pleurisy,

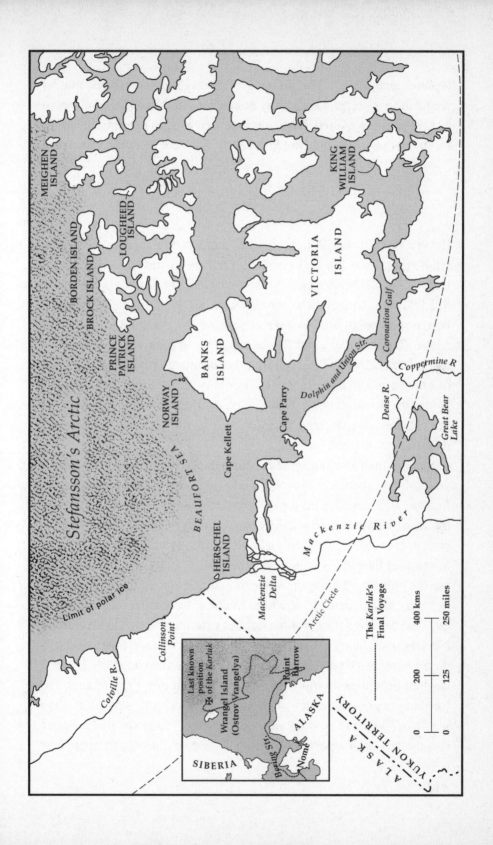

Stefansson's Arctic

MEIGHEN ISLAND

BORDEN ISLAND

BROCK ISLAND

LOUGHEED ISLAND

PRINCE PATRICK ISLAND

KING WILLIAM ISLAND

VICTORIA ISLAND

Coronation Gulf

Coppermine R

NORWAY ISLAND

BANKS ISLAND

Dolphin and Union Str.

Dease R.

Great Bear Lake

Cape Parry

Cape Kellett

BEAUFORT SEA

Limit of polar ice

HERSCHEL ISLAND

Mackenzie River

Mackenzie Delta

Collinson Point

Colville R.

Arctic Circle

The Karluk's Final Voyage

400 kms

250 miles

200

125

0

0

Last known position of the Karluk

Wrangel Island (Ostrov Vrangelya)

Point Barrow

ALASKA

SIBERIA

Bering Str.

Nome

ALASKA

YUKON TERRITORY

typhoid, pneumonia. The police at Herschel were convinced that he would die and shipped him off by dogsled to Fort Yukon, Alaska, where he eventually recovered. Finally he was well enough to leave the North. He did not realize it then, but his years of Arctic exploration were over.

—THREE—

Robert Borden was delighted with Stefansson's discovery of new lands; that, after all, had been the premise of the Canadian Arctic Expedition. The Geological Survey was less enchanted. Budgeted at $75,000, the expedition eventually cost the government half a million. At one point, Stefansson had promised to give Anderson control of the Southern Party, but that never came to pass. His resistance of authority, his habit of disregarding government orders, his dismissal of science as less important than discovery ensured that the Canadian government would never again employ him. It is significant that of the six honorary degrees awarded him in the course of his career, only one came from Canada.

Stefansson had taken no salary from the government during the six years of the expedition. Now he had to find some means of support. In London, before setting off for the Arctic, he had met Ernest Shackleton, the Antarctic hero, who told him to get an agent and go on the lecture circuit. He took Shackleton's advice. Lecturing appealed to him, and not just for the money at three hundred dollars a lecture; he wanted to use the platform to promote some of his ideas about the North.

It was an exhausting schedule. In one twenty-three-day period in 1921, he delivered twenty-three lectures in as many towns in California, Nevada, and Utah. He was a gifted speaker, never used notes, and seldom knew exactly what he was going to say until he started, often beginning with something he had read in that day's newspaper. He liked to grab his audience with a provocative opening statement. One was "An adventure is a sign of incompetence," followed by his belief that the leader of a good expedition should be able to anticipate and prepare for anything that might go wrong—advice he did not always follow himself.

One of Stefansson's weaknesses, if it can be called that, was his impatience with detail and his disinclination to follow any rule that he did not lay down for himself. All this time, the government was trying to get from him the official report of the Northern Party's six years with the Canadian Arctic Expedition. But Stefansson, who had written so romantically about the Arctic on his own terms, balked at the idea of turning out a dry-as-dust official document. This, of course, was the understanding he originally had with Ottawa, and it certainly would have been a valuable addition to the meagre store of knowledge available about the High Arctic. But the report was never written, which meant that the activities and scientific findings of the Northern Party did not appear in the fourteen-volume published report from the expedition, which dealt solely with activities of the Southern Party.

Something had changed Stefansson since those early days when he had been an enthusiastic young anthropologist. Certainly it had been necessary to use the media and the lecture platform to arouse interest in the Arctic and to raise funds for his northern ventures. But there was more than that. One cannot dispute Anderson's conviction that Stefansson loved the attention. He loved to see himself extolled in the press. He enjoyed the applause of the large audiences that turned up to hear about his adventures and his philosophy. Certainly he wanted to find new lands and to explode old accepted theories. But he also wanted to be known as the greatest of the Arctic explorers. In the end, that became his primary goal. Popular books took precedence over unexciting official reports. As a contemporary anthropologist, E. S. Burch, has pointed out, while praising Stefansson's exploratory work, "His results were far below what one has a right to expect, given his training and the extraordinary opportunities he had. . . . Stefansson was just too interested in being an explorer and an iconoclast . . . and not interested enough to put together a systematic ethnographical account of what he had learned."

Stefansson's response to Ottawa's repeated requests was to announce that he was preparing his own book on the subject—and that seemed to be that. The book was *The Friendly Arctic,* a 784-page tome published in 1921 that portrayed the North as a kind of polar Mediterranean and brought choruses of praise and damnation from his supporters and critics. Robert Borden himself supplied the introduction, in which he wrote, "As a result of the Expedition many thousands of square miles have been added to the territory of Canada, much interesting material of great scientific value has been secured, unknown areas of vast extent have been explored, and many illusions with respect to Arctic conditions have been dissipated."

Two of America's greatest living explorers, Adolphus Greely and Robert Peary, praised the book. "By combining great natural, physical and mental ability, with hard practical common sense," Peary wrote, "he has made an absolute record." Greely was equally enthusiastic.

Balanced against this testimony were the comments of another world-class explorer, the navigator of the Northwest Passage, Roald Amundsen. "Of all the fantastic rot I have ever heard this comes close to the top," Amundsen told the press. The book, he declared, was a "dangerous distortion of the real conditions. . . . [His] foolish tale also injured the prospects of more serious explorers."

Stefansson admitted that sometimes he "oversold the merits of Arctic lands and seas." As an explorer, he was as much a journalist as a scientist (when as a young man he had served briefly as a reporter on two newspapers, one the venerable *Boston Evening Transcript*). He knew a good story when he saw one and must have been torn by the need to keep his narrative readable and exciting while at the same time maintaining his thesis that a white man could survive in the Arctic if he lived like an Inuk. That, of course, ignored the truth—that the Inuit themselves often starved, were injured on the ice, or fell through the crusted surface.

The very title of the book betrays him. It certainly helped the sales, but there were times when the Arctic was distinctly unfriendly, as the survivors of the *Karluk* could testify. It was true that fresh caribou meat eaten half raw was an antiscorbutic, but there were times when the caribou didn't come. It was true that Arctic weather had been given a bad name; it was often just as cold or colder in Minnesota. But it was also true that sometimes the dogs froze or starved to death.

114

Both *My Life with the Eskimo* and *The Friendly Arctic* are optimistic books. But Stefansson could not conceal the hardships and the danger in his kind of Arctic travel. There were times when men and dogs were forced to go on half-rations. Stefansson wrote of several narrow escapes from falling through the ice. In May of 1916 he broke through the snow cover into a crevasse, an accident that left him black and blue with a sprained ankle. That set his plans back by nine weeks and confined him to a sledge for thirty-seven days.

His thesis was simple (and some would say simple-minded): anyone could live in the Arctic if he adopted the methods of the natives who had been doing just that for hundreds of years. Yet he was ignoring the implications and contradictions of his message. He wanted those Inuit who had not been corrupted by white influences (such as the Copper Eskimos) to be left alone to live their traditional lives and at the same time seemed to be advocating the very opposite: more and more people thriving in the North. He believed that anyone could live off the land, and he certainly proved it in his own case. But there was one bitter truth that he brushed aside: living off the land is also time consuming. The ceaseless hunt for food interferes with ethnological and anthropological studies. Even a crack shot must wait for and stalk his prey. To catch a seal takes infinite patience; one must sit quietly beside the breathing hole in the ice and wait until the animal appears. Nor did Stefansson consider the likelihood that hundreds of potential hunters would wreak havoc on the caribou and muskox herds in the North. In my day in the Yukon, you could buy wild venison from the butcher and order it from a restaurant menu, but the time came when the herds were so diminished that the laws had to be changed to prevent its sale to the public in the interests of conservation.

The Friendly Arctic was Stefansson's most popular book. Its real value lay in the light it shed on an unknown land and a misunderstood people. His readers were no doubt surprised to learn that the Inuit are just as susceptible to cold as white men; that only 10 percent of them live in snow houses; that the average snowfall in the Arctic is less than half, and in some places less than a quarter, of that in Montreal,

Petrograd, Chicago, Warsaw, northwest Germany, or the Highlands of Scotland; and that the Arctic seas, which Clement Markham, a former president of the Royal Geographical Society, referred to as "the polar ocean without life," have as much life per cubic mile as any other ocean.

The most controversial aspect of Stefansson's iconoclasm was his advocacy of an all-fat-and-meat diet. Fresh meat, cooked rare with plenty of fat, he insisted, was a better antiscorbutic than the traditional bottled lime (rarely lemon) juice the British navy had been using since the days of Captain Cook. But Stefansson went further. Man, he insisted, can thrive forever on an all-fat, all-meat diet. This was the diet of the Inuit with whom he had lived and thrived. It bears a certain similarity to a number of present-day diets that also eschew carbohydrates.

Challenged by a group of doctors at the Russell Sage Institute of Pathology, Stefansson agreed to test his dietary theories for a year. He and a young Danish disciple, Karsten Andersen, entered Bellevue Hospital in New York, were carefully examined by doctors there, and set out on a supervised all-meat-and-fat diet for a year. They were at first confined to the hospital under supervision and allowed no cereals, vegetables, or fruit, and only water as a beverage. After six weeks they were allowed to venture out but always under the supervision of an orderly or a nurse—human guinea pigs, each with his own keeper.

During this experiment, Stefansson continued to lecture, often arriving on stage with a couple of lamb chops in his pocket. The pair took regular runs in Central Park, and it was noticed that during this period their stamina increased. After a year both men were tested again and showed no ill effects from the all-meat diet. "I never felt better in my life," Stefansson announced, and for the rest of his life continued to concentrate on meat. As one dietitian put it, "he made an enormous stride toward liberalizing our ideas about diet," a statement with which today's committed vegetarians might take issue.

In 1921, Stefansson was planning another expedition to the Arctic under the sponsorship of the Canadian government. But Ottawa dithered. It developed that Ernest Shackleton wanted to head any new expedition, claiming that Stefansson had told him he did not intend to lead it. Stefansson was convinced that Shackleton had double-crossed him; at any rate, the proposal came to nothing. Always a controversial figure among the bureaucrats, Stefansson had his enemies in the Geological Survey. He had, indeed, been blackballed when he tried to join the prestigious Rideau Club in Ottawa, an astonishing development considering his accomplishments and the fact that Borden himself had sponsored his application, with the Speaker of the House seconding it. His attempt to settle Lapland reindeer on Baffin Island in 1920 ended in failure because the lichen that grew on Baffin turned out to be unsuitable for the herds. Nobody, apparently, had thought to test it.

These were not good years for Stefansson's reputation, though he continued to look ahead with his usual confidence. In *The Northward Course of Empire,* published in 1922, he foresaw the changes that would come to Arctic exploration through air and undersea travel. The book did poorly but his predictions would turn out to be on the button.

That year the *Karluk* disaster returned to haunt him. His old *bête noire*, Anderson, kept it alive until his critics publicly re-examined the tragedy. There were some who charged, wrongly, that Stefansson had left the ship to save his own skin, knowing she was doomed. That jibe was far-fetched, but some *Karluk* survivors continued to be critical, especially William Laird McKinlay, who spent a lifetime working on an anti-Stefansson book that he finally published in 1976. McKinlay believed that the expedition was ill-conceived, carelessly planned, badly organized, haphazardly manned, and almost totally lacking in leadership.

Piled on top of all that was a new tragedy centring again on Wrangel Island, the spot from which some of the *Karluk* survivors had been rescued. Stefansson wanted to claim the island for Canada and in 1921 applied for permission to do so from Prime Minister Arthur Meighen, Borden's successor. There were objections, and when the government stalled, Stefansson, with his usual impetuosity, decided to go ahead anyway—a fateful decision. He formed the Stefansson Arctic Exploration and Development Company for the purpose of exploring the island and claiming it for Canada with a view to colonization.

On September 9, 1921, four young men and one Inuit seamstress led by Allan Crawford, a twenty-year-old University of Toronto science student, set off for Wrangel Island by way of Nome on the schooner *Silver Wave*. For the next two winters, nothing was heard of the expedition.

In April 1923, Stefansson appeared before the Canadian cabinet, but the cabinet dithered. Was Wrangel Island part of Canada? On May 23, the explorer left for London to meet with the Minister for the Colonies and to raise funds for a rescue attempt. There matters moved with glacial speed. The Foreign Office wanted to sound out other nations about the sovereignty of the island. Nothing more could be done, Stefansson was told, until the Canadian prime minister arrived for the Imperial Conference of Prime Ministers in September. On September 1, he received the tragic news that all four men had perished—three in a vain attempt to reach the Siberian shore, the fourth of scurvy on Wrangel Island. Only the seamstress, Ada Blackjack, and the inevitable ship's cat survived.

The young men who set off so enthusiastically to occupy a distant Arctic island did not heed Stefansson's instructions to take along a little umiak (a wooden boat covered with animal skin) and more than one Inuit companion to do duty as seamstress and hunter. The tragedy, as Stefansson was to write, was "a fearful blow." It played hob with his "friendly Arctic" theory. But it can also be argued that Stefansson's own impetuosity in mounting the expedition before being sure of the island's sovereignty contributed to the tragedy. It would have made more sense to get those essential details cleared up before embarking on what proved to be another wild goose chase. As for Wrangel Island, Russia claimed it, and nobody raised objections—the Canadians because they thought it worthless and the British because they did not want to jeopardize relations with the new Soviet Union. Four young men had gone to their deaths on a distant speck in the ocean that nobody really cared about—and also because nobody really seemed to care about them.

Throughout these unfortunate events, Stefansson continued to write and lecture on the North, apparently unruffled by Canadian criticism and certainly buoyed up by American hero worship. His literary output was prodigious: no fewer than thirty-nine books and close to four hundred magazine and newspaper articles, some for popular publications such as *Harper's, Maclean's,* and *Physical Culture* but others for scholarly publications including the *Geographical Journal,* the *Quarterly Review,* and *Nature.* He was elected president of the Explorers' Club, received medals from half a dozen geographical societies, and attained the supreme journalistic accolade—a two-part profile in *The New Yorker* magazine.

The North continued to hold him in thrall. He never stopped preaching the advantages of living as the Inuit did and even published an entire book on diet. He was for thirteen years adviser to Pan American Airlines, which was pioneering trans-polar flights. When the Second World War broke out he became an adviser to William J. Donovan, coordinator of information for the United States, and, through him, produced a memorandum regarding Alaskan petroleum resources. From this came the notorious Canol enterprise to pump oil by pipeline from Norman Wells on the Mackenzie River to Whitehorse. Stefansson, ever the iconoclast, damned the development as "the worst possible route." It turned out he was right; the Canol project was a boondoggle that gobbled tax money to no great purpose and was allowed to fall into disrepair after the war.

By this time he was married. The nuptials took place on April 10, 1940, when he was in his sixty-second year. The bride, Evelyn Schwartz Baird, whom he met in Greenwich Village where he was living at the time, was a vivacious, dark-eyed, twenty-eight-year-old divorcee and sometime folksinger. She was, in her new husband's view, "a perfect human being" and one who coaxed him out of what had been a confirmed bachelorhood. Bachelor, yes, but by no means unattracted to women. He had enjoyed a passionate five-year affair with Betty Brainerd, whose father had helped boost Seattle during the Klondike gold rush. "I love you with every atom of my being," she once wrote to him. Stefansson, on his part, told her that "the only thing that I care to know about you is that you love me." Alas, the romance faded in

119

New York, partly because of Stefansson's indifference to the letters she sent him. "Silence is not an alarm, but a rebuff," she told him.

Stefansson was exceedingly discreet about his several attachments. He enjoyed a seventeen-year love affair with Fannie Hurst, by far the best-selling woman novelist in the country (if not the world). But in his autobiography he scarcely mentioned her; she was little more than a name in passing, although he did dedicate one book to her.

The subject of Stefansson's "marriage" to Pannigabluk always remained off limits. Evelyn Stefansson tried to breach her husband's wall of discretion but failed. Her intense curiosity about Pannigabluk led her to question Richard Finnie about her. On one occasion when Stefansson's mixed-breed grandchildren wrote him a letter, his only instruction to his wife was not to answer it. Gisli Palsson, an Icelandic anthropologist, suggested a possible explanation in *The Intimate Arctic,* pointing out that Pan, as Stefansson called her, often travelled with Rudolph Anderson and might well have had an intimate relationship with him, too, a speculation that would have infuriated the explorer.

Stefansson and his young wife moved to a picturesque brownstone house in Manhattan and also acquired a farm in Vermont. There, Stefansson continued his voluminous correspondence with a wide variety of prominent figures on both sides of the Atlantic, ranging from Orville Wright, the first man to fly an airplane, to Sir Arthur Conan Doyle, the creator of Sherlock Holmes. He never threw away a scrap of paper and made carbon copies of every letter he wrote, many of which he sent off to friends. By the time he was eighty, his letters to such prominent figures as the playwright Sir James Barrie, former president Theodore Roosevelt, and the poet Robert Frost, whom he resembled physically, occupied no fewer than one hundred vertical files. As a book lover, Stefansson had few peers; he bought so many they kept him poor. In his Village days he had had to occupy two apartments, the walls of both lined from floor to ceiling with shelves crammed with thousands of books and pamphlets—a private library that was one of the largest in the country. When he moved to a house, he was forced to buy a second one next door to contain it.

In the immediate post-war years, with the support and financial backing of the United States Office of Naval Research, Stefansson embarked on a monumental project that was close to his heart. He would oversee, edit, and contribute to an Arctic encyclopedia—twenty volumes, six million words—dealing with every aspect of the world north of the Arctic Circle. Because of his reputation as an explorer he was able to enlist the support of prominent scientists, historians, civil servants, and museum directors and to secure the co-operation of major universities and such business enterprises as the Hudson's Bay Company and Pan American Airlines.

It was an ambitious but worthwhile venture, doomed, alas, by the international politics of the post-war era. By 1949, he and his wife, who was his chief assistant, had put in two years of work on the project and shipped manuscripts for the first two volumes to the Johns

Stefansson and his wife, Evelyn, supervising the unloading of his Arctic collection at Dartmouth College. The explorer kept a copy of every letter he wrote.

Hopkins University Press. Suddenly, without explanation, Washington cancelled Stefansson's contract and the project was abandoned. Why? He was never able to get a reason for the disaster.

Evelyn Stefansson was convinced, with good reason, that McCarthyism and the Cold War were to blame. Stefansson, who had secured the co-operation of both the British and the Canadian governments, had been hoping to enlist the USSR, which controlled 49 percent of the Arctic. The political situation made direct contact impossible, but he was able to subscribe to a good many Russian-language and English-language Soviet publications. When he hired a young American translator who had spent his final undergraduate year studying in Moscow, Washington wanted the assistant fired. Stefansson, with the backing of General George Marshall, refused. That, together with his long friendship with Owen Lattimore, the target of McCarthy's most vicious attacks, was certainly behind the debacle.

Stefansson was devastated by this body blow. The encyclopedia was to have been his monument, the culmination of his ambitions, the crowning achievement of his career, and would have confirmed for all time his reputation as the greatest of all polar experts. "There was nothing to do but reduce our staff, give up what we could of our New York accommodations, and thereafter do practically nothing except type, file and otherwise try to salvage manuscripts, notes, maps and pictures."

He could no longer afford the expense of housing this accumulation of research or his huge library. His only recourse was to turn the Stefansson Collection over to Dartmouth College in New England. There the explorer became a conspicuous figure on campus, hatless and coatless in spite of the New Hampshire winter and easily recognizable because of his shock of white hair. He put his final frustrations behind him. Always soft-spoken, he would lard his conversation with epigrams such as "False modesty is better then none," and also with an enviable store of jokes. He was fond of quoting his youthful hero, Robert Ingersoll: "My brain may not be the best in the world but it is so conveniently placed for home use." To those who wondered why he had never gone to the North Pole, he would reply: "I'm a scientist, not a tourist." Richard Finnie described him as "ceaselessly expounding, but informal, jovial, trusting, warm-hearted, considerate, and generous." Stefansson did not hold grudges in spite of the calumny visited upon him. He never spoke harshly of anyone, even his arch-enemy, Anderson. In *The Friendly Arctic*, Stefansson had high praise for Anderson and played down the mutiny at Collinson Point.

Evelyn Stefansson did her best to heal the breach between the two. She had been told that Anderson had been heard talking wistfully of a reconciliation. When she saw him at the first Alaska Science Conference, she noted that "he looked stooped and sad."

Stefansson on the Dartmouth College campus showing students how to build an iglu. In one sense, he never really left the North.

"Suppose he wants to make up?" she told her husband. "Wouldn't it be a pity if he had no opportunity? Help him, Stef. Go over and say hello." Stefansson was reluctant, but to please his wife he walked across the room to Anderson. She followed in his wake, "slightly exalted in my new role as peacemaker." But when her husband extended his hand, Anderson turned on his heel and walked away. "I wanted to die," she remembered. It was the only time she saw Anderson and the last time her husband did.

Stefansson loved a party—an enjoyment he had picked up from the Inuit. At a dinner in late August 1962 for an old Greenland friend, his wife found him in marvellous form, merry and witty and stimulated by his guest. They discussed falconry, and warmed by good wine, took their coffee into the living room. Stefansson reached for a cup; his hand trembled, and the coffee splashed from the cup before he painstakingly replaced it on the table. His wife went to him at once and found that he was unable to speak, felled by a massive stroke with accompanying paralysis. It seemed physically impossible for him to stagger from the room, but, Evelyn Stefansson remembered, "his enormous dignity, which would not permit him to ruin a perfect evening by collapsing in front of his guests, combined with a strong act of will, had powered his exit and enabled him to do at the close of his life what he had often done during it—the impossible!"

Dignity, certainly, but also a fair measure of pride. He had, after all, successfully cultivated his image as the most rugged of the polar explorers, the one who always seemed to return from the dead, even in Fort Yukon when his end seemed certain. Through the eyes of a younger generation we get a final glimpse of him, bending over on the snow-covered Dartmouth campus, cutting out snow blocks and fashioning a miniature iglu—a blond Eskimo to the last and still a prisoner of the North. He could not bear to have anyone see him fail or falter, and so he struggled with the stroke only to fall into a deep coma until, less than a week later, on the morning of August 26, 1962, his doctors reported that in his eighty-third year, the last of the old-time explorers had finally gone to his rest.

CHAPTER 3
The Persevering Lady

Jane Griffin, the future Lady Franklin, at twenty-four.

From *Portrait of Jane* by Frances J. Woodward, Hodder and Stoughton, 1951

—ONE—

In September 1859, when Leopold M'Clintock's little schooner *Fox* entered the English Channel from the mists of the Arctic labyrinth, Jane, Lady Franklin, hurried back from her mountain-climbing expedition in the Pyrenees to resume her role as one of the best known and most venerated women in England.

Her husband's fate and that of the 134 men he commanded in his search for the Northwest Passage had finally been established as a result of her own determined quest. Her twelve-year struggle to accomplish his rescue and, when that failed, to enshrine his memory as the greatest of all Northern explorers had touched off the most intense decade of Arctic exploration in history and caught the imagination of the world. It was now her purpose to ensure that posterity would hail him as the discoverer of the elusive Passage.

In that determination she did not lack for supporters. "She now holds the highest position of any English woman," her brother-in-law exclaimed, and that assessment was echoed by more independent observers. As Francis Spufford has written in *I May Be Some Time*, "No other nineteenth-century woman raised the cash for three polar expeditions, or had her say over the appointment of captains and lieutenants."

The *Daily Telegraph* called her "our English Penelope"—a reference to Odysseus's chaste and faithful wife, the heroine of the *Odyssey*. Benjamin Disraeli, referring to the successful discovery of her husband's expedition by M'Clintock on King William Island, noted that "these are deeds that will claim the pages of history and the name of the true heroine of the tale will never be forgotten."

"What the nation would not do," an Aberdeen editor wrote, "a woman did." The plaudits were indeed worldwide as she discovered when a group of natives paddled her up the Fraser River in the colony of British Columbia. The citizens of the town of Yale had hung a banner across the narrows emblazoned with the words "LADY FRANKLIN PASS." In the Sandwich Islands, Queen Emma sent her own chariot complete with footmen to convey her to her lodgings. In London, the Royal

Geographical Society awarded her its Founder's Medal, the first ever offered to a woman.

The object of this veneration was then approaching seventy. Since 1845 her life had been centred on the Canadian Arctic. Though she had never personally experienced the frozen world, she could not escape it. Now, as she prepared herself one more time to ensure her husband's place in history, she remained its prisoner.

She did not seek celebrity for herself; it sought her. Nor could she avoid it, much as she might have wished. She suffered from a shyness that made her shrink from personal publicity. She refused to have her photograph taken and was afflicted by recurring headaches that, in her youth, she described as "an excess of nervousness." She left no personal memoir, and there are only two portraits of her, both in chalk. The first drawing, made when she was twenty-four, shows a pleasant, if placid, young woman with a studied countenance, "artificially tranquil," to use her own expression. Indeed, she told the artist that "tranquility if not sadness was the habitual expression of my countenance for I feared she would give me a false, artificial simper which I would hate to see."

The second chalk drawing, made two decades later, shows a still attractive woman with only the suggestion of a double chin and no simper. John Franklin's wife was certainly not one to simper, but the drawing fails to reveal the steel in her character. She kept her looks well into middle age. One acquaintance remembered her shortly before she turned forty as "the most beautiful woman she had ever seen." At about the same time she attended a party where she produced "an extraordinary sensation" and "there was not a gentleman in the room who did not go up to ask Mr. Le Maistre [the host] in a whisper who that very pretty young lady was sitting on the sofa by the fire." This she reported in a letter to her fiancé, Captain John Franklin, explaining that he must not think it an instance of excessive vanity but related only to please him. It was one of close to two thousand letters that she turned out, often at great length, in her cramped and spidery handwriting. This vast collection is housed at the Scott Polar Research Institute in Cambridge and amplifies an astonishing shelf crammed with some two hundred hand-written journal-diaries, the main resource that Frances J. Woodward used in her brilliant and scholarly *Portrait of Jane,* the only biography of Lady Franklin ever written and one that can honestly be described as "definitive." I have seen this long shelf of journals and can only applaud the biographer for working her way through them. Much of this essay is based on her painstaking research.

Jane was late when it came to marriage, although that was not for lack of suitors; one of them was Peter Roget, whose name was later immortalized on the title page of his famous *Thesaurus.* Perhaps it was her innate shyness that held her aloof; equally likely might have been the prospect of losing her independence. At the age of twenty-eight, with no suitable husband in sight, she consoled herself with the resolution that "*whenever* I marry, *whoever* I marry, I will open my whole heart to him who will then possess supreme & exclusive dominion over it." In the same year she wrote: "Shall I really make a good wife as I intend to be? Or is it one of my romantic fancies to think that the supremest bliss of a woman is to be found in her sanctified affection towards her husband?" She was longing to be married but had no intention of marrying without love, and as her biographer has noted, "none of the numerous offers she received fulfilled that indispensable condition."

As the daughter of a well-to-do silk weaver she was able to travel and did so with her family—all travellers—to the Netherlands and the south of France. For all her life she was an inveterate wanderer, a kind of professional tourist to whom travel was a form of education. She wrote it all down in her journal, complete with tables of distances covered, lists of sights seen and sights unseen and of souvenirs bought and not bought, not to mention mountains climbed and unclimbed.

At home, she attended the lectures at the Royal Institution for the Advancement of Science, a series of subjects that ranged from magnetism and electricity to mechanics and optics. She dabbled briefly in phrenology, a great fad of the Victorian era, and did her best to learn French, Italian, shorthand, and even a few words of Arabic. She was an active member of the Book Society and read as many as three hundred books a year, but no novels.

When she first encountered Captain John Franklin in 1824 at the age of thirty-two, she was plain Jane Griffin. He was married to her friend Eleanor Anne Porden, a poetess of some consequence, the author of a prodigious epic, *Richard Coeur de Lion,* a two-volume tome of sixteen cantos. Eleanor was a fellow member of the Book Society and also of the Royal Institution's lecture series. She was also tiny, frail, and sickly, and therein lay her tragedy.

Even as John Franklin was preparing for his third voyage to the Arctic, his wife was dying of tuberculosis. It is difficult to know whether Franklin understood the seriousness of her condition. Certainly he was prepared, if necessary, to scrap his plans and remain at her side, but she would have none of it. She insisted that he carry on, and carry on he did. One week after he left, she succumbed.

When Franklin returned in 1827, the Griffin family, who had, as usual, been travelling about, this time in the Scandinavian countries, discovered that he had named Cape Griffin in their honour. That led to closer relations, which developed into an intimacy between the two and led to a dinner party with Jane seated at Franklin's right. The details seem to have been torn out of the notes she made for her journal "by some misguided relative." As Frances Woodward writes: "It is a great loss that we do not know how these diverse personalities grew to love each other."

"Diverse" is certainly the word. Franklin, in middle-age, was plump, balding, and bovine, scarcely the image of a dashing polar explorer or even a staunch sea captain. But it must be remembered that in this age of exploration, when the English were unlocking the secrets of darkest Africa, the mysterious East, and the chill channels of the Arctic labyrinth, they had an aura about them that made them instant celebrities like the movie stars and sports heroes of our own day. Franklin was as stolid as they come—conventional, unimaginative (at least in his letters to Jane), and ill at ease in the company of those outside his own tight circle. "One is even tempted to believe," Ms. Woodward has written, "that the most interesting thing about Franklin is his choice of wives."

What was it, then? What drew him to these two remarkably gifted women, and, more to the point, what was it that drew them to *him?* There was about Franklin a certain human kindness that was rarely apparent in the martinets who rose to command in His Majesty's navy. Franklin, quite literally, would not have hurt a mosquito. There was, as he put it, room enough for both of them in his world. Men were rarely flogged aboard the ships he commanded in that age of corporal punishment, and that speaks greatly in his favour. It was said that on those few occasions when he was reduced to using that form of discipline, he trembled from head to foot. He was highly moral without being prissy and actually believed in the principles of honour and duty that came with his calling. He was, in the best sense, a good man and a genuinely likeable one. Above all, as his biographer has put it, "he had essential nobility of character." If his honour was impugned, as it certainly would be within a few years of his marriage, he would not rest until it was restored, even if it meant returning, in advancing age, to the white hell of the Arctic maze.

In choosing Jane Griffin as his second wife, Franklin made an inspired choice. It was through her and because of her that this plodding and unexceptional explorer was hoisted to the pinnacle of the polar pantheon. It is interesting to speculate how things might have turned out had he remained a widower or chosen a different sort of woman as his consort. He is in the school books today, when many of his colleagues are half forgotten, through the stubborn and unceasing campaign of the indomitable Jane.

He had made three unimpressive forays into the Arctic. The first, in 1818, was an abortive attempt to reach the North Pole in which he served as second-in-command to David Buchan. That was called off as the result of a storm so savage that the expedition, instead of advancing toward the Pole, ended up two miles farther from it. The second was an unmitigated disaster. Franklin's task was to take a party overland from York Factory on Hudson Bay to Great Slave Lake and on to the mouth of the Coppermine River. From there its task was to map the unexplored Arctic coast using small boats.

Franklin's own published story of that second ghastly journey had caught the imagination of the English public. Yes, he had lost eleven men through starvation and in one case murder—a record in Arctic exploration—because of his dalliance and his reluctance to turn back when starvation faced him. He had done that without producing any tangible result. But of these dead men only one was an Englishman. Nine were French Canadian voyageurs while another was an Inuit, and they didn't really count. By this time he was the embodiment of the tragic hero that the English doted on: the man who had eaten his own boots, who had faced death with resolution and conquered it. On his third expedition, the one from which he had recently returned, he and his party explored and mapped more than a thousand miles of Arctic coast. For that he received the inevitable knighthood.

The Franklin search stands at the core of the age of exploration that marks the Victorian period. Without his wife's twelve-year campaign to seek out his fate and memorialize his achievements, would he now be a familiar name in the history books, outclassing such half-forgotten but more eminent fellow explorers as Parry, Rae, and Ross?

As Francis Spufford has written in his analysis of the effects of polar exploration on the English imagination, " . . . in her hands the network of sympathy and sentiment she inspired became a tool of redoubtable influence . . . she could blight or accelerate careers, bestow or withhold the sanction of her reputation. . . . When the Admiralty seemed torpid, or reluctant to act, she pushed; when search ships were dispatched on directions she disapproved of, she launched whispering campaigns against their commanders, and when, critically, the news from the Arctic threatened the moral image of Franklin's party, she fought to preserve the ground on which the ideals of womanhood and those of polar exploration coincided."

They were married in England and spent most of their honeymoon in Paris—a period she later deplored as a "career of vanity, trifling, and idleness"—while they waited for John to get his next command. Jane Griffin was "Mrs. Franklin" for a few short months. After her husband was knighted in 1829 she would be Lady Franklin. She gave herself to him, heart, soul, and pocketbook. There would be no marriage settlement; she had decided, with her usual firmness, that everything she had (it came to about £10,000) would be at her husband's disposal.

Before they married she had gone off to Russia on one of her many peregrinations with her father and two friends, and Franklin had wanted to accompany her. Her Victorian sensibilities, however, caused her to refuse "from a strong sense of impropriety in the arrangement, as well as from a conviction that we should all be placed in a number of awkward and disagreeable situations during long and rough voyages and journeys." Instead, she arranged to meet him in St. Petersburg. Had she been a little too assertive for a wife-to-be? She hastened to assure him in writing that she would always be a submissive spouse and suggested that he "put this letter by and turn it to account at some future time when I am in a rebellious mood; and upon this consideration I think you ought to feel infinitely obliged to me for furnishing you with so valuable a document."

Franklin turned down a commercial offer in Australia and stuck with the navy even if it meant languishing at half pay. At last, in the autumn of 1830, he was appointed commander of the twenty-eight-gun frigate *Rainbow* bound for Malta in the Mediterranean. It was a minor post, Jane thought, but it might be one he could use for his advancement. She urged him to use his new position "to resume your chieftainship in your own peculiar department." If he stuck with it, she suggested, and came back with an increase in credit and fame, "surely a ship when you liked to ask for it would be the least, and a natural reward for your services."

As the captain's wife she could not travel with him on his own ship, but she intended to follow him to the Mediterranean and eventually meet him in Malta. There she would be able to see him as much as possible even if war came. "I had much rather be in the midst of it, than sit brooding over disaster and bloodshed at home." She wouldn't be in anybody's way, she assured him, and "you will never find me any hindrance to the most strenuous, and energetic exertions you can make in your country's cause."

En route to Malta, she indulged her passion for visiting the odd corners of the foreign world, "doing what no European lady had done within living memory," Ms. Woodward wrote, penetrating North Africa as far as "the snow-white city of Tetuan" and living in a small, windowless Moorish house. This wanderlust never left her, and she pursued it during Sir John's many absences.

Invigorated by "the amazing tonic power of great excitement," she set off for Egypt and the Holy Land, riding on a donkey to Rosetta, and later to Nazareth. In all the time her husband was at the Mediterranean post, she never seemed to stand still save for her months on Malta with him: up the Nile from Alexandria to Cairo (where she visited a harem); by Austrian brigantine to the Holy Land; on a mule's back from Smyrna (Izmir) to Constantinople; on a mattress on the deck of a converted yacht out of Smyrna, where she lost her binoculars and handbags to the sea. She toured the Greek islands, climbed Mount Olympus, experienced an earthquake in Zante, picked a branch on the Mount of Olives, made a private expedition to the island of Cephalonia—ignoring the smallpox raging there after surviving the plague raging in Constantinople, walking the streets with vinegar up her nose and a parasol across her waist "to keep off all contact with stragglers."

"You have completely eclipsed me," her husband wrote admiringly at one point, "and almost every other traveller—females certainly."

His ships were always known as happy ships, and this one became famous throughout the navy as "the Celestial Rainbow" and also, with envy, as "Franklin's Paradise." That was not enough for Jane. In her many and detailed letters to her mate she continued to urge him to make more effort to achieve an Arctic command.

When his term of service ended in 1834, Franklin returned to England without her. He had no sooner landed than he put in an application for another ship. "Will you not give me credit for this premature application?" he asked in a letter to his wife, who did not join him for another year. He told her proudly about his audience with the King to report on Greek affairs. He also waited upon the First Lord of the Admiralty and the President of the Royal Society. "On reading all these details," he wrote to her a little proudly, "you will fancy my dearest, that your shy timid husband must have gathered some brass on his way home, or you will be at a loss to account for his extraordinary courage. What will you say on learning that I have done all but the truly official part principally because I knew you would have wished me to do so. . . ."

But then, in a later letter, he added a few soft words of reproach. Yes, of course he would rejoice to be sent north again, but there was also the matter of honour to be considered. With war against Russia on the distant horizon, this was not a time to leave his homeland on a mere adventure that would put him out of the Admiralty's reach. He did not want to go, he told her, "for the mere desire of travelling and still less for the mere empty shadow of increasing my fame."

He was eager for a command, but no command was offered. In March 1836, the Colonial Secretary dangled the prospect of a new post before him: lieutenant-governor of Antigua, a speck of an island in the Caribbean. He was flattered but insisted on consulting his wife, who was not flattered at all. To her, it was an unworthy assignment: close, indeed, to an insult. At her insistence he turned it down and, to the surprise and delight of both, received an immediate offer at twice the salary to become governor of Van Diemen's Land, now Tasmania, a large island off the southeast coast of Australia.

They embarked in August with high hopes. How could they foresee that the next six years would be the most painful they had known? On shipboard, Lady Franklin bustled about, running a Sunday School class for children, organizing evening lessons on natural history, practising shark fishing with a harpoon in hand. During a three-week stopover at the Cape of Good Hope, she climbed Table Mountain—four thousand feet, in a five-hour ascent—went off with a wagonload of tourists to investigate the South African interior, and studied everything from Hottentot burial customs to the Kaffir method of constructing the assegai.

After a "brisk but rather stormy passage" from the cape, they reached Van Diemen's Land on January 6, 1837. Their arrival was greeted with enthusiasm—a triumphal entry with three hundred horsemen and seventy carriages. But behind all this pomp and ceremony lay trouble. Van

Diemen's Land was a prison, and John Franklin now found that he was its reluctant warden. Some 40 percent of the population consisted of convicts, while large numbers of "free citizens" were former convicts. Under the transportation system, three thousand more arrived every year. The previous administration had gone along with this procedure, under which convicts worked out their sentences by being assigned to one of the colonists for a period of time under penalty of having to return to prison if they broke the rules. That was a form of slavery, but it had suited the previous governor, George Arthur, very well as it had his powerful colonial secretary, Captain John Montagu, who had married Arthur's niece. In this cozy, hidebound Tory establishment, Sir John and Lady Franklin stood out as disturbers of convention.

She was in no sense your typical governor's wife, content to turn up at public affairs in a fashionable frock and indulge in vapid conversation. She threw herself into a whirl of activity, visiting prison hospitals, forming a ladies' committee to reform female convicts, turning the governor's mansion into a veritable museum full of stuffed birds, aboriginal weapons, petrified fossils, and the like, and trying to launch an agricultural settlement for bona fide immigrants in the hope that Van Diemen's Land might eventually become a real colony and not a jail.

In all these varied ventures she got little encouragement from the political establishment and found herself thwarted time and again by the implacable Montagu. When she tried to start a college in New Norfolk the Colonial Secretary balked, insisting that public money could not be squandered on such a project. "A more troublesome interfering woman I never saw," he declared privately.

She could not escape criticism. When she tried to rid the island of snakes by offering a shilling a head out of her own pocket, her opponents sniffed that she was "puffed up with the love of fame and the desire of acquiring a name by doing what no one else does." A section of the press sneered at her as the power behind the throne. One newspaper went so far as to call her "a man in petticoats." There was an uproar when Franklin, on Montagu's advice, dismissed a popular surgeon for dereliction of duty. The doctor's friends, convinced that the

Lady Franklin at fifty-one.

From *This Errant Lady* by Penny Russell, National Library of Australia, 2002

dismissal was unjust, lobbied to have it reversed. Franklin vacillated—the same kind of vacillation that had postponed his decision to turn back in time on that earlier Arctic journey. Finally he recanted, to the fury of Montagu, who believed, probably rightly, that Jane Franklin was behind the move.

During this period, Lady Franklin indulged her prodigious wanderlust. She became the first woman to climb the four-thousand-foot Mount Wellington and the first to travel overland from Melbourne to Sydney. Her last expedition, to travel overland with a small party to McQuarrie Harbour on the island's west coast, was far more strenuous than anything she had ever attempted. The only white men who had tried it were escaped convicts, who perished in the attempt. The party followed a narrow foot track through jungle and forest, over gullies, river torrents, swamps, and morasses. After they left the last post of civilization they were faced with the six-mile valley of the Acheron River, which they were forced to cross at least twelve times.

She could face the natural obstacles of Van Diemen's Land with equanimity, but she could not deal with the campaign of obstructionism that the wily Colonial Secretary was waging against her husband and herself. The matter came to a head after Montagu wrote a pompous memorandum that came close to calling Franklin a liar and a weakling. Franklin fired him—"an act of public virtue" in his wife's view—or thought he had; but he soon realized that Van Diemen's Land was not a self-governing state. The matter could be settled only by an appeal to Lord Stanley, the Secretary of State for the Colonies. But on the same ship that carried Franklin's report on Montagu to England there was a special passenger—Montagu himself, armed with a sheaf of documents and memos telling his side of the story. His friends in the press backed him. One paper published an article titled "The Imbecile Reign of a Polar Hero"; another blamed the polar hero's wife: "Can anyone for a moment believe that she and her clique do not reign paramount here?"

In England, Montagu's careful manoeuvring paid off. As Montagu himself made clear, his line of defence with Lord Stanley was "that he was the victim of Lady Franklin's hatred, and she alone was the cause of his suspension." Stanley sided with Montagu and shot off what one observer called "a public horsewhipping" to the embattled explorer. Montagu got a copy and rushed it to Van Diemen's Land, where it was lodged in the Derwent Bank and its contents unofficially disseminated before Franklin himself saw it.

Franklin wanted out but was subjected to a further embarrassment when a newspaper arrived from England reporting that a new lieutenant-governor had been gazetted to replace him. It was two months before an official dispatch (already six months old) arrived to inform him that his term was at an end. By then his replacement had arrived. A lackadaisical colonial office and the primitive state of the overseas postal system had put him in an impossible position.

"GLORIOUS NEWS!" the *Colonial Times* exulted. That was the reaction of the establishment's anti-Franklin press, but the people of Van Diemen's Land did not agree. In January 1844, a crowd of two thousand well-wishers cheered the pair off when they embarked for England; more than ten thousand signed an address of farewell. A decade later, when Jane Franklin appealed for funds to help search for her lost husband, the Tasmanians contributed seventeen hundred pounds.

The entire experience had devastated them both. Franklin himself was close to a breakdown, and Jane was in a state of nervous prostration. How they must have wished they had accepted the lesser posting in Antigua! Now nothing would do but that the polar hero should tell his own side of this sorry tale in a pamphlet that few bothered to read. In England his Tasmanian troubles were small potatoes. He was still a hero to the public and to his Arctic cronies. But that wasn't enough for him and it wasn't enough for Lady Franklin. His honour was at stake, or so he believed. Some new feat of exploration was required to remove the stain of Montagu's perfidy. He had reached the nadir of his career, and his sixtieth year was approaching; he could not rest until he had redeemed himself. On his return to England he would, with his wife's exuberant support, launch a new expedition to discover the Northwest Passage.

Had Sir John Franklin accepted the original offer of a governorship in the Caribbean, the history of Arctic exploration might be remarkably different. The Great Search for his missing expedition, much of it instigated by the importunity of his persevering wife, dragged on for more than a dozen years. More than fifty ships were engaged in that search, untold funds were squandered, and lives were sacrificed in a hunt that covered the frozen world from Alaska to Baffin Bay. The Great Search also lifted the curtain over a labyrinth of islands that had been unexplored before it began.

Franklin's return to England in 1844 coincided with a new flurry of interest in the Northwest Passage, stimulated by John Barrow, Jr., the Admiralty bureaucrat responsible for England's great age of naval exploration. For fifteen years, from 1818 to 1833, no fewer than nine expeditions had been mounted by the Royal Navy to seek out this will-o'-the-wisp, making Edward Parry, John Ross, and Franklin the heroes of their days. None had been successful and interest in polar exploration was fading when James Clark Ross (John's nephew) and Francis Crozier returned in 1843 from a record-breaking voyage to Antarctica in two vessels especially built for polar travel, *Erebus* and *Terror.* They had penetrated farther south into the Antarctic region than any before them and were the talk of England. Barrow seized on the interest raised by this expedition to prepare detailed plans to use the same vessels to renew the search for the fabled Passage before some other nation beat the British to the prize.

The hope for some sea route linking the Atlantic to the Pacific went back to the fifteenth century, when it was seen as a shortcut to the riches of the Orient. As new discoveries caused the search for it to be moved farther and farther north, its practical value dwindled. What Barrow was seeking was an essentially useless channel (or series of channels) blocked by formidable barriers of ice and virtually unnavigable. As Francis Spufford has pointed out, more expeditions have managed to travel safely to the moon and return than had been able to navigate the Passage from sea to sea.

Sensible considerations did not weigh on Barrow, to whom the Passage was a symbol of all that was pure, noble, and courageous in Arctic exploration. Spufford quotes from Barrow's digest of exploration narratives, which he published in 1846 after his retirement. In it he singled out the moral accomplishments of the explorers—the way officers "exhibited the most able and splendid examples of perseverance under difficulties, of endurance under afflictions, and resignation under every kind of distress." That fitted the Victorian attitude toward morality. The Passage was seen as a glittering prize, but no longer for sordid commercial reasons. Discovery was venerated for its own sake. The Passage was to be conquered simply because it was there.

Franklin pushed hard to lead the proposed new expedition to search out the Passage, and his friends pushed too. His honour was at stake; the only way to restore it would be action in the pure, clean environment of the Arctic channels. As Parry put it to the navy, Franklin would die of disappointment if he didn't get the job. James Clark Ross was the logical choice, but he bowed out on what looked like a thin excuse: he didn't want to be separated from his new bride. That said, Jane Franklin did not lose the opportunity to play upon Ross's friendship for her husband and his sympathy with his situation. "If you do not go," she wrote to him, "I would wish Sir John to have it . . . and not to be put aside for his age. . . . I think he will be deeply sensitive if his own department should neglect him. . . . I dread exceedingly the effect on his mind. . . ."

Franklin was now an old man by the standards of the day. The Admiralty was doubtful, but the explorer's old Arctic comrade from an overland expedition, Dr. John Richardson, offered to sign a medical certificate indicating that his health was sound enough for any journey through frozen channels. Franklin admitted that he was too plump for overland travel but pointed out that the entire voyage would be by ship. His superiors sympathized, and in the end the Arctic explorer got the job because his friends felt sorry for him.

In February, Franklin's appointment was confirmed. The *Erebus* and the *Terror* would be the first ships in Arctic records to operate using adapted railway locomotive engines of twenty horsepower each and screw propellors. On board would be ample provisions for three years, which, Franklin claimed, could be stretched to five if necessary. There was no attempt to plan for unforeseen emergencies. No relief expeditions were contemplated since Franklin feared if they were the Admiralty might scrap the whole idea.

In the exuberance that marked the venture only two critical voices were raised. Old John Ross, the crusty Arctic survivor, wondered why so many men were needed to trace the Passage. This was the largest expedition so far to invade the polar world—134 men on two big ships. Ross thought one smaller steam vessel would be cheaper and more efficient, and he was right. When the Passage was finally conquered just over half a century later, Roald Amundsen succeeded with a single small schooner and only seven men. Ross urged Franklin to leave depots of provisions and perhaps a boat or two at various points, should he be trapped or wrecked, a sensible piece of advice that Franklin dismissed as an absurdity.

An eccentric surgeon-naturalist, Richard King, who had written a book on the Arctic coast, also had his reservations. The best way to find the Passage, he insisted, was to take a party of no more than six men overland along the coastline from the mouth of the Great Fish River. But King was ignored by the naval hierarchy who were committed to cumbersome sea voyages in large ships—the larger the better.

On May 19, 1845, the expedition set off. Aboard the *Erebus,* John Franklin's daughter by his first marriage, Eleanor, noticed that a dove had settled on one of the masts. "Everyone was pleased with the good omen," she told her stepmother, "and if it be an omen of peace and harmony, I think there is every reason of its being true."

Jane Franklin's niece, Sophy Cracroft, was beside her aunt on the pier to wave one last goodbye as Franklin signalled his farewell with a handkerchief. His only worry was his wife. Could she endure his absence? From Sophy he had extracted a promise: that she would stay by her side until he returned. For the next thirty years the faithful niece rarely let her aunt out of her sight, travelling in her footsteps from Hong

Sir John Franklin as he looked at the height of his fame.

Kong to Sitka, Alaska, and rejecting all suitors who might have interfered with what she considered a higher cause.

And so they waited, spending their winters in England, expecting news from the Arctic, and their summers abroad: in France (whose government listed Franklin's name at the Rouen Customs House as among the world's most famous navigators), and in the West Indies and the United States, where Lady Franklin performed her usual round of inspecting hospitals, schools, factories, and other institutions and also managed to climb Mount Washington.

In spite of this hectic itinerary she could not take her mind off the Arctic. "We have now given up all expectation of hearing from Papa this year," Eleanor wrote to a friend. "In October or Novr next I trust we shall either see or hear from him."

To old John Ross, Jane wrote, "I dare not be sanguine as to their success—indeed the very thought seems to me presumptuous, so entirely absorbed is my soul in aspirations for their *safety* only." And, if they didn't come back as planned, would Ross be the man to go in search of them?

Ross, whose earlier skepticism in 1844 had caused him to promise Franklin that he would mount a search if needed, wrote to the Lords of the Admiralty that if Franklin hadn't managed to reach Bering Strait by this time, his ships must be imprisoned in the ice. He wrote again the following month suggesting that it was time to take steps for relief; but the Admiralty fobbed him off, declaring that they would offer rewards to Hudson's Bay traders and whalers to be on the lookout for the expedition, and that was all.

In June, the difficult Dr. King again entered the picture. He asked the Colonial Secretary for permission to follow the Great Fish River and guide members of the missing expedition who might have, he thought, been forced to abandon their ships, to depots of food. King, not being a navy man and considered a bit of a nuisance, which he was, got nowhere. "I do not desire that he be the person employed," Jane Franklin told Ross, who had volunteered to lead a rescue expedition that the government was belatedly considering. At the very least, she hoped, the

Sir John Franklin in middle age, an old man by the standards of his day.

government would authorize the Hudson's Bay Company "to explore those parts which you . . . cannot immediately do." As Ms. Woodward has argued, if King's experience and Jane's instinct had been immediately followed, some of Franklin's men might have been rescued.

But though time was running out, the navy dawdled. Franklin had three years' supplies when he sailed for the Arctic in 1845. Belatedly, in January 1848, the little supply ship *Plover* set off for Bering Strait carrying more supplies for the missing ships, only to be delayed for a year in transit. With *Plover* went a letter from Jane, who warned her friends not to write anything "that can distress his mind. . . . Who can tell whether they will be in a state of body or mind to bear it." The letter was returned as were the others she dispatched over the next several years. Meanwhile, Sir John Richardson was heading off on an overland expedition to examine the north coast of the continent from the Mackenzie estuary to the Coppermine. She wanted to accompany him but was dissuaded from that venture. "It would have been a less trial to me to come after you," she wrote to Franklin in a letter that was returned, "as I was at one time tempted to do, but I thought it my duty & my interest to remain, for might I not have missed you & wd it have been right to leave Eleanor—yet if I had thought you to be ill, nothing should have stopped me." Instead, she put up her own money—three thousand pounds—as a reward to any whaler who might find the lost expedition.

In May 1848, the government's own search expedition—two big ships, *Enterprise* and *Investigator*—finally set off under the overall command of James Clark Ross, who had reversed his firm decision never to go north again. As usual it carried a letter from Jane: "My dearest love, May it be the will of God if you are not restored to us earlier this year that you should open this letter & that it may give you comfort in all your trials. . . . I try to prepare myself for every trial which may be in store for me, but dearest, if you ever open this, it will be I trust because I have been spared the greatest of all. . . ."

For all of 1847 she had made no entries in her journal; the next year her comments were entirely bound up in the search. She was now a public figure, a state she accepted in spite of her shyness. As Francis Spufford writes, "Knowledge of her name established rules for conversation with her; it stipulated an attitude of reverent attention to her story." By November, the faithful Sophy Cracroft found her "much out of health & in deep despondency." The nation, caught up in the drama and suspense of her vigil, felt for her. New Year's Day opened with public prayers in sixty churches for all absent in the Arctic.

But the new year also brought its own measure of discord. Eleanor was in love and wanted to marry the Reverend Philip Gell, whom she had met in Van Diemen's Land. Jane had considerable property from Franklin's first wife, but her husband had made no provision for his daughter. Jane held his power of attorney. With the two young people about to be married, she arranged for a settlement, which, for them, was not enough; Franklin was almost certainly dead, but his wife stubbornly refused to acknowledge that lamentable fact. For the first time she had to think about money: she would need funds to support her continuing search for *Erebus* and *Terror*. Thus was opened a breach in the family at what was also the worst time in her life.

She lived in hope. In April, she wrote to the president of the United States, Zachary Taylor, pointing out that the Admiralty was now offering a reward of twenty thousand pounds to any ship of any flag that brought help to the missing vessels. "I am not without hope that you will deem it not unworthy of a great and kindred nation, to take up the cause of humanity which I plead, in a national spirit, and thus generously make it your own. . . ."

The letter, which suggested that by helping in the search the Americans might get credit for discovering the Northwest Passage, was "the most admirable letter ever addressed by man or woman," in the words of a British member of parliament. As a result, the American secretary of state wrote to her pledging "all that the Executive government of the United States in the exercise of its constitutional powers can effect."

She went back to the Admiralty, which she felt had not made much effort to carry the search into those regions where the missing expedition was likely to be found. Franklin's orders had been to sail west and south from Cape Walker and, if blocked by ice, to explore Wellington Channel to the north. Neither of those areas had been given much attention. What the Navy wasn't prepared to do Jane Franklin was willing and ready to attempt.

She had learned that two suitable vessels—dockyard lighters—were available and that "with some alterations in the rigging, would be well adapted for my purpose, and being very strong, they could soon be made ready for me." Now she asked the board of the Admiralty to either lend her the two ships or sell them to her outright. "I cannot attempt to conceal from the Board, that it is only by the sacrifice of all my private property . . . and by the additional aid of borrowed capital, that I shall be able to effect my object, if unassisted."

The Admiralty was less than enthusiastic. They had sent a supply ship, the *North Star,* to support Ross's expedition, and that was enough. In the suite of rooms she had taken in Spring Gardens because it was close to the Admiralty, Jane saw a steady stream of visitors, anyone who might have a clue or suggestion about the missing ships. She even went so far as to visit a clairvoyant, and later that year there was the curious case of "Little Weasy," a four-year-old child who had died of gastric fever and kept "appearing" to his brothers and sisters, once, apparently, with a vision of the missing expedition from which he scrawled a crude map of the search area. Poor Lady Franklin, whom a friend described as in "a restless excited state of feeling," was reduced to grasping at straws.

She did not give up. In the summer of 1849, she and Sophy travelled north to the Shetlands to meet the whalers returning from the Arctic, hoping for news of the lost ships. En route she consulted William Scoresby, an acknowledged Arctic expert, and took tea with the mother of John Rae, the Hudson's Bay trader and explorer. She was becoming an Arctic expert herself and at Stromness in the Orkneys talked to the member of a whaling crew who claimed to have seen her husband and his ship that year. Her hopes rose but were quickly dashed when the tale was discredited.

Back in London, she found that both Richardson and James Clark Ross had returned to report they had found no trace of the missing ships. For Jane Franklin, this was a body blow. All her hopes had been centred on Ross, whose early confidence had buoyed her up. But she persevered. She wrote to an acquaintance in New York, Silas Burrows, to assess the possibility of raising funds in America "so as to enable me to send a small vessel or 2 small vessels of not above 100 tons each, with boats to those especial parts where I am persuaded the lost ships and crews are most likely to be found." She would be happy to come to the United States, she told him, to outline her views to any group of "sturdy young adventurers" ready to join in the search.

She had written to the czar of Russia for help, and he had replied by announcing an expedition to search for Franklin on the north coast of Siberia. It was unlikely that Franklin had got that far; nevertheless, the Admiralty was already planning to send the *Enterprise* and *Investigator* on a second expedition in that very direction—westward to Bering Strait. She herself leaned toward the eastern Arctic as the most fruitful setting for the search, and in that she was right. To John Rae, whom the British government had sent to Wollaston and Victoria Lands, she made a tentative suggestion: "I do not know whether you consider that the mouth of the Great Fish River should be examined. . . ." Nobody had bothered to examine it and here was a bitter irony. When in 1854 Rae came upon the first clues to the fate of the Franklin expedition, the Inuit indicated that many of his men had died at the mouth of the Great Fish River.

By 1850, the mystery was tantalizing the public. No fewer than six expeditions—fifteen ships—were sent off that year to probe the frozen channels of the Arctic archipelago. *Enterprise* and *Investigator* got off in May. Their captains, Richard Collinson and Robert McClure, would be out of touch with the world for four and five years respectively.

Most of the activity that fevered year was the direct result of Jane Franklin's campaign. She had brought in a seasoned whaling captain, William Penny, to command her own expedition in spite of the Admiralty's objection to a non-naval officer and then convinced the Admiralty to underwrite the entire cost of the enterprise. They had no choice, for by this time public opinion was solidly behind her. She got her way when in April the two ships, appropriately named *Lady Franklin* and *Sophia,* set sail for the Arctic. Her impassioned pleas to Sir George Simpson also brought dividends. The *Felix* and the *Mary,* which sailed a week after Penny under the command of the seventy-three-year-old John Ross, were financed by Simpson's Hudson's Bay Company and by public subscription. The following month, the British government mounted the biggest expedition of all—four ships under Captain Horatio Austin, followed shortly by an American expedition with the unofficial support of Congress and the financial backing of Henry Grinnell, a prosperous New York shipping merchant who had become obsessed with the search because of Jane Franklin's appeal to President Taylor. At Jane's behest he bought two ships and turned them over to the U.S. government so that they might be placed under naval discipline.

The last ship to sail to the Arctic that year, in June, was the ninety-ton ex-pilot boat *Prince Albert,* which had belonged to another of Jane's friends, the Cowes shipbuilder Robert White. It was equipped by Jane herself and some of her friends, and its captain, Charles Forsyth, was ordered to probe the section of the Arctic that had been ignored by others and, she believed, was the likeliest spot of all for the search. But when September came, to her despair none of the searchers had returned.

That fall by way of carrier pigeon she had some sketchy news. Austin reported evidence of a Royal Navy encampment on Beechey Island at the entrance to Wellington Channel. Penny revealed the presence of the graves of three of Franklin's men on the same spot.

Apart from this, nothing seemed to be going right. She had squandered her savings outfitting the little *Prince Albert*, but when it came back in October the captain had little to report. Charles Forsyth had not taken the search where she had asked him. Disobeying her instructions, he had ignored Peel Sound, believing it to be blocked by ice, and turned west and north. It was generally believed that Franklin had gone west and north. But Jane Franklin knew her husband better. He was a stickler for detail, and if it were at all possible, he would have followed his orders.

The Investigator, *commanded by Robert McClure, trapped in the ice pack north of Banks Island during the Franklin search. The expedition failed to find any clues.*

151

The *Prince Albert* made a second search, the only ship to set off for the Arctic in 1851. Lady Franklin spent the first five months of that year reorganizing the expedition. To replace Forsyth, she chose a tough Canadian mixed-blood, William Kennedy, son of a Cree woman and a Hudson's Bay Company factor. He had come to London on his own as had his twenty-four-year-old second-in-command, Joseph René Bellot, who jeopardized his career in the French marines to dedicate himself to Jane's service. He was her favourite, and she called him her "French son," insisting that the French flag be hoisted beside the Union Jack. When *Prince Albert* finally sailed in June, he was so overcome he sobbed like a child. "I must supply your mother's place," she had told him. "Well, then," he wrote in his journal, "I will be for you a son and the inexhaustible devotedness of a son who is in search of his father."

Where had Franklin gone after Beechey Island? He had left no written clue, but five of the eight Arctic authorities asked to predict his route believed he would be found north of Wellington Channel—in direct opposition to the orders he had been given and tragically, as it turned out, opposite to his own inclinations. Thus, when a new expedition—three sailing ships and two steamers under Sir Edward Belcher—was mounted the following year, it set off again in the wrong direction. A report from John Rae confirmed this error when he discovered two pieces of wood, almost certainly from the Franklin ships, on Victoria Island. That was a long way from Wellington Channel and in the opposite direction from Belcher's vain search.

These tantalizing clues served to spur Jane Franklin on. In spite of recurring illnesses, she renewed her efforts to push for further searches. She wrote anonymous letters to the press and appealed to the French and the Russians as well as her benefactor Henry Grinnell, trying to revive the flagging interest in the United States. The correspondence she received was voluminous and much of it ridiculous, such as the offer from a Mr. Henry Moore of Pennsylvania, who said he could tell her how to save her husband if she would introduce him to Queen Victoria and send him seventy-five pounds. And there was verse, too:

My Franklin dear long has been gone
To explore the northern seas,
I wonder if my faithful John,
Is still battling with the breeze;
Or if e'er he will return again,
To these fond arms once more
To heal the wounds of dearest Jane,
Whose heart is griev'd full sore.
My Franklin dear, though long thy stay
Yet still my prayer shall be,
That Providence may choose a way,
To guide me safe to thee.

In May 1853, two more ships sailed for the Arctic, the *Phoenix* and the *Advance*. The second-in-command of the latter was young René Bellot. Lady Franklin was unable to bid her favourite goodbye because his ship sailed one day ahead of schedule. Three months later he was drowned in the Wellington Channel while bringing dispatches to Belcher.

That was tragedy enough, but in January 1854 there was a worse one. The Admiralty informed her that, as of March 31, the names of the officers and men aboard *Erebus* and *Terror* would be struck from the books. She was too ill, or more likely too sick at heart, to reply, but she gathered her strength and a week later shot off a blistering letter attacking the decision as "presumptuous in the sight of God as it will be felt to be indecorous, not to say indecent . . . in the eyes of men." With that she refused to claim her widow's pension, and while the rest of the family wore black, she switched from deep mourning to bright colours of pink and green as soon as the Admiralty's notice was gazetted. As she wrote to her sister-in-law, "it would be acting a falsehood & a gross hypocrisy on my part to put on mourning when I have not yet given up all hope. . . . Still less would I do it in that month & day that suits the Admiralty's financial convenience."

The Arctic Council during the Franklin search. The object of that search is portrayed in a painting in the background.

154

155

—THREE—

John Rae was in no sense a Royal Navy man. The Orkney-born physician and explorer for the Hudson's Bay Company was one of the few people who believed that Franklin had turned south and not north, as the majority insisted. In his view, Franklin was to be found well west of Boothia Felix in the vicinity of King William Land. This was uncharted territory. Nobody knew whether Boothia was an island or a peninsula; the same uncertainty applied to King William Land. In April 1854, Rae led a small party of six in a trek across the neck of Boothia, which turned out to be a peninsula. On the return trip he was able to establish that King William Land was indeed an island. The stretch of water between the two, now known as Rae Strait, was an alternative part of the Northwest Passage, but Franklin would have had no way of knowing that.

On April 21, at Pelly Bay on Boothia, Rae met a party of Inuit who told him a tale that would eventually be worth ten thousand pounds to him and his men. They had heard stories from other natives about thirty-five to forty men who had starved to death some years before to the west of a large river, perhaps ten or twelve days' journey away. Rae had no idea who the men were, and since his job was to chart the Arctic coast for the Company, he got on with it. But at Repulse Bay that fall, several Inuit gave him more details about the dead men, and Rae soon realized that their bodies must have been found near the mouth of the Great Fish River—the very spot that the persistent Dr. King had argued the Franklin Party would head for and the very spot for which Jane Franklin herself had tentatively but unsuccessfully advocated.

Rae's report to the Admiralty was a shocker. "I met with Esquimaux in Pelly Bay from one of whom I learned that a party of 'white men' (Kabloonans) had perished from want of food some distance to the westward. . . . Subsequently further particulars were received, and a number of articles purchased, which places the fate of a portion (if not of all) of the then survivors of Sir John Franklin's long-lost party beyond a doubt; a fate as terrible as the imagination can conceive. . . ."

Rae would not bring himself to use the word "cannibalism" in his report, but he certainly made it obvious. The Inuit had walked among the bodies and the scattered equipment of the expedition, and "from the mutilated state of many of the corpses, and the content of the kettles, it is evident that our miserable countrymen had been driven to the last resort. . . ."

Rae did not publicize his findings, but the Admiralty distributed his report to the press. A vast public controversy ensued, with Rae the villain—a clear example of shooting the messenger. The real impact of Rae's report was that it demolished the universally held image of Arctic explorers as noble and highly moral creatures, unsullied by any human weakness. In *Household Words,* the periodical that Charles Dickens had launched in 1850, a contributor wrote that the narratives of the naval explorers "supply some of the finest modern instances of human energy and daring, bent on a noble undertaking, and associated constantly with kindness, generosity, and simple piety. The history of Arctic enterprise is stainless as the Arctic snows, clean to the core as an ice Mountain." He ended his essay with these words: "Let us be glad . . . that we have one unspotted place upon this globe of ours; a Pole that, as it fetches truth out of a needle, so surely also gets all that is right-headed and right-hearted from the sailor whom the needle guides."

Rae's report was based on hearsay evidence, and the public, clutching at that straw, simply refused to believe that Englishmen would eat each other. *The Times* expressed the prevailing sentiment: "All savages are liars." Rae was excoriated because he had stood up for the natives, insisting that their stories were believable. The controversy cost him a knighthood. Dickens entered the lists in his own periodical when he described the Inuit as "Covetous, treacherous and cruel . . . with a domesticity of blood and blubber." He simply did not believe, *could* not believe, that "the flower of the trained adventurous spirit of the English navy, raised by Parry, Franklin, Richardson and Back," had descended to what was the most dreadful crime in the Victorian mind. "It is in the highest degree improbable that such men would, or could, in any extremity of hunger, alleviate the pains of starvation by this horrible means." But

John Rae, with the "odious beard" that Lady Franklin decried after Rae's reports of cannibalism among the Franklin crew brought widespread condemnation.

158

later evidence found on or near King William Island was to establish incontrovertibly that cannibalism had occurred among Franklin's crew.

Rae was still at sea when the controversy was raging. On his return he paid the mandatory visit to Lady Franklin, where the atmosphere was decidedly chilly. She gave vent to her feelings in her journal in what can only be described as a catty attack on the appearance of the explorer that had nothing to do with the subject at hand. She had quite liked Rae before this, but now she wrote, "Dr. Rae has cut off his odious beard, but still looks very hairy & disagreeable. . . ."

The Admiralty had asked the Hudson's Bay Company to send a land party down the Great Fish River. Its leader, James Anderson, came back with some scanty remains: part of a snowshoe with "MR STANLEY" on its back and a leather backgammon board which Jane remembered putting on board the *Erebus*. There was no doubt now that her husband was dead, but for her that did not end the matter; she simply switched the effort that she had expended trying to save him to a new direction.

She intended to make it absolutely clear to the world that he had been the first to discover the Northwest Passage. Anderson had told her that what was needed was a ship from the north from which sledge parties could reach King William Island. "I am about to make a last effort to solve this mystery before the curtain falls forever over their unburied remains," she declared.

On January 22, 1856, the government announced that Rae and his men would receive the award of ten thousand pounds for establishing the fate of the lost expedition and that Robert McClure and his crew would receive ten thousand for being the first to negotiate the Northwest Passage. As far as the Admiralty was concerned, that search was ended.

Jane was having none of it. In April she dispatched a voluminous letter—25,000 words—to the Admiralty contesting both awards. But the Admiralty was obdurate, and in spite of appeals to Parliament, the prizes were approved.

Still she did not give up. "Though it is my humble hope and fervent prayer," she wrote, "that the Government of my country will themselves complete the work they have begun, and not leave it to a weak and helpless woman to attempt the doing that imperfectly which they themselves can do so easily and well, yet, if need be, such is my painful resolve, God helping me."

That was laying it on pretty thick. *Weak?* She who had climbed mountains in South Africa, America, and Australia? *Helpless?* She who had the ear and the support of the leading figures of the day, including the Prince Consort himself? In June a bevy of famous names was placed on a memorial addressed to Lord Palmerston, pleading for another expedition. One can only conclude that Jane's appeal to the Admiralty had a whiff of blackmail about it.

Sir Edward Belcher, the least competent of all the Arctic officers during the Franklin search, had foolishly abandoned one of his ships, *Resolute,* which an American whaler later discovered floating about in Davis Strait. Congress bought her for $40,000, had her refitted, and offered her to the British Admiralty as a hands-across-the-sea gift—or perhaps as a piece of naval one-upmanship. Jane's friend Henry Grinnell wanted the Admiralty to lend the ship to her for a final expedition. At a speech to the Royal Geographical Society by the American ambassador, she primed the chairman, Sir Roderick Murchison, who in turn primed the speaker, who inspired a round of applause when he referred to *Resolute* as "a consecrated ship" with the implication that the Franklin quest was commensurate with that for the Holy Grail.

At the same time, the weak and helpless woman was arranging through friends at the Admiralty for *Resolute* to receive a royal salute. She even arranged for a *Resolute* party for the officers and crew of the consecrated ship—with gifts for all—with the aim, through the careful behind-the-scenes work of others, of having it reserved for her own expedition. She was moving heaven and earth to get her way. Some of her friends in the Commons pursued the idea while another prepared an approving article for the *Illustrated London News.* She herself offered a prize of five hundred pounds to whalers who might investigate a rumour that the missing ships had fallen into the hands of the Inuit.

160

In addition, she arranged to have Henry Grinnell call a meeting in New York and sent yet another address to the Admiralty urging her right to have *Resolute*. She left nothing to chance, writing the address herself, which she then quoted in a letter of her own to the First Lord with a copy to the Prince Consort. Such was her campaign that even *The Times* argued that the ship should be placed at her disposal. But all her considerable efforts were in vain. The Admiralty demurred.

Still she did not give up. Foreseeing that refusal, Jane had already asked a friend in Aberdeen to examine the screw schooner yacht *Fox,* whose owner had just died. When the report was favourable, she bought the *Fox* for two thousand pounds and put Leopold M'Clintock, an experienced naval man, in charge of her own expedition to explore King William Island, the one corner of the Arctic that had been bypassed.

She gave M'Clintock two objectives: the rescue of possible survivors and the recovery of any records that might confirm the claim that her husband had been the first to discover the Northwest Passage. Time was of the essence; the expedition must sail no later than July 1857, which gave her two short months to organize the expedition, a task that included replacing the vessel's velvet furnishings and equipping her for the Arctic. To that end she thought nothing of working nights.

She was prepared to spend ten thousand pounds of her dwindling fortune, an outlay that a public subscription reduced by three thousand. M'Clintock and his officers refused to take a penny for the "glorious mission," which M'Clintock called "a great national duty." His sailing master, Allen Young, not only served without pay but also contributed five hundred pounds of his own to the public subscription. And when Lady Franklin tried to insist on a deed of indemnity, which would free M'Clintock of all liabilities, he refused it along with the gift of the ship itself, with which she tried to reward him.

Early in July 1857, *Fox* set off on the final mission to solve the ten-year-old Franklin mystery in the only part of the Arctic that had not received any attention but which the persevering Lady Franklin had more than once urged upon the navy. *Fox* was half the size of Franklin's ships and by no means as sturdy. Until April 1858, it was beset for

Leopold M'Clintock, whose successful discovery of Franklin relics on King William Island brought an end to the great search. He is shown here as a rear admiral.

250 days in the implacable ice of Melville Bay, being pushed 1,385 miles in the wrong direction—an inauspicious start that delayed the expedition for a year.

In July 1858, M'Clintock at last reached Beechey Island where the graves of three of Franklin's men had been found. He erected a suitable stone tablet in their memory and set out to manoeuvre his little yacht down Peel Sound in the direction he was sure Franklin had taken. When a dike of ice barred his way, he headed instead down Prince Regent Inlet, hoping to make his way into the sound through the narrow channel of Bellot Strait. Six times he tried to force his way through; six times the ice pushed him back. In September he got through as far as the western mouth of the strait when another belt of ice blocked his way. He spent the winter of 1858–59 in a sheltering inlet at the eastern end.

That winter he laid out depots for three sledging expeditions. One would explore Prince of Wales Island. Another would scour the delta of the Great Fish River and the western shore of Boothia. The third would search the north coast of King William Island. Somewhere in that chill and treeless region M'Clintock was certain they would find evidence of the lost expedition.

He was right. Tantalizing clues began to turn up—first an Inuk wearing a naval button, then an entire village where the inhabitants had buttons, a gold chain, silver cutlery, and knives fashioned of wood and iron from the wrecked ships. One native had seen the bones of a white man who had died on an island in the delta of the Great Fish River; others recalled a ship caught in the ice to the west of King William Island. M'Clintock and his deputy, Lieutenant William Hobson, were told of two ships the Inuit had seen, one sunk and one badly broken. White men had been seen, too, hauling boats south to a large river on the mainland.

Soon on their sledging forays they came upon further evidence: silver plates bearing the crests of some of the officers and tales of white men who had dropped in their tracks as they headed for the Great Fish River. In late May, M'Clintock came upon a human skeleton, the body face down, as if its owner had stumbled and dropped forward where his bones lay. And finally, there was a note from Hobson, who had discovered the only written record ever found of the lost Franklin expedition.

In a cairn at Victory Point, Hobson had found a message written on a naval form dated May 28, 1847. It showed that the lost ships had indeed gone up the Wellington Channel, circled around, and wintered at Beechey Island. They had been beset in the ice stream just northwest of King William Island. Lieutenant Graham Gore had taken a party ashore and left the message, certain that their ships would shortly be freed to make their way through the Passage.

Scrawled in the margin of this cheery note, a second message, written a year later on April 27, 1848, told a more sober tale. Franklin had died the previous June; the ships had been trapped in the ice for nineteen months; and nine officers, including Gore, and fifteen men were dead. This added to the mystery. No other polar expedition had suffered such a devastating loss.

The survivors had abandoned their ships and were now trying to reach the Great Fish River. Most didn't make it. On King William Island's northwest coast, M'Clintock came upon a massive sledge with a pitiful load of useless articles: books, soap, sheet lead, crested silver plate, dinner knives, a beaded purse, watches, and a cigar case, "a mere accumulation of dead weight, but slightly useful and very likely to break down the strength of the sledge crews" in M'Clintock's description. On top of the sledge was an eight-foot boat and inside it, two skeletons. Thus far had they stumbled and no farther.

When they set off in May 1845, Franklin's two ships had been stocked with three years' supply of provisions that could easily be stretched to five. What had happened? In the intervening years, three causes have been identified as the roots of the mass disaster: scurvy, lead poisoning, and botulism.

Scurvy, brought on by a deficiency of Vitamin C, had been recognized since the days of Captain Cook. It was traditionally cured by regular doses of lemon or lime juice (which was the reason that Englishmen were universally known as "limeys"). What was not known, however,

164

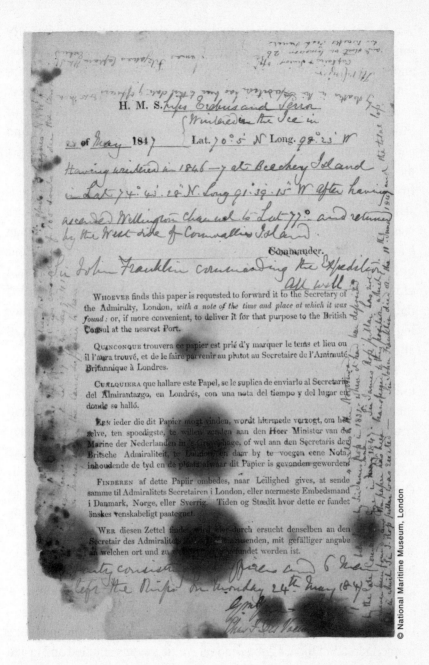

H. M. S. *ships Erebus and Terror*
{ *Wintered in the Ice in*

28 of May 1847 Lat. 70° 5' N Long. 98° 23' W

*Having wintered in 1846-7 at Beechey Island
in Lat 74° 43' 28" N Long 91° 39' 15" W after having
ascended Wellington Channel to Lat 77° and returned
by the West side of Cornwallis Island.*

Commander.

Sir John Franklin commanding the Expedition.

all well

WHOEVER finds this paper is requested to forward it to the Secretary of the Admiralty, London, *with a note of the time and place at which it was found :* or, if more convenient, to deliver it for that purpose to the British Consul at the nearest Port.

QUICONQUE trouvera ce papier est prié d'y marquer le tems et lieu où il l'aura trouvé, et de le faire parvenir au plutot au Secrétaire de l'Amirauté Britannique à Londres.

CUALQUIERA que hallare este Papel, se le suplica de enviarlo al Secretario del Almirantazgo, en Londrés, con una nota del tiempo y del lugar en donde se halló.

EEN ieder die dit Papier mogt vinden, wordt hiermede verzogt, om het zelve, ten spoedigste, te willen zenden aan den Heer Minister van de Marine der Nederlanden in 's Gravenhage, of wel aan den Secretaris der Britsche Admiraliteit, te London, en daar by te voegen eene Nota, inhoudende de tyd en de plaats alwaar dit Papier is gevonden geworden

FINDEREN af dette Papiir ombedes, naar Leilighed gives, at sende samme til Admiralitets Secretairen i London, eller nœrmeste Embedsmand i Danmark, Norge, eller Sverrig. Tiden og Stœdit hvor dette er fundet önskes venskabeligt paategnet.

WER diesen Zettel findet, wird hier durch ersucht denselben an den Secretair des Admiralitäts ... zusenden, mit gefälliger angabe an welchem ort und zu ... gefundet worden ist.

*... consist ... officers and 6 men
left the Ships on Monday 24th May 184*

Found on King William Island, this form provided the only written clue to the fate of the Franklin Expedition. The scribbled phrase "all well" was premature.

was that the citrus juice lost its potency after a year or so. Equally important was the lack of fresh meat or fat aboard the navy ships, another source of Vitamin C, which Stefansson learned from the Inuit but which the British, who believed in meat preserved in salt, ignored.

A second cause of death was indicated when the bodies of three of Franklin's men were exhumed from their graves on Beechey Island and subjected to scientific investigation. Owen Beattie and John Geiger discovered that all three had suffered from lead poisoning, apparently from badly soldered tins, a suspicion confirmed by some three thousand empty tins surrounding the Franklin camp. The canning process was in its infancy; tins were soldered not by machines but by human hands. The percentage of lead found in the dead men's bones was four or five times that of a normal Englishman of the day. The three men did not die of lead poisoning; it was probably pneumonia that killed them. Nonetheless, they would probably have suffered the debilitating physical and mental effects that lead can cause had they survived after Beechey.

The third cause of death was botulism, present in badly tinned and undercooked provisions. The two villains here were the victualler, Stephen Goldner, who cut every corner possible in order to underbid competitors, and the navy itself, which in the interests of saving money did little to inspect the tinned meats, soups, and vegetables that were being supplied to it, usually at the last moment, by the rapacious Goldner. Bones and offal went into tins with meat. Horsemeat was often a substitute for beef. Quantities of dust entered the tins along with the vegetables. Gravy was diluted and all efforts at preservation were frustrated by inadequate cooking. As a parliamentary inquiry later established, little or no attempt was made to look into Goldner's shoddy methods.

Botulism is an invisible killer—tasteless, colourless, odourless—that can strike suddenly and unexpectedly. It can taint food and make it smell rank, but then, all the food on Arctic vessels smelled and tasted foul after a few months. The toxin can be killed by heat—by hard boiling or hard frying—but when the ships were held up by the ice pack, coal for cooking was the first sacrifice made. It is thus clear why so few men died in the first years of the expedition. Later, the sledge parties that left the ships used what fuel was available to melt snow, leaving little to heat up tins of Goldner's tainted supplies.

"The canning provisions—supposedly advanced—were a chimera," Scott Cookman reports in *Ice Blink,* after poring through the records of the select committee of the House of Commons that finally investigated Goldner's contracts and eventually put him out of business. "The latest patented methods leached them of nutrients but left them tainted with bacteria and viruses. The canning process contaminated them with lead and arsenic. Soldered shut to prevent admittance of the 'atmospherics' believed to cause spoilage, they were in fact death capsules packed with *Clostridium botulinum.*" Franklin himself had probably not succumbed to these afflictions but died of pneumonia or some similar ailment typical of advancing years. In a postscript to a letter to Jane Franklin on his return, M'Clintock went out of his way to assure her that her husband had clearly not suffered long and had died just as success was in sight.

On hearing the news of M'Clintock's finds she had returned from the Pyrenees, where her doctor had sent her for her health, to find herself famous. The *News of the World* published one of the many letters her admirers sent in, this one titled "The Good Wife's Expedition":

> Since the beginning of the world, it has been considered that a good woman is the best thing to be found. . . . This is not a frothy compliment, for the world has before it at the present moment the living woman who deserves it, to contemplate, to admire and to bow down to with all the homage and devotion that a human being may bestow. There is a Lady Franklin to extol. . . .

With her husband's death firmly established, the widow accelerated her campaign to ensure his place in history as *the* discoverer of the Northwest Passage. She had wanted a national monument to the crews of the lost ships placed in Trafalgar Square, but apart from what her biographer calls "a niggardly tablet" at Greenwich, the government declined to act. One thing, however, was certain: any memorial or monument must record the fact that Sir John had been the first to discover the Passage. Meanwhile she spent her time badgering Members of Parliament to make sure that the officers and the crew of the *Fox* would be reimbursed. Her behind-the-scenes efforts were successful; Parliament voted them five thousand pounds. When the Royal Geographical Society presented M'Clintock with its Patron's gold medal and Lady Franklin with its Founder's gold medal—the first to a woman—the inscriptions made it clear that her husband's expedition took precedence as the discoverer of the Passage.

This was her crowning achievement. Everything she had struggled for was now accomplished. For more than a decade her ambitions for her husband had held her captive. Now, it was as if she had been released from a long incarceration. At last she could indulge in the one passion she had denied herself. She could travel the world (at least to the warmer climes, for she had no interest in frozen landscapes) and gratify her wanderlust. She would go to America at the behest of Henry Grinnell, with whom she had conducted a warm correspondence for a decade.

She set off with the faithful Sophy Cracroft in tow in July 1860 on what might be described as a triumphal tour—a succession of banquets, state dinners, presentations, and receptions. They crossed the Atlantic; stopped at New York; went on to Canada, where she had an audience with another visitor, the young Prince of Wales; sailed from New York to San Francisco; then on to Rio de Janeiro, where she met the Emperor of Brazil; then to Chile, where she rode about in a bullock cart; back up the coast, through Panama, to San Francisco again; and then on to British Columbia, where a group of Indian paddlers took her by canoe up the turbulent Fraser.

On their return to California, she and Sophy embarked on the liner *Yankee* for the Sandwich Islands (Hawaii), which she had visited following her husband's departure from Van Diemen's Land. Here she was the guest of King Kamehameha IV and his queen, Emma, who was so entranced that she could hardly be induced to step into the carriage before Jane, of whom she declared, "With Lady Franklin I would go anywhere—even as a servant." Jane and Sophy toured the islands, the king himself providing his own boat and crew to use as they wished. They clambered down the great crater of Kilauea and paid their homage at Captain Cook's monument before returning to a well-appointed state dinner in their honour.

Everywhere she went, Lady Franklin was treated with regal pomp. On Maui, the people believed she was the queen of the English. At a royal reception held to mark the anniversary of Queen Victoria's accession, the guests were presented to her as if she were royalty; the bows made to her were even lower than those for royalty themselves.

Hawaii was not the end of her peregrinations. The Far East beckoned, and off she went with Sophy to Yokohama and Nagasaki and then on to Hong Kong, Shanghai, Singapore, and Penang. Their last stop before returning home was Calcutta, where they dined with Lord Elgin, the new viceroy of India.

When Jane Franklin returned to England in the summer of 1862, just before her seventieth birthday, she had been away for two years. Those long months of travel had not exhausted her; on the contrary, she had thrived. A friend reported that he had never seen her looking "so well, young and blooming." Now for the first time she had a house of her own—in Kensington, complete with a little garden that gave it a charm unique in London. A celebrity herself, "the most extensively travelled Lady in Great Britain," in the words of the publisher John Murray, there were few of the famous she could not meet if she wished, for she was considered "the great gun of the season."

Now in her eighth decade, she was still active. Queen Emma, at her invitation, had arrived on a visit that occupied much of her attention. Then, in 1865, there was "a fearful working up of the slumbering past," in Sophy's words. News came from the Arctic that Charles Francis Hall, the Cincinnati newspaper-publisher-turned-explorer, had learned from the Inuit at Repulse Bay that some of the members of the lost expedition were still alive. There was considerable argument among the Arctic experts about this report, but she could not dismiss it. "It is our bounden duty, as it is an impetuous instinct," she wrote, "even though we may feel shocked at the sight of skeletons rising in their winding-sheets from their tombs. . . . I believe Hall is doing exactly what should have been done from the beginning, but which no Government could *order* to be done." But since Hall was still in the North and out of touch, nothing for the moment could be accomplished. She herself, at the age of seventy-five, was on her way to India.

For the English she continued to be a major attraction. She was late for her train at Charing Cross; no matter—it was held for her. At Dover, Sophy noticed that men were continually taking off their hats to her aunt. Her Indian sojourn, exacting as it was, came as a tonic. She travelled from place to place, often by bullock cart and once on the back of an elephant. On one day she made a thirteen-hour journey with only a half-hour break. En route home from Bombay, at the site of the half-finished Suez Canal she met its builder, Ferdinand de Lesseps, who himself took her and her niece on a tour of the big ditch.

She was back in England with Sophy in time to watch the unveiling in November 1866 of a national monument to her husband at Waterloo Place. The following year she was off again on what her biographer calls "a breathless career of sightseeing," the highlight of which was an audience with Pope Pius IX at the Vatican. "There had been difficulties in giving an audience to my Aunt on Thursday," Sophy confided to her diary, "but it was felt that every possible favour shd be done to the widow of the good Sir John Franklin." His Holiness even paid her the striking compliment of advancing a few steps to meet her and "expressed his great pleasure in receiving her who was so well known & honoured as a devoted wife. . . ."

In England she was pressed to follow up Hall's reports by organizing a new British expedition to Repulse Bay, but she confessed to "a dread of future heart-rending revelations whether true or false." One gets the impression that she had finally put that obsession behind her. Instead, she set off for India once more, riding through the narrow streets of Benares on the back of the Rajah's monstrous elephant. At

Delhi, she and Sophy made a four-hour drive to view the red sandstone minaret Kutb Minar, 238 feet high. "I need not say," Sophie admitted, "that we went to the top." Jane walked determinedly around the topmost small platform, but that, Sophy confessed, "my head would not bear."

On Jane's return to England the past again awaited her. She was startled by a small paragraph in *The Times* reporting that Charles Hall, after five years in the Arctic, had discovered the skeletons of several of Franklin's men on King William Island and had brought numerous relics with him to the United States. Once again she was moved to take action. She wanted another search made with Henry Grinnell's help, and she wanted to see Hall herself: "Having failed in my last effort to get any experienced Arctic officer to examine him personally we are compelled to feel that we must go now to America ourselves."

By late April she was back, with Sophy, in San Francisco, which she detested, and taking a ship to the formerly Russian town of Sitka on an island off the Alaska Panhandle, the most northerly point in all her travels. She had apparently retained some hope that documents from her husband's expedition might somehow have reached the old Russian capital. She and her niece arrived on May 19, 1870, at the charming and picturesque little community (as it still was when I visited it in 1932), recently acquired from the Russians by the United States.

In Sophy's journal there is no word about any missing documents and no suggestion that they even searched for any. Was that really their reason for travelling north? Or was it simply a vague excuse to justify Jane's wanderlust? She wasn't much more than a year away from her eightieth birthday and still on the move. They spent an enjoyable month in the former headquarters of Alexander Baranov, the rum-swilling Lord of Alaska, and then moved on, this time to Salt Lake City, where she indulged her fascination with Mormonism, especially its polygamous aspects. From there they moved on to Cincinnati to meet with Charles Francis Hall in July and then to New York in August with Hall to visit Henry Grinnell, who, she hoped, would persuade Hall to change his plan to go to the North Pole and instead join in "the so holy and

171

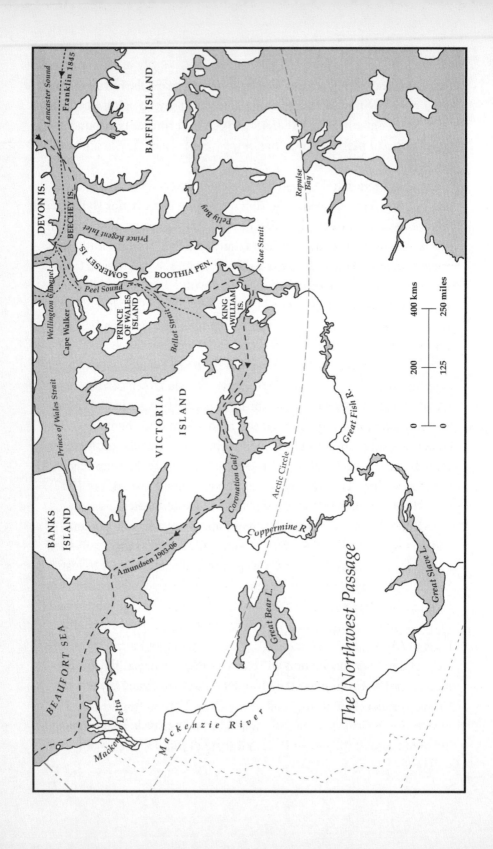

The Northwest Passage

BEAUFORT SEA

BANKS ISLAND

VICTORIA ISLAND

Prince of Wales Strait

DEVON IS.

BEECHEY IS.

Lancaster Sound

Franklin 1845

BAFFIN ISLAND

Wellington Channel

Peel Sound

Cape Walker

SOMERSET IS.

Prince Regent Inlet

Pelly Bay

Repulse Bay

PRINCE OF WALES ISLAND

BOOTHIA PEN.

Bellot Strait

KING WILLIAM IS.

Rae Strait

Amundsen 1903-06

Coronation Gulf

Coppermine R.

Arctic Circle

Great Fish R.

Great Bear L.

Great Slave L.

Mackenzie Delta

Mackenzie River

400 kms

250 miles

200

125

0

0

noble cause as the rescue of those precious documents from eternal sepulture in oblivion." Hall was prepared to help her but only after he had achieved the Pole, a triumph that eluded both him and those who followed for forty years.

Sometime after she returned to London, the occasion of the death of Robert McClure revived an old controversy. In October 1850, McClure had actually seen the Passage, or more accurately, *a* passage, following his exhausting sledge journey along the eastern shore of Banks Island to Prince of Wales Strait. There, as his colleague Alexander Armstrong declared, "the highway to England from ocean to ocean lay before us." It had generally been assumed but not proven that some of Franklin's dying crew had viewed one of the routes through the frozen passage from King William Island, but McClure's discovery was indisputable. Now, at the age of eighty, it behooved Lady Franklin to support her claim that her husband was the real victor in the long search. Allen Young, who had been sailing master on the *Fox,* was preparing an expedition of his own to accompany the North Pole expedition of Sir George Nares. His plan was to break away from the major expedition and turn south to Peel Sound, seeking records of *Erebus* and *Terror.* But money continued to be a problem. Jane Franklin reminded the whaling fleet that a three-thousand-pound reward she had put aside earlier as a prize for the recovery of such records was still in force. Her well-publicized announcement contributed to a new wave of excitement on both sides of the Atlantic and the usual spate of crank letters, including "a proposal from a Mr. Ralph Scott to carry out an invention of his for rising into the air."

It also brought an offer from James Gordon Bennett, Jr., of the New York *Herald* (the paper that had sent Stanley after Livingstone) to put up five thousand pounds for Allen Young's expedition if one of his correspondents could tag along. In May 1875, Young's expedition set off, financed largely by Bennett and Lady Franklin herself. By this time, however, she was seriously ill of "a decay of nature" and prayers were being said at her request in both America and England.

She was not a model patient, although the press described her condition as "sinking." She refused flatly to take her medicine, and when a glass was offered to her, she flipped it away, settling back on her pillow with the ghost of a laugh. She hung on for three more weeks and went to her grave in a casket borne on the shoulders of six Arctic explorers. She died a fortnight before the memorial to her husband could be unveiled in Westminster Abbey, too weak to compose the inscription on the cenotaph. Her uncle, the poet laureate Alfred Tennyson, did it for her:

> *Not here! the white North has thy bones;*
> *And thou, Heroic sailor-soul,*
> *Art passing on thine happier voyage now*
> *Toward no earthly pole.*

Hers was a remarkable achievement. Through her own obstinacy and firm will, she transformed a plodding and unexceptional naval officer into a British saint.

To the left of Franklin's bust, the dean, S. P. Stanley, had arranged for an inscription:

> To the memory of Sir John Franklin, born April 16, 1786, at Spilsby, Lincolnshire: died June 11, 1847, off Point Victory, in the Frozen Ocean, the beloved chief of the crews who perished with him in completing the discovery of the North-west Passage.

That was what she had fought for—that the memory of her husband would be tied irrevocably to the achievement of what had been called "the greatest prize in the history of maritime exploration." With that accolade engraved in stone, the persevering Lady could truly rest in peace.

CHAPTER 4

The Hermit of the Tundra

John Hornby in the Great Bear Lake country, 1912, consuming endless cups of tea.

—ONE—

John Hornby, who died slowly of starvation in April 1927 in the heart of the Arctic desert that Samuel Hearne dubbed the Barren Ground, is perhaps the most frustrating figure in the history of the North. If he is a legend today it is largely because he worked at it— worked at being an eccentric, worked at being an outsider, worked hard at portraying himself as a rugged survivor who welcomed hardship and laughed in the face of danger. Who else would choose to spend a winter in the most inhospitable corner of Canada just to be able to boast that he had done it?

He had no other purpose in his life. He wasn't a prospector and could hardly tell a gemstone from a chunk of granite. Nor was he an explorer; he was not interested in seeking out new lands and was wary of those who did because he feared they would import civilization into his untrammelled wilderness. He was a competent trapper, but he made scarcely a nickel from furs because he couldn't concentrate on his traplines and was too slovenly to take proper care of the hides he did garner.

The Barren Ground obsessed Hornby. In his mind, it was his property, and like a lovesick suitor he was jealous of anyone who tried to invade that land above the treeline. But what did he see in this desolate domain? Where was the attraction? Indeed, only a handful of explorers have crossed this empty plain that stretches from the forests that screen the Mackenzie to the shores of Hudson Bay, a "monotonous snow-covered waste," in the words of Warburton Pike, one of the earliest of the tundra explorers, "without tree or scrub, rarely trodden by the feet of a wandering Indian." In Pike's description, "a deathly stillness hangs over all, and the oppressive loneliness weighs upon the spectator until he is glad to shout aloud to break the awful spell of solitude."

This is the domain that Hornby chose for himself, the one in which he felt secure from a world he thought had gone crazy. It is a topsy-turvy land that has not yet recovered from the ebb and flow of the overwhelming ice sheets that dislocated the ancient drainage pattern, diking lakes with mounds of rubble, gouging out new rivers, choking others,

176

and scattering debris from one end of the North to the other until the whole lake and river system was out of kilter. From the air, the Barrens in summer are an endless rolling desert of brown suede, stippled with thousands of tattered little lakes and marked by the occasional cyclopean boulder, as big as a house, dragged for hundreds of miles to rest on the slopes of the western mountains.

They call it a "cold desert" because the precipitation is less than five inches a year and the evaporation almost non-existent. If the permafrost that imprisons the little lakes should ever thaw, the Barrens will be another Sahara.

Here, too, as Hornby discovered, one finds the bizarre geological formations known as eskers—high ridges of sand and gravel looking like railway embankments, some a hundred feet high and a dozen miles in length, their crests flattened by the hooves of thousands of migrating caribou. These snake-like ridges, which provide the only shelter from the winds that howl across the treeless plains, are deposits of sediment made by streams of meltwater that flowed in tunnels under the ice when the glaciers were decaying. It was in a dugout in one of these eskers that Hornby and a companion took shelter for an entire winter.

The Barrens made him and in the end the Barrens destroyed him. He would have had it no other way. As an early biographer has put it: "Without the Barrens there could have been no Hornby. Without them, he would have been a misfit—one of society's drop-outs." The settled world was not for Jack Hornby. "You can fully realize how miserable I feel here," he wrote from England to a former partner between forays into the tundra. "This senseless life is detestable. How can people feel justified in leading an aimless existence?"

Yet Hornby himself led an aimless existence, wandering about the North without any real objective, usually ill-prepared and ill-equipped for misfortune or disaster. He liked it that way. As his erstwhile companion Captain James Critchell-Bullock put it, "No argument could persuade Hornby that any Arctic or sub-Arctic explorer was worthy of consideration unless the principals have gone out on a shoestring and returned by the skin of their teeth."

Hornby, on the edge of the Barrens, travelling light with his dog, Punch.

Many of those qualities he had absorbed from the native Indians, with whom he had a love-hate relationship and to whom, at times, he showed the generous if impulsive side of his nature. They might steal from him; but when they were starving he shared his meagre rations with them, and when he was close to death they brought him food. It was the same with his trail mates. In periods of stress he was not above carrying the heaviest loads on a portage or cutting back on his own rations to sustain a comrade. Hornby remarked more than once that he wished he had been born an Indian, and a good many of those who knew him tended to think of him as an Indian. He walked in a kind of crouch, and he learned to move quickly through difficult country, keeping his loads to a minimum, living off the land, and making himself an expert on the movements of the caribou. Max Cameron, chief

178

geographer at the Department of Mines, who had little sympathy for the natives, once remarked that Hornby "was remarkable for his Indian characteristics: improvidence, periods of intense energy, alternating with slovenly, lazy slipshod."

"Slovenly" may not apply to Indians, but it did apply to Hornby, who was in the habit of cracking open caribou bones with a hammer and sucking out the marrow, who used a single knife, which he never washed, for every operation from eating to butchering, and who cleaned his rump with a stick after relieving himself. He took the English love of tea to extremes, brewing himself a potful on every conceivable occasion, waking his fellows at two in the morning when necessary to heat the water over fires fuelled by anything combustible—a side of bacon, books or newspapers, fox fat, his own filthy trousers, or the shirt off his back.

More than one observer described him as Chaplinesque, a gaunt little man, only five foot four, weighing no more than one hundred pounds. He had a swarthy complexion, a prominent beak of a nose, a head of long, tangled, matted black hair, and intensely blue eyes. He would never travel with a brown-eyed man, he said; they were not to be trusted. He dressed like a street beggar in ragged trousers, an old shirt, and a grubby overcoat; yet at the bottom of his pack he carried a dinner jacket, black bow tie, dress shirt, two hairbrushes mounted in monogrammed silver, and two silver-capped bottles of cologne—indispensable, no doubt, for a man who rarely washed.

His remarkable stamina contributed to his legendary status in the North. A powerful and relentless walker, he had once run a hundred miles between Edmonton and Athabasca Landing on a bet. On another occasion he had managed to keep up with a galloping horse at fifty miles an hour and had even run side by side with a speeding locomotive. Once in Edmonton, he had decided to visit his cousins in Onoway, fifty miles distant, only to learn that the train would not leave until the following morning. "No good for me," he declared, and headed off in moccasins, without an overcoat. The next morning he headed right back. These are legends, told over the years, and no doubt built up in the telling. But no one disputed the claim of the *Edmonton Journal*, which declared that he "could outrun any Indian on the trail, could out-last any Indian in endurance, and could outstarve any Indians when there was nothing left but starvation." Hornby relished this kind of praise and encouraged it. It sustained him in those wan moments of cold, starvation, and despair that he made his lot.

Much of what we know about Hornby comes as a result of the care-ful research and investigative skills of George Whalley about half a century ago. Whalley was able to cover the actual ground as well as to interview the most prominent actors in the Hornby drama who were still alive. Hornby wrote no memoir, though he had planned a book about the Barrens to be called *The Land of Feast and Famine;* fortu-nately, Whalley was able to uncover some of Hornby's correspondence, especially with his friend and comrade George Douglas, for his biog-raphy, *The Legend of John Hornby,* an eloquent work that is essential reading for those who want to delve further into the land of the cari-bou and muskox.

Hornby, Whalley tells us, came to Canada in 1904 on a whim—he seemed to do everything on a whim—with no particular purpose in mind. He came of a family of wealthy cotton merchants and was edu-cated at Harrow. His father was a champion cricketer, one of the most famous in England, and a Rugby Blue. The evidence suggests that Hornby, at twenty-three, was running away. From what? The settled, upper-middle-class life was clearly not for him. He had no need to scrabble for funds. One suspects that Hornby was bored and that to him Canada represented adventure. But he chose Edmonton as a des-tination only because he had a cousin in the area and not because the city was the gateway to the Canadian North. In fact he did not seem to have any burning desire to travel farther than Athabasca Landing. He had no plans for the future—he never seemed to have any plans—and hung around Edmonton for the next four years taking occasional jobs (a railway gang, a survey party) and lounging about in the town's hotel bars.

Much of this early period is a blur, enlightened by occasional rem-iniscences such as those of Yardley Weaver, with whom he shared a survey tent in the Athabasca country. One night they heard a movement outside and Hornby sat upright in his blankets to declare that the pack horses were trying to get water from a nearby creek. He plunged out immediately into the freezing cold, bare-headed and bare-footed, chopped a hole in the ice so that the animals could drink, came back to his blankets, and immediately fell asleep. It is a revealing story; Hornby was an animal lover who was forced in trying times to hunt for food but never for sport. One thing that bothered him was the thoughtless and inhumane treatment that the natives dealt out to their dogs.

Edmonton in those days was the jumping-off point for the Canadian Northwest. A steady wave of trappers, prospectors, and miners moved in and out of the community, which buzzed with tales of the hinterland, some true, some apocryphal. Yet there is no evidence that Hornby had any desire to experience the frozen world. He was simply lolling about Edmonton when he encountered a big-game hunter named Cosmo Melvill who changed his life. The six-foot son of a Shropshire cotton merchant, Melvill was fascinated by the Barren Ground muskoxen, mysterious and little known animals in those days. He was mounting an expedition to the Arctic to hunt for this dwindling species and invited Hornby to come along. They set out in May 1908, travelling by York boat and sternwheeler down the Mackenzie as far as the Great Bear River.

Melvill's party of four struggled up the Bear, "the swiftest stream I have ever seen and also the clearest," for seventy-five miles. After all the back-breaking portages, it must have been a relief to enter the navy blue waters of Great Bear Lake. Here was a vast biological desert, one quarter the size of England, so cold that no plankton could live in its deepest waters and no fish could stray far from the shoreline. "It is rather a hard thing to describe Bear Lake; it looks like the sea," Melvill said. Like the other great inland seas of Canada, it lies on the rim of the Precambrian Shield, rent by subglacial valleys, gouged deeper and broader by the rock-shod ice sheets. Into these great hollows the melting glaciers spilled their runoff. Great Bear is always bitterly cold. Its transparent waters never rise more than a few degrees above freezing.

Here, on the extreme northeast corner of the huge lake, not far from Caribou Bay at the mouth of the Dease River, the Melvill party built a camp and trading post. This would be their home for the winter of 1908–9. Caribou Bay (which would come to be known as Hornby Bay) was well named, for here were thousands of Barren Ground caribou, migrating west from the tundra for the winter. On November 17, Melvill estimated that one thousand or more had passed their camp in the course of twenty-four hours.

The caribou migration—*la foule,* the throng—is an awesome sight that I remember from my own northern days: thousands of animals flattening the birch and poplar saplings as they thundered through the woods and tumbled down the high banks of the Yukon River, slipping and sliding, the does pushing the fawns forward with their snouts and the whole valley pungent with the sickly smell of rotting flesh from those who had not survived the crossing. A century ago in Hornby's day, the caribou made the difference between life and death for whites as well as natives. When they changed the pattern of their migration, as Hornby himself would discover, it could mean death on the Barrens.

The following April, with the weather growing warmer, the Melvill party with four Indians set out from the Coppermine River to look for muskoxen. The river, which had been explored by Samuel Hearne, had never been mapped, and they could not be sure exactly where they were. They had reached a country into which even the Indians would not venture.

But white men had been there, for among the trees they found the ridgepole of a tent, something the Indians never used. One of the party, Pete McCallum, examined the old cuttings in the trees and, comparing them with the later growth, figured that they must be sixty years old, suggesting that this could have been the site of one of the camps of John Richardson, Franklin's partner.

For Hornby, drifting down the Coppermine with the others, these were happy, carefree pre-war days, and he would remember them fondly. This was storied ground, for it was here that Hearne, to his horror, witnessed

182

the massacre of an entire Inuit village by his Indian followers. "The shrieks of the poor expiring wretches were truly dreadful," Hearne wrote, "and my horror was much increased at seeing a young girl, seemingly about eighteen years of age, killed so near my feet that when the first spear was struck into her side she fell down at my feet and twisted round my legs, so that it was with difficulty that I could disengage myself from her dying grasps." Hearne was helpless to intercede, but the memory of what had happened here at Bloody Falls prevailed, which explains why the Melvill party saw no Inuit on their journey.

They found no muskoxen either, though they came upon a pile of bones from some sixty of the mysterious animals. At this point they climbed one of the round-topped hills above the river and, to the north, looked upon a spectacle that must have brought a shiver of excitement. It was a corner of the Arctic Ocean, rimmed by the dark bulk of Wollaston Land, sharply visible against the cloudless skies. But the next day was foggy and the Indians indicated they had no intention of going farther north. Melvill had two choices: go on alone without the Indians or return to Great Bear Lake.

Had Hornby been in charge they might have plunged on north impetuously, but Melvill was both sensible and cautious. "I expect most people will think us awful cowards," he wrote, "but the fact was that we had no dog food and unless we got plenty of caribou going back, not only the dogs but ourselves would be on pretty short commons." They had come to the Arctic not as explorers but to get muskoxen, and since the Indians intended to take them back by a different route where muskoxen had actually been encountered, discretion was wise. Indeed, a few of them were spotted on the way back—a small band of seven that Melvill was able to glimpse for a moment, noting that the animals ran like sheep. They had been on the way for the best part of a month but had not managed to take any muskoxen or been able to encounter any Inuit.

For the next three years, Hornby spent his time in the Great Bear Lake area. The record here is vague, but one thing becomes clear. In this empty country, much of it unexplored, Hornby was remarkably

Hornby's friend and long-time correspondent, George Douglas, in his cabin.

reluctant about helping the occasional explorer or trader who came his way. George Douglas, who headed a meteorological expedition bound for Coppermine, remarked on Hornby's attitude when he asked him specific questions about the area. Hornby's answers were misleading, often facetious, and sometimes incoherent as he chatted away "just like a monkey." At first Douglas thought that the wiry little man was bushed, a not uncommon problem with those who had been confined for months or years in the savage land. At last he realized that Hornby was purposely holding back information. Why? Douglas could not know that this oddball was attempting to distract him from his purpose: to invade what Hornby considered to be *his* territory.

Hornby knew the country well. He had been down the Coppermine and the Dease for short trips and through the screen of trees that bordered those rivers had been able to view the Barrens in all their starkness. In that vast and gloomy expanse of clay and rubble, scoured clean of its topsoil by the advancing ice sheet, he had been given a brief view of what to him was something close to paradise—a lone land unmarked by the hand of civilization. Seen from the air, the Barren Ground is undeniably haunting, as I myself can testify. The claw marks of the ancient ice sheet are still visible, radiating out, like spokes of a wheel, from the original glacial core. It was this formidable realm, glimpsed by Hornby on his travels northeast of Great Bear Lake, that began to obsess him and that would in the end consume him. He could not accept the prospect of all this tranquility being disturbed by the intrusion of strangers.

There was a childlike aspect to Hornby's character, which though it undoubtedly appealed to many who encountered him also created difficulties. He was not able to stick to any task for long. This was apparent in his relations with the newly arrived Oblate missionary Father Jean-Baptiste Rouvière, who was intent on establishing a mission to the Inuit of Coronation Gulf. Hornby established a firm friendship with Father Rouvière, with whom he whiled away many an hour over a chessboard. Hornby had attached himself to the mission, unofficially, and the two had started work on a small cabin on the north shore of Dease Lake (later renamed Lake Rouvière). Yet the job was scarcely underway when Hornby drifted off, leaving the priest to finish it himself over the following month. Where he went and why no one could tell, but in the coming years, his unexpected departures followed a pattern.

Hornby was easily bored and would lose interest in any project, abandoning it without any explanation, only to return later without a word. In this case there may have been a plausible reason for his actions. About this time he built another cabin for a young Sastudene Indian widow, Arimo, a charming and intelligent woman who was for a time his native "wife." Hornby, if not in love, was certainly attached to her; she was one reason why he stayed so many months in the Dease Lake country.

By the spring of 1913 he had been five years in the North, out of touch with civilization. The events of the outside world—the death of Edward VII, the sinking of the *Titanic*—reached him long after the fact. His friends the Douglas brothers, George and Lionel, had departed, and a new priest, Father Guillaume LeRoux, had arrived, ostensibly to work under Father Rouvière in establishing the mission to the Inuit. LeRoux was a different creature from the easygoing and likeable Rouvière—hard-headed and hot-tempered, quick to flare up and confident enough to assume authority over the older priest, who was actually his senior. When LeRoux learned about Hornby's dalliance with Arimo, he made his strong disapproval of the arrangement so clear that he managed to alienate her from Hornby.

With the priests occupying cabins at Hodgson's Point, Hornby withdrew to his own domicile six miles away. It was not a happy winter, marked by a further quarrel between LeRoux and Hornby over a quantity of stores left behind by George Douglas for Hornby's use, which LeRoux refused to let Hornby take from the storehouse.

Alone and lonely, Hornby, who had from time to time yearned for the solitary life, now found it oppressive. His disenchantment with the Great Bear country was beginning. On October 8, the two priests set off for the Coppermine, having learned that the time was ripe for establishing

Arimo, Hornby's one-time mistress, and her son Harry, on the Dease River, 1909.

their mission on the northern coast. It was late in the season, and they were inexperienced travellers, badly provisioned and ill-clothed. Most of all, they had little understanding of the Inuit temperament.

Hornby, who had had a run-in with two Inuit, apparently had told the priests before they left that the natives were "getting ugly." It was a prescient warning. Neither priest was ever seen again, but their decomposed bodies were found in 1916 at Bloody Falls. The two Inuit who had earlier threatened Hornby, Sinnisiak, and Uluksuk, were eventually brought to trial for murder, found guilty, and given the death penalty. That was quickly commuted to life imprisonment, and with good reason, for these were Stone-Age people with a limited knowledge of the white man's law. In the end they served two years of light detention in the Royal North West Mounted Police post at Fort Resolution and were then released to their own people.

None of this, of course, was known to Hornby, who had his own disaster to cope with in the fall of 1913. That October, he set off across the lake in the York boat *Jupiter* with an eclectic collection of Inuit artifacts he had put together during his years in the Dease country that he intended to present to the Edmonton Museum. It included a quantity of Inuit tools and clothes as well as a variety of specimens—flowers, bones, insects, and whatever furs and skins he had gathered. As he travelled down the lake a vicious gale blew up, buffeting the frail craft and throwing sheets of water into the boat, which was finally washed onto the shore and wrecked with the loss of most of its unique cargo.

It was perhaps the last straw. That winter Hornby decided to leave the North and, after nearly six years, venture into the Outside. He was a disillusioned man. The loneliness of his life, the loss of his precious specimens, and, most important, the tension between himself and the overbearing priest were all contributing factors. He was not the same man who had arrived at Great Bear Lake in 1908. The North had turned him into a creature who differed from those who had not experienced it as he had. Hornby was not one to plan his future, but it must have concerned him to realize that he was one of Service's "men who don't fit in."

188

Inuit from Coronation Gulf with Hornby (background) on the edge of the Barrens.

He had no plan for what he would do once he left the Great Bear Lake country. He spent a short time in Edmonton and went on to Lakefield, Ontario, where he was reunited with George Douglas. There and at Northcote, Douglas's birthplace, the two friends had much to talk about, with Hornby relieving his frustrations.

At least he finally knew where his immediate future lay. World events made up his mind for him. The Great War had broken out; every able-bodied man was needed, and certainly Hornby, who thought nothing of packing 125 pounds on his back, was able. Douglas suggested he go to England, join the Imperial Army, and take a commission. Instead, in September 1914 Jack Hornby took the train to Valcartier, Quebec, and joined the 19th Alberta Dragoons.

However, as George Whalley has pointed out, "There can have been few men worse suited for army life than Hornby—by habit, tempera-ment and desire." The disciplined life of the parade ground and bar-rack room was as far from the free and easy vagabond existence as it was possible to get. Hornby didn't look like a soldier, especially on leave. He turned up at the Royal Paddington Hotel in London to meet Douglas and was saved from rejection only by the timely interference of his friend. "He looked like a tramp—dirty trousers, a dirty pale blue silk shirt with pale yellow attached collar with ragged lace ribbon bands across the breast, and heavy moth-eaten astrakhan fur collar and cuffs." Hornby was totally out of place, and Douglas steered this lost soul into the darkest corner of "a very gloomy dining room."

Hornby's unit embarked for France just in time to go into action in the second Battle of Ypres, notorious for Germany's first use of poison gas. According to his commanding officer, Lieutenant Colonel F. C. Jamieson, "Everybody liked him. He was cheerful and never com-plained" and was also willing to go out on patrols. Inwardly, however, he had no heart for the military life. "My thoughts are forever of the North," he wrote to Douglas. " . . . I have lived too long with what here one calls the uncivilized races . . . to ever get accustomed to the con-tinual wrangle & utter selfishness of the white races. . . ."

Douglas had written to tell him that no one had had any word of the two priests Rouvière and LeRoux. Hornby impulsively replied that he would try to get away and outfit a search expedition—a naive suggestion for a soldier in action at the front, especially one who had already applied for a commission. He was eventually gazetted as a second lieutenant in the South Lancashire regiment and must have seen considerable action, for he was mentioned in dispatches, then awarded the Military Cross for bravery, and wounded a month later. He told a friend that he did not expect to come out of the war alive and, as a result, was careless of danger.

Reports of his war service and subsequent activities are vague and confusing. A local newspaper near his hometown reported that he had been shot through the shoulder and was in hospital in London, which suggests his wounds were serious. But a fellow traveller who later crossed Great Slave Lake with him reported that "he had seven machine gun bullets through his body under his ribs and could get out of his sleeping bag only by hauling himself up by the tent pole." Did he take convalescent leave from the hospital in London or did he just walk out, as Colonel Jamieson suggested? One thing is clear: though the war was still raging, he did not return to the trenches but took passage on a ship for Canada, ended up in Vancouver, and was posted Absent Without Leave.

The military authorities tried to track him down through George Douglas's sister, but he proved elusive. He didn't draw his pay and left no clue as to his whereabouts. Finally he turned up in Edmonton for a medical examination and was allowed to relinquish his commission on grounds of ill health caused by his wounds. He was granted the honorary rank of second lieutenant, an unusual reward for a flouting of army rules that might have led, had he gone AWL in action, to a firing squad.

The Great War affected many men, but the changes it wrought in Jack Hornby were deep and permanent. He was never quite the same man again. Flanders Fields were about as far from the limpid waters of Great Bear Lake as the moon itself. For half a dozen years Hornby had experienced the silence of the North, an eerie quiet broken only

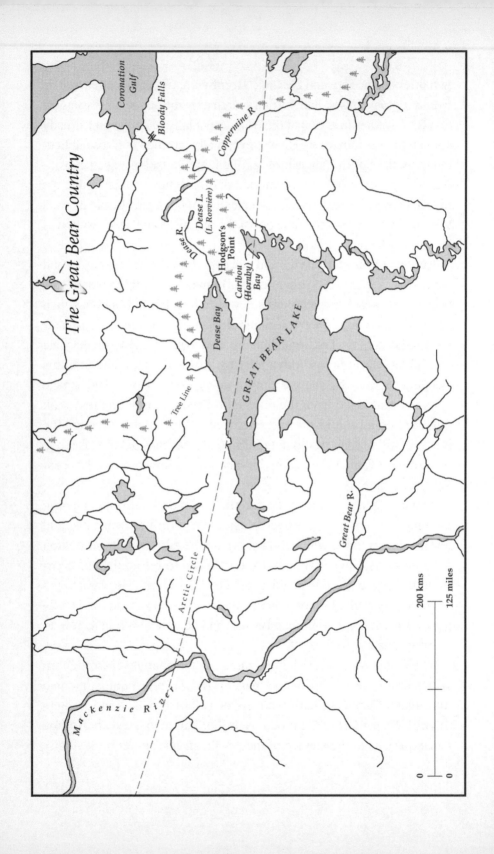

The Great Bear Country

Coronation Gulf

Bloody Falls

Coppermine R

Dease R.

Dease L.
(L. Rovrière)

Hodgson's
Point

Caribou
(Hornby)
Bay

Dease Bay

Tree Line

GREAT BEAR LAKE

Great Bear R.

Arctic Circle

Mackenzie River

200 kms

125 miles

0

0

by the spectral laugh of the loon, the lonely howl of the wolf, and the whistle of the wind. In Flanders, his ears were assailed day and night by the cacophony of cannon and mortar, the chatter of machine guns, and, what was worse, the haunting cries of dying men. And there was more: the wretched trenches were filthy and sodden, the colourless landscape was pocked by shell holes and a confusion of mud and wire that bore no relation to the white world he had grown to love.

Mentally and emotionally, he was in bad shape. The noise of the guns, he told a friend in Edmonton, had driven him crazy. Worse, in his view, the army had turned him into a murderer. Civilization had gone mad. His only solution was to retreat again to the Far North; he was unfit for anything else, couldn't work under others, and felt himself unable to take a job. "I wish I had never gone to the army nor had ever left the North," he wrote to Douglas, who was working on an engineering job in Mexico. He asked at the same time for a loan of a hundred dollars. Douglas responded with a cheque.

"I'm going back home," Hornby told the *Edmonton Bulletin.* "Along the Barren Lands and in the Arctic is my home." Off he went, with only the money he had borrowed and very little equipment. The hotel keeper at Fort Smith described him as "this desperate man running away from civilization . . . making the tremendous trip in a little boat no better than a broken down packing case." Hornby's loathing of the civilized world and his obsession with the untrammelled North had reached the point where some who encountered him thought him out of his mind. His last gloomy winter on the big lake plus his war experiences had increased his eccentricities.

Hornby reached Dease Bay in September 1917, but it was not the hospitable place he had originally encountered. Once he had taken a proprietary interest in it; now it was "his" no longer. A new personality, Darcy Arden, a respected trader and prospector, had replaced him as the key figure among the Indians and had married Arimo, his one-time mistress. Hornby made his way across to Caribou Bay to the cabin he and Melvill had built, and here he crippled himself with an axe to the point where he could only crawl.

Though it was six months before he could stand upright, he was faced with struggling every second day to get a fish net through the ice, three miles from his cabin. This was his only source of fresh food. It turned out to be the coldest winter on record with the temperature reaching –70 degrees Fahrenheit. In a letter to Douglas written the following summer, Darcy Arden described Hornby's plight: "He is not fit for this country now. The war has affected poor Hornby very much and he is not the man like he was when you were here before. Some time last March I went over to see him and found him starving and completely out of his head. I think if he stays at the lake this winter something will happen to him."

Hornby welcomed hardship and put himself, apparently deliberately, into situations where the absence of food became a way of life. "No one but Hornby would live in such discomfort in the Northland," Denny LaNauze, the Mountie inspector, once remarked. Hornby's movements during the winter of 1918–19 were driven by aimless hunts for caribou, ranging from various points in the Great Bear Lake area to the big bend of the Coppermine. But he was finally finished with Bear Lake; he never wanted to see it again; it invoked too many unhappy memories. In the spring he left it for good. He headed out to Edmonton but got no farther. "The post-War flurry irked me," was the way he put it. He dawdled before going north again, this time by way of the Peace, but he had left too late in the season and found himself frozen in near Chipewyan. He spent that winter in an enlarged wolf den.

The Barrens continued to engross him, to occupy his imagination, and to haunt his mind. Why? What was it about this bleak and friendless land that bewitched him? Apart from the few glimpses caught during his trips down the Coppermine, he had very little knowledge about the tundra and virtually no experience. Yet here he was, musing about spending a winter alone in an unforgiving realm that even the native Indians avoided. That, one suspects, was its appeal for Jack Hornby. He would do something few men had ever done in the history of the North, and if his ambition was fulfilled, he would be applauded for it. Hornby belonged to those among us who have a dream. With some it is an acceptable vision: to make a million, to write a masterpiece, to swim the English Channel, to scale a mountain peak. Hornby's dream was unique: to live alone in the Barrens—alone and free—to thumb his nose at civilization, to seek out and revel in all the hardships this bleak and windswept terrain had to offer.

When spring came his plan was to travel east by way of Great Slave Lake from Fort Resolution to Fort Reliance at its eastern end, a distance of some two hundred miles. After that he would make his way by Artillery Lake to the tundra. At Fort Smith he organized supplies for the venture—two outfits, one for trapping white fox or valuable furs, one for trading. He set out in June and reached Fort Reliance in September. The Indians were off on their seasonal caribou hunt, leaving Hornby to build his winter quarters, a small cabin, six by eight feet, directly across the bay from the chimneys of the original fort put up by the Arctic explorer George Back in 1833.

He really had no firm idea of what he would do or how he would fare after he left the shelter of the treeline. He was supremely confident that he could live off the land, but he had made no preparation to do so. He did not even understand the migrations of the caribou, which are the key to existence on the Barren Ground. He did not take into account the possibility of accident or injury, nor did he realize that he had chosen an unlikely region in which to justify his theories. He had settled upon a poor place for caribou and also for fishing. Worse, with winter coming on and his cabin yet unfinished he was taken ill, unable to lay out his nets. When at last he had recovered enough to finish his new quarters and had just started trapping, the accident-prone hermit fell against his small tin stove and burned his leg badly.

Ill luck continued to bedevil him. He finally managed to mount a four-day caribou hunt, but that proved fruitless. When he returned he found the Indians had come back in his absence and looted his cabin, leaving him only a meagre supply of food and one pair of snowshoes. He and his dogs were reduced to living on bannock and the small trout that he found in his nets.

"I am now practically destitute," he told his diary in January. In order to get enough bait for his traps he would have to hunt for caribou. But that took time and energy, and in the meantime he was forced to feed his dogs from his supply of staples. Now he admitted, "The urge to get fur blinded me to the consequences of running short of supplies." At that point he was down to fifteen pounds of flour and only enough fish from his nets and hooks to feed the dogs and himself for a single day. To stay alive he would need between twelve and fifteen pounds of fish each day, but his right arm was partly paralyzed and his right hand badly swollen from a neglected injury. Chopping wood was painful and his fishing ground was three miles away.

It was bitterly cold. He had no skin clothing, and he was losing the body fat that might have kept him warm: he was little more than a walking skeleton, reduced to skin and bones. His dogs were also growing weak on a starvation diet. On February 23, he scrawled a wan note in his diary: "No trout, no bait, no caribou, nothing." And outside his cabin a fierce blizzard was blowing.

The bad weather continued, making it impossible on certain days to visit his trapline or his fishing ground. When he did, he often found nothing. On March 6, two days after his biggest dog died, he told his diary: "At times this life appears strange. I never see anyone, no longer have anything to read, and my pencil is too small to permit me to do much writing. It is not surprising that men go mad." There is no self-pity here, no wail of despair; Hornby was merely examining a way of life he had chosen for himself and commenting upon it.

A few Indians came and went. They too were starving: that was their way of life. Hornby fed them fish when he had any. On March 11, he came in from examining his rabbit snares and collapsed on the cabin floor, too weak to reach his bed. Yet his powers of recuperation were remarkable. Two days later he was out again and after twelve hours returned to his cabin with a whitefish and a fox. In this hand-to-mouth fashion the days dragged on. Spring came; the fishing improved. On June 17 he gorged himself on a thirty-pound trout, but there was no way in which he could accumulate enough for the daily hundred pounds he would require for the next season. Although his plans to establish himself on the Barrens by way of Artillery Lake were dashed, he still clung stubbornly to his original dream. Now that the ice was breaking up he would return to Fort Resolution for more supplies; then, perhaps, he could set out and reach his destination in the fall.

Of course he couldn't. Exposure and long periods of starvation had turned him into a wraith. "It is a bad business having to go back to semi-civilization in such a shocking physical condition," he scribbled in his diary with the last bit of his stubby pencil. "But it can't be helped. I shall avoid the people I know as much as possible."

He left his camp on June 21 and reached Resolution by July 10, so famished he could not put down solid food. For the rest of the day he slept under the Hudson's Bay woodpile. He had survived a terrible winter but had accomplished nothing. As government surveyor Guy Blanchet said, "A normal man would not have got into such a situation but, if he did, neither could he have come through as Hornby did."

Incredibly, in spite of all the trials he had faced, he planned to return to the east end of Great Slave for a *second* winter. He had learned little from his experience. He built another cabin not far from the site of the original one. He must have known by now what the winter held. It is hard to discover exactly what he planned to do; the record is clouded. Perhaps he didn't know himself. He had written to George Douglas from Fort Resolution that he would like to spend a winter on the Thelon River at the very heart of the Barrens. That was wishful thinking. The winter that followed was a repeat of the one he had survived; he emerged once again emaciated and exhausted by the experience and with very little to show for it. For the moment, Hornby had had enough of the North. He went out to Edmonton, made a little money guiding for a group of big-time American game hunters, and drifted about until one day he met a man who would change his life. Or, more to the point, he met a man whose life would be changed nearly to the point of suicide by the year he spent with Hornby in the Barrens.

If you searched the country over, you would be hard put to find two characters who differed from each other as much as did James Critchell-Bullock and John Hornby. In matters of temperament, personality, outlook, and habit they were opposites. To confine the pair of them to a cave in the Barren Ground might be forecast as a folly, and a murderous one at that. Yet that would be their home for much of the winter of 1924–25. That they survived was largely because Hornby, ever the wanderer, was absent from the cave for days, even weeks, at a time.

They met, accidentally, at the King Edward Hotel on Front Street, Edmonton, in October 1923: two figures that fitted the images of "Mutt and Jeff," a leading comic strip of the day. Hornby, at five foot four, was Jeff; Bullock, at six foot two, was Mutt (and twenty years younger than his new acquaintance). As they were both public school boys with appropriate accents, they fell into conversation. Bullock wrote to his brother that "for some unearthly reason [Hornby] . . . has taken a fancy to me."

Bullock was an army man who had served as a subaltern with the Bengal Lancers in India and also with Allenby's desert mounted corps in Palestine. Now he was an honorary captain, retired from the army after a bout of malaria. He was everything Hornby was not: fastidious, disciplined, punctual, well scrubbed, and well tailored. Before he quite realized it, Hornby had talked him into a vague scheme to study the Barren Ground, its flora and its fauna, and to trap white fox. He had no idea what he was getting into. Hornby, who was never one to downplay his own wilderness background, intrigued him and undoubtedly flattered him by offering him a partnership on such short acquaintance. He could be charming and open-hearted, as many who encountered him remarked. To Bullock, searching about in Edmonton for a new career in the Canadian North, he must have seemed the ideal companion and mentor.

In November 1923, Hornby, to test his companion's stamina, took Bullock on a three-week excursion into the Rockies to gather specimens of mountain sheep and goats for the Edmonton Museum. That

James Critchell-Bullock was first entranced, later disillusioned by Hornby.

last purpose was abandoned as so many of Hornby's plans were, but from his new partner's viewpoint the trip was a success. He gained a boundless respect for Hornby, who packed the heaviest loads despite his small stature, showed less fatigue, and endured the bitter cold with only two blankets.

Their expedition to the Barrens was planned for the following summer. It would take three years and had two purposes. Bullock, who had been Allenby's photographer in the Middle East, planned to make a motion picture of his Barren Ground experiences; Hornby hoped to get a government grant to study muskoxen and caribou. It would also be a business trip, one that Hornby claimed would bring them a gross profit of thirty thousand dollars in white fox furs. For a retired army man looking for some type of challenging enterprise in the colonies, it seemed attractive, even entrancing: a well-planned, well-ordered, and highly profitable venture with the added benefit of exploring an obscure but romantic corner of the country—and all in the company of an experienced and trusted guide. Bullock wrote to his brother that Hornby was held in high esteem "above everyone else in the whole North country," but added, offhandedly, that "success only depends on getting him to be business-like." That was like saying that success only depends on getting a one-legged man to run the hundred-yard dash.

In the interim, Hornby had befriended a vivacious Welsh woman, Olwen Newell, a recent arrival in Canada some twenty years his junior. It was his idea that she would go north with the expedition and write an account of his travels. She had responded with enthusiasm and soon found herself employed in the expedition's office under Bullock, who was acting as a pro-tem business manager. It was obvious that she was attracted to Hornby, whom she found "a chivalrous man, fastidious in conversation and in his attitude to women . . . an unassuming man, conservative in dress." A close friend warned her, however, that Hornby was not the marrying kind. Hornby saw her as "clever but a simple, affectionate and rather highly strung girl."

He left early in February for Ottawa hoping to raise funds for his projected expedition, but there he met with a cool response. In his absence, Bullock concluded, wrongly, that Hornby and Olwen Newell were engaged and intended to marry. That would put an end to the expedition. He fired Miss Newell, and a flurry of letters and telegrams ensued between Hornby, Bullock, and Hornby's friend Yardley Weaver, now an Edmonton lawyer. Hornby did his best to make it clear that he had no intention of marrying anyone. "I candidly told her, that I had never loved any girl," Hornby told Weaver. "Besides I mentioned she was young & I am old."

Bullock, with the military efficiency that was his nature, continued to prepare for the journey, collecting stores and equipment, studying meteorology and geology, practising photography with various cameras, and pestering civil servants in Ottawa to subsidize the project. "I am entering upon this expedition . . . because Mr. Hornby has honoured me by saying that in me he has found a perfect assistant and partner," he wrote in April. "Unknown to him I am assisting the enterprise financially in such a manner that its failure will leave me penniless." Bullock, in short, was staking everything on a man whom he had known for only a few brief months. The former Bengal Lancer had not done his homework.

Neither of these two adventurers who looked forward with such eagerness to travel to the very heart of the Barrens really knew very much about the other. Bullock was mesmerized by his older partner to the point where he had invested his savings in the proposed expedition, believing that the payoff in white fox pelts and the proceeds of his documentary film were as good as money in the bank. Hornby, after all, had agreed to underwrite his share of the costs that Bullock was incurring. He had also undertaken to raise funds for the expedition in Ottawa and New York—or so he said. Actually, Hornby had no intention of contributing anything. After Hornby met a dead end in Ottawa there was no further talk about New York. Instead, he went off to England to see his parents and ostensibly to raise money, although there is no evidence that he tried.

Ottawa finally came up with a pittance for Hornby—three hundred dollars a year and rations to study the Barren Ground caribou and muskox—but nothing for Bullock, who was still forking out thousands to launch what he thought would be a major scientific expedition. Hornby made a fetish of travelling light. His usual equipment, even on a journey of months, seldom cost more than two hundred dollars. Malcolm Waldron, who based his narrative *Snow Man* on Bullock's diaries, wrote that Hornby would have writhed to see Bullock's list of "necessities." Here were thousands of feet of motion picture film; a standard motion picture camera as well as a portable motion picture camera; a Graflex camera and three hundred reels of Graflex film; a complete developing outfit; a portable darkroom; a botanical outfit with presses to preserve specimens; an entomological outfit with preserving fluid for small mammals and insects; a series of thermometers, theodolites, and three watches for surveying; a surgical kit with anesthetic, sutures, and dressings; and a small library of books on natural history and the Barrens.

In England, Hornby was maddeningly indecisive. His elderly parents were pleading with him to stay with them while Bullock was asking him for an estimate of what the expedition would cost, as Ottawa required. Hornby's response was a blunt cable: "CANCEL EXPEDITION." "I certainly wish now I had not crossed to England," he wrote in the explanatory letter that followed, "so you can realize how miserable I feel here. This senseless life is detestable. . . . How can people be justified in leading an aimless existence?"

This decision was a body blow to Bullock, who had become enmeshed in the expedition's plans psychologically as well as financially. He had every intention of carrying on alone. With the venture already publicized in the Edmonton press, he could not bear the shame of now dropping everything. He would need a helper and so advertised for a fellow adventurer to go with him to the eastern end of Great Slave Lake and then down the Thelon to Chesterfield Inlet on Hudson Bay. He cabled Hornby for permission to use his old cabin on the edge of the Barrens and was astonished to receive an immediate reply: "RETURNING NEXT STEAMER. WAIT FOR ME."

What had caused Hornby to change his mind? Bullock was not yet aware of his would-be partner's jealousy of those who would invade "his" domain. Nor had it occurred to Hornby that Bullock would go off without him. After all, Bullock was his responsibility. What would become of him, a stranger, in that unfriendly territory?

On Hornby's arrival in Edmonton on June 15, 1924, the *Journal* hailed him as a man "who prefers life in the Barren Lands to anything that civilization has to offer" and hinted at the haziness of his plans by reporting that he "isn't very particular whether the party spends one year or two in their efforts to secure the pictures." The paper mentioned that Hornby had lived for several years in the area "and knowing every mile of the country, it will be like going home for him." This public attention marked the real beginning of the Hornby legend in the North.

Hornby baited Bullock about the extravagance of his equipment, which the captain had spent some four months assembling. He was more than suspicious of Jack Glenn, the strapping ex-policeman who had answered Bullock's newspaper advertisement and had signed a contract to join the expedition. Hornby insisted that Bullock fire Glenn, largely, he said, because he would never trust a man with brown eyes, but really because he resented a stranger exploring the Barrens. He temporized when it was agreed that Glenn would bring his wife and that the pair would settle in one of Hornby's cabins near Fort Reliance to remain as a kind of backup, a good distance from the treeless tundra.

As usual, Hornby's planning was haphazard. When the day came for the expedition to leave for the North, he held back, suggesting that Bullock and the Glenns go ahead by canoe and wait for him at Fort Smith. That caused a major delay. The short summer season was advancing and every day counted if they were to establish themselves in the Barrens before freeze-up. Hornby was expected to arrive by July 7 but to Bullock's frustration did not turn up. Bullock and the Glenns went on to Fort Resolution without him.

They were in for a long wait. Bullock was beside himself; apparently Hornby had changed his mind again about the expedition. Bullock had depended on his partner to bring along several articles of equipment including an engine and gasoline, which, in Hornby's absence, he had been forced to buy himself.

Hornby arrived at last—six weeks later—with a party of four acquaintances in an old scow whose engine was continually breaking down. He had picked up two brothers, Malcolm and Allan Stewart, both trappers, an older trapper, Al Greathouse, and a youth known simply as Buck for his last name, Buckley.

This loose group headed off from Fort Resolution to the far eastern end of the lake. There they dropped the Glenns at Hornby's old cabin—dubbed Fort Hornby—directly across from the ruins of Back's Fort Reliance. Also, under Hornby's direction and with help from the trappers, they put up a small log cache (on poles to keep out wolverines) to hold their surplus supplies. By this time Bullock the ex-cavalryman had begun to realize something about Hornby—that his only interest lay in existence from day to day and that any aim of keeping records, gathering statistics, or planning ahead was foreign to his nature. All of Bullock's scientific gear was to be left behind in the cache (save for one still camera and a portable movie camera) to be sent to him when the need arose. The outfit had cost Bullock something close to four thousand dollars. When he protested this waste of money, Hornby simply asked if money was of any ultimate importance.

With the northern winter fast approaching, the various members of this party of convenience began to shuttle their gear and their canoes— some five tons in all—across twenty-five miles of short carrying places that go under the name of Pike's Portage after the big-game hunter and explorer Warburton Pike. That led them to Artillery Lake, a fifty-mile-long finger of water that reaches into the Barrens.

For Bullock, packing 110 pounds on his back was misery enough, but Hornby's shiftless conduct made it worse. "Cannot understand him," Bullock told his diary. "He becomes more untidy and hopeless every day. He is obviously more in favour of supporting schemes of commercialism than our own scientific endeavours." A fortnight later he noted: "Hornby regularly eats raw caribou marrow, cracking bones noisily with a large dirty hunting knife sitting among a most awful mess of blood, sinew, and untidiness imaginable. Apparently the dirtier the

204

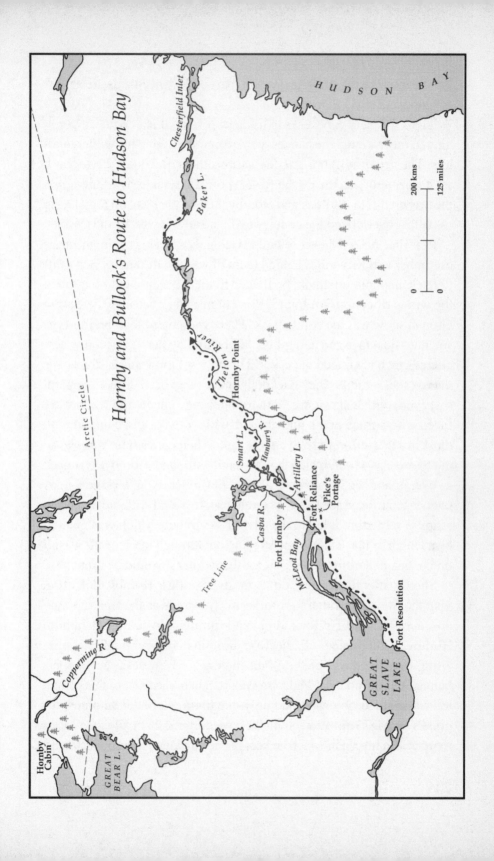

Hornby and Bullock's Route to Hudson Bay

HUDSON BAY

Chesterfield Inlet

Baker L.

200 kms

125 miles

0

0

Thelon River

Hornby Point

Arctic Circle

Smart L.

Hanbury R.

Artillery L.

Fort Reliance

Pike's Portage

Casba R.

Fort Hornby

Tree Line

McLeod Bay

Coppermine R.

Fort Resolution

GREAT SLAVE LAKE

Hornby Cabin

GREAT BEAR L.

job the more he relishes the product, particularly his hands are a mess of blood and hawk entrails."

It took the party two weeks to navigate Artillery Lake. With ice beginning to form around the canoes, it was time to arrange for winter quarters. The group split up. The Stewart brothers dug out a shelter built with frozen turf on the Casba River (now the Lockhart) where it met the timbered area. Bullock and Hornby pitched their tent on top of a big esker that overlooked the country to the north and west of the Casba.

But what kind of shelter to build? Certainly not a log cabin; the nearest timber was fifty miles behind them. It was too distant for dog sleds to fetch, and logs could not be floated to them because the river ran in the wrong direction. An Inuit iglu wouldn't work because the Barren Ground snow was too soft to pack. There was no sod for a prairie-type sod hut—just the sand and gravel left behind by the subglacial watercourse that had created the esker. The only solution was to dig a cave in the esker's flank. They hacked it out of the frozen ground, ten feet by seven, with a six-and-a-half-foot ceiling. The inside walls were faced with spruce brush and ground-willow twigs and caulked with moss in a vain effort to keep out the sand. Their canvas tent was spread out to serve as a roof, which they covered with sand. Hornby, as rugged as ever, made the long trip to a stand of timber to cut a ridgepole. A twelve-foot trench served as a storehouse. Covered with old hides and strips of tarpaulin, it led to the cavern's entrance, which was marked by a length of black stovepipe sticking out through the snow. It wasn't much, this makeshift hovel, but for that winter it would be home.

Shortly after the job was done, the ever-restless Hornby took off to visit the Stewart brothers six miles away. That was the first of many absences that left Bullock alone and fuming. He could not fathom Hornby, as the variety of adjectives used in his diary suggests: "puzzling" . . . "irresponsible" . . . "disgusting" . . . "tireless" . . . "superhuman" . . . "profound." Malcolm Waldron, in his account of this period, tells us that Hornby, who had only one tooth, wore dental plates for pride's sake in civilization but in the cave dropped them into the nearest receptacle, a tin can in which he kept his freshly killed mouse specimens.

206

In the cabin, he ate without teeth, tearing at his meat with his single incisor, "giving it a perfunctory prod or two with his gums, and swallowing it at a gulp."

Hornby had a pet aluminum spoon, twisted and dented, that he stuck in the sand by his bed and never washed. Each time its use was called for, he picked it up and scooped out the grease and sand with his thumb. "He would drag a whole carcass into the cave and squatting on his sleeping bag, disembowel it, creating a frightful mess."

Ribald talk was of no interest to him. Any time the conversation with Bullock verged on sex, Hornby cut him off. Bullock suffered tortures trying to keep himself clean with a shallow pan full of freezing water, but Hornby never bathed and, to Bullock's chagrin, did not seem to need any kind of a wash. It was as if the dirt fell away from him as soon as it was formed.

By November the nights were sixteen hours long and the makeshift candles provided scarcely enough illumination to allow them to read and re-read the crumpled six-month-old newspapers that had served as wrappings. Hornby again set out, this time for Fort Reliance, on an absence that left Bullock alone in the cave for three weeks. Hornby's purpose, ostensibly, was to bring back the weather instruments that Bullock needed to make his observations. In fact, the puckish Hornby had decided to play a trick on Bullock—at least that was how he saw it—a capital jest in which he would spread a rumour that Bullock had gone off his head and was trying to murder his partner. In his bizarre reasoning, Hornby, who was always concerned about his public image, believed that the rumour of Bullock's mental condition would shine a spotlight on the expedition, which he thought needed to be called to the public's attention. It would be Hornby's way of presenting himself as a rugged adventurer, meeting and overcoming all odds.

Because of the rumours of Bullock's madness, Hornby reckoned that when they finally reached Hudson Bay a large crowd would be waiting for them, astonished and overcome with admiration that they had come all the way from Edmonton. But Bullock must not know his scheme. That would spoil the joke.

To his partner's frustration, Hornby returned from Fort Reliance without any of the instruments that had been the one reason for his hundred-mile journey. ". . . Poor Hornby is becoming more untidy," Bullock complained to his diary. "His only care is in setting traps, cutting up meat, and chasing and talking about caribou. Apparently my elaborate equipment is going to be wasted."

Hornby always seemed to be on the move, visiting the trappers, looking for vagrant bits of timber to prop up the roof, or hunting for caribou, while Bullock languished in the cave. Then one bitterly cold December day, Hornby collapsed. Bullock dragged him inside, believing his partner to be on the point of death. But after forty-eight hours the tough little man recovered.

The days grew shorter, the cold grew worse, the wind rose to a velocity of sixty knots. Now they were sleeping for fourteen hours; what else was there to do? The weird cacophony of the Barrens intruded upon their rest: the eerie wail of the wolves, the whining of the endless blizzards, and the sudden explosive cracking of the earth as the sand and gravel in the esker expanded and contracted. It was so cold that even with a fire in the stove they were forced to wear their winter clothing when in their sleeping bags.

Two days before Christmas, the restless Hornby set off in the midst of a blizzard to visit the Stewart brothers, and once again Bullock was alone. He realized that without dogs he could not forage for fuel—and Hornby had taken all the dogs except one lame animal. There was plenty of caribou meat stored in the tunnel, but it was frozen rock solid and he needed fire to thaw it. During that night the roof sank further under the weight of the snow. Now it was scraping against his head.

All the fuel that remained was a pile of twelve twigs, none more than an inch in circumference. There were also spruce needles in the walls, and he gathered a few handfuls of these. He managed to start a brief fire to heat the water pail, solid with ice, and the frozen slabs of caribou meat, which he put into a pan with some grease. He gulped his tea—mixed with sand from the walls—and gnawed away at the meat until the fire died. Exhausted, he crawled into his sleeping bag, over which he piled all of Hornby's bedding. When he woke on Christmas Eve, he found that his beard was frozen solid to the blanket. His lone entry for that day is a cry from the heart: "Alone this Christmas Eve on the Barren Lands of the Sub-Arctic of America. . . . Alone in a dugout beneath the sand and snow. . . . Alone in this awful shack of continual discomfort with its subsiding walls and crazy roof likely at any moment to fall and entomb me in a living grave. Alone with sufficient wood to make only one more fire. . . . Alone with but the whole of the blizzard outside to cheer me and the thoughts of peace and happiness and the faces of loved ones coming to mind only to remind me more and more of my deep loneliness. . . ."

The incredible monotony of the Barrens preyed on his mind. Earlier in Edmonton, Hornby's enthusiastic descriptions had invested them with a kind of mystique, even glamour. But here, in the actual environment, the magic was gone. The flat, featureless land stretched off in every direction to a hazy horizon, devoid of tree or shrub and unmarked by any physical feature—not a ravine or a hill or even a slope, not a knoll or a depression or a fold in the ground—nothing save for the esker in which he huddled. One is reminded of the recent photographs taken on the red surface of Mars, but the Barrens were even devoid of colour: only a greyish white to match the sullen sky above.

Bullock realized that he would have to move, and with the blizzard abating, he staggered off at last with the lame dog leading the way. He managed to follow the half-obliterated trail for six miles and arrived exhausted at Malcolm Stewart's shack, where Hornby greeted him laconically. Following a ten-day period for Bullock to recuperate, the two went back to the cave.

Understandably, Bullock's early admiration for his new partner was fading. In November he had written to Yardley Weaver that Hornby was "the most delightful of companions & what more could I wish for?" By January Hornby was getting on his nerves. In Edmonton, Bullock had been fascinated by Hornby's tales of his northern adventures. Now his endless boasting, his refusal to indulge in what Bullock considered serious conversation, and his self-aggrandizement were too much. Years later, Bullock described the tenor of Hornby's talk: "If I were King there would be no wars. There is no man living who could beat me in a straight fight. The Government ought to give me Artillery Lake as compensation for all the hardships I have endured on behalf of the North. The North has never known such a traveller as I. Hardships and the ability to starve like a gentleman are the only criteria of a good traveller. My name will live in history as I have made the greatest of all contributions to the North Country. I am the only white man with whom the Indians and Eskimos know they can safely leave their women."

The winter dragged on, with Hornby coming and going, setting traps, gathering wood, shooting the odd caribou, and disappearing for ten days at a time. "Cannot imagine what H. is up to," Bullock confided to his diary in mid-March. "Here we are, dozens of foxes behind the other people, and he is still wandering about. . . . Again he will set a line of traps, spend days doing it and never trouble to look at it." Several days later, he wrote: "Never would I allow H. to arrange for my welfare again. . . . One day's wood left, but I will get through somehow. Damn everyone and the fates included."

On April 1, 1925, a police patrol from Fort Resolution, guided by Hornby and Malcolm Stewart, arrived at the cave. Corporal Hawkins of the RCMP and his companion, Constable Baker, seemed perplexed to find Bullock in good spirits and apparently in the best of health. Although they had brought forty-eight letters for him, Bullock was baffled. What were the Mounties doing out here in the Barrens? They certainly hadn't come merely to deliver the mail. And why was the corporal regarding him with such attention? In the gloom of the cave, he sensed that the visitors were not at their ease. The conversation was desultory: only Hornby was enjoying it. As they conversed in whispers, Bullock noticed a gleam in his eye but could make no sense of it. After a brief two-hour visit, the patrol declined his invitation to lunch, made their way out through the labyrinth of poles now holding up the sagging roof, and tendered their goodbyes, leaving Bullock to read his mail and wonder why they had come three hundred miles just to bring it. Haphazard patrols were not part of their regular procedure. And why were their explanations so brief?

That is the story that Waldron tells in *Snow Man* from his reading of Bullock's diary. The visit is a murky business. At Malcolm Stewart's dugout, the police explained that they had received a note from Jack Glenn, Bullock's erstwhile partner, quoting Hornby as saying that Bullock was dangerously insane. Hornby denied that he had told Glenn to report Bullock's condition to the police. But now he admitted that in his view, Bullock had been acting strangely, had talked of committing suicide, and was despondent because the long winter nights frustrated him in his goal of making a motion picture of the Barrens. Again and again Hawkins asked Hornby if he was afraid of Bullock. Again and again Hornby denied it.

It was not unusual for two men, especially as different in temperament as this pair and confined to close quarters, as Hornby and Bullock were, to resort to violence, suicide, or even murder. But Hornby had been away from the cave for days, even weeks, at a time. If Bullock was despondent, and he certainly was, it was because he was confined twenty-four hours a day while his cave mate alleviated his restlessness by periodic forays to Fort Reliance or the cabins of his trapper friends. In a letter to his friend Weaver on the same day the police arrived, Hornby had reported that "Bullock is now in fine condition, but I was certainly at times afraid that his rather too vivid imagination might lead him to act stranger than he has done."

Was all this a practical joke by Hornby at Bullock's expense? Or was Hornby really alarmed that his partner was going off the deep end? Whalley writes, "Hornby himself probably didn't know," but he adds, "it is difficult to avoid the conclusion that at times Hornby was deliberately tormenting, frustrating and humiliating Bullock."

There were two sides to this maddening partnership. Although Hornby might be infuriating to live with, Bullock was still in awe of his considerable abilities. He could not remain at odds with him for long. Hornby had all the guile of a naughty little boy, but there were moments when, like a naughty little boy, he was lovable. Writing to Glenn three years later, Bullock eulogized him as "the bravest man I ever knew and the finest friend that any man ever had on a backwoods trail. Out in the bush, Hornby was the real Hornby, and [a] better man never lived."

These qualities were evident when at last they left their cave after burning all non-essentials in order to make their way east by way of the Hanbury and Thelon rivers—a torturous journey that would add up to seven hundred miles of back-and-forth trekking. They could have returned to civilization the easy way—back through Artillery and Great Slave lakes. Indeed, Corporal Hawkins had advised Hornby against using the Thelon route, but, perversely, Hornby rejected his counsel. He wanted to be known as the first to cross the Barrens from west to east—the hard way. On his arrival at Chesterfield Inlet a crowd would gather and ask where he had come from. "Edmonton," he would reply casually, and already he was hearing in his mind the cries of astonishment that would greet his words. Hornby was building himself a legendary reputation, block by block.

They had sent some fox furs out by the police patrol but had 150 more—half a ton—to take with them across the Barrens. Bullock finally made the long trip himself back to the cache at Fort Hornby only to realize, to his dismay, that most of the expensive equipment stored there for him would be an unwanted encumbrance. He had invested his meagre savings in that outfit, and Hornby, before he left for Ottawa to raise money, had agreed to pay half the cost. Now he was making it obvious that he had no intention of paying a cent. As Bullock wrote later, "He feels that I spent unwisely & that such elaborate equipment was unnecessary. He fails to understand that I bought it for the precise reason that I had every faith in his promise to make the expedition an extensive thing." The best he could hope for would be the thirty thousand dollars Hornby had claimed they would make when they sold the furs.

They tried their best to lighten their burden for the coming trek. Even without the goods left behind at the cache, they could not get the weight of the staple food, canoes, cameras, and film below one ton. That done, they piled the unnecessary gear into the cave and, using fox fat for fuel, burned it all.

Hornby's scheme to gain publicity by casually remarking that he had come all the way to Chesterfield Inlet from Edmonton was achieved only at serious mental and physical cost. They faced an epic ordeal, and an unnecessary one. They set off on May 19 over the crusted snow with all their supplies including their two canoes lashed to a single sled—the two men and three dogs straining away on the ropes and harness. Ahead lay tortuous canyons, seething rapids, and portages of sand, muskeg, and slippery rock. The task would not be easy, with each man handling a canoe entirely on his own. Their immediate goal, the junction of the Hanbury and Thelon rivers, was at least one hundred laborious miles away and the going was slow. They drove themselves and their dogs eighteen hours a day, but they had to move the heavy load forward in stages, packing and unpacking, loading and unloading as they advanced toward their goal. For every mile of portage they were forced to travel fifteen. As spring advanced, water from the melting snow ran into a lake, and its weight depressed the ice on the edge so that a channel was created near the shore that ran three feet above the frozen level. They had to unload the sled, move everything into the canoes, and pole or paddle their way along the margin.

For almost two weeks in that confusion of small, ragged, unknown lakes, they were hopelessly lost. "We do not know where we are," Bullock wrote. "We are both trying to appear unconcerned." Where was the Hanbury? In what direction were they now headed? Bullock made a fifteen-mile reconnaissance and almost drowned breaking through the thin ice at a lake's edge. Here were long reaches of water not on the maps and, in that flat country, very little drainage. The day after Bullock's accident, Hornby set out to get some hint of a route to the Hanbury. He finally succeeded by chopping a hole in the ice and tossing in some bannock crumbs to find which way the current flowed. The movement was almost imperceptible but observable. They followed it eastward, and by June 10 they reached Smart Lake, which is in fact part of the Hanbury. Their destination, the trading post at Baker Lake on Chesterfield Inlet, still a convoluted five hundred miles to the east, was the only human habitation on that route.

The time had come to again reduce the weight they were carrying. Bullock was in agony from an injury to his back incurred on his last trip to Fort Reliance. Hornby, who had opposed lightening their loads, now gave in to his partner's condition. They stood their sled on end and anchored it with some rocks at the base to mark their cache. Then they dumped twelve thousand feet of motion picture film and most of their winter equipment, including heavy parkas and extra blankets, on top of the sled, lightening their load by two hundred pounds.

They moved on east, paddling and portaging. Hornby quietly took on the heavier loads to ease Bullock's suffering. In mid-June they saw their first muskoxen. Finally, on the twenty-third they reached the point where the Hanbury flows into the Thelon. Here, after five weeks on the trail, Bullock could at last begin filming.

Things were looking up. They camped at a bend in the river that would later be called Hornby Point. That day they managed to cover forty miles, a record for the trip. But that night Bullock cut his foot so badly with an axe that they could not move for two days, and by then they had lost the last of their dogs. On August 2, they were able to move twenty-five miles, with Hornby acting as nurse and filling his partner with doses of caribou soup.

The following day, with Bullock unable to handle a canoe and on the verge of collapse, they began a three-day recess. Bullock now faced another concern. He was dead broke because of his expenditure on the discarded equipment. What would he do when they reached civilization without funds? The howling winds and incessant rain that night increased his despair.

A new problem nagged at them. By August 21 they were out of meat, half starved, their bodies skeletal, subsisting on whatever fish they could catch. In this condition they entered the lower Thelon. In spite of a recurring blizzard, Hornby managed to kill a caribou "that just about saved our lives." They took a day off and feasted, gulping down an enormous meal: all the caribou liver, both kidneys, all the fat they could gather from the carcass, four one-pound steaks, and thirteen pounds of fish. Bullock felt so lively that in spite of the storm, he took

214

a bath in ice water. It was at this point that Hornby, finding his partner in good spirits, confessed why the police had come to the esker cave. There is no record of Bullock's reaction.

A few miles out of Baker Lake, with their goal almost in sight, they had another near disaster. There were rapids ahead, but in the bright sunlight Bullock didn't see them and was swept forward in his canoe. He looked back and to his horror saw his partner standing up in his own canoe trying to get a better view of the rocks and shoals. He too had missed seeing the rapids. Now, as Hornby teetered in the canoe, the waters seized it and he dropped onto one knee. "I'm all right, Bullock!" he shouted over the roar of the rapids. Both craft struggled with the waters for a mile and a half until calm was reached, but it had been a near death thing. Hornby could not swim; once again he had survived through pure luck.

They reached the Hudson's Bay post at Baker Lake on August 27, 1925, having travelled 535 miles in 107 days on a journey only a handful of men had made before them and one that future travellers would not find necessary. With the coming of the airplane and the parallel improvement in electronic communication, Hornby and Bullock's feat of endurance would not need to be repeated. They had crossed the Barren Ground at the end of an era that began with Samuel Hearne. It is ironic that Hornby, who wanted to keep the land of the tundra virtually untrammelled, would serve as a reminder of the passing of the old ways.

The Hudson's Bay Company's post and that of Revillon Frères stood side by side on the slope above the point where the Thelon empties its waters into Baker Lake, which is connected to the great bay by Chesterfield Inlet. A curious group made its way to the water's edge to greet the newcomers, who were tying up their canoes. Here was a puzzle. No canoes had gone up the Thelon that summer. How could two be coming down? The Hudson's Bay factor held back his curiosity until the canoes were properly fastened. Then he asked: where did they come from? This was the moment that Hornby had been waiting for. This was the reason why he had chosen to go back to civilization the hard way; this would add another chapter to the legend he had helped create about himself.

"From Edmonton," he remarked nonchalantly.

"From *where?*" the factor asked.

Oh, yes, Hornby repeated. They'd had a fine trip. Couldn't be better.

Up at the trading post, the factor repeated the question again. Just where had they come from? Hornby repeated his answer, to general bewilderment. Then he and Bullock told their tangled tale.

At dinner that night at the neighbouring Revillon Frères, Bullock noted that Hornby seemed ill at ease and realized that the little man was sorry the trip was over. "A week of this, Bullock," he said, "and we'll wish we were back in the Barrens. They live by routine at these posts." Routine had no part in Hornby's way of life.

The Hudson's Bay motorboat took the pair to Chesterfield Inlet. The schooner *Jacques Revillon* took them across Hudson Bay to Port Harrison, and the steamer *Peveril* brought them to St. John's, Newfoundland. Here Bullock suffered a devastating blow. The fox pelts they had brought out were worthless. When the candles in the cave had run out, wolf and fox fats had had to be used instead, providing such poor light that careful cleaning was impossible. During the summer's heat the residue of animal grease boiled into the hide and loosened the fur. Seasoned trappers were aware of this problem and knew how to deal with it. Once again Hornby's slapdash methods, together with his partner's inexperience, had nullified the commercial aspects of the onerous trek across the Barrens. It had all been in vain.

As one Arctic expert, Lawrence Millman, noted in his introduction to Malcolm Waldron's *Snow Man*, "Hornby and Bullock courted misfortune like a pair of dogs rooting up truffles." The long, hazardous journey had added nothing to science, resulted in no new maps being drawn up, and produced no new ethnographic data on the native peoples. No documentary was ever made of Bullock's Barren Ground footage: the lack of a telephoto lens and the absence of proper light were to blame.

Bullock himself was unable to get backing for another Arctic expedition. He lived a purposeless life in England, emigrated to Kenya, and invested in a local asbestos mine, which failed. Both his marriages failed, too. In 1953, he checked into the elegant Norfolk Hotel in Nairobi and put a bullet through his head. "The last of the Bengal Lancers," *The Times* called him, making no mention of his trip with Hornby. As Whalley wrote, "Bullock is an interesting phenomenon: he was the only person who ever proceeded on the assumption that Hornby was a competent Northern traveller, and survived that curious assumption."

All true. And yet in spite of Hornby's many deficiencies—his refusal to plan ahead, his inattention to detail, his devil-may-care attitude to danger—his Barren Ground trek had a positive and lasting legacy. After his return he sent to the Department of the Interior at Ottawa a sixteen-page single-spaced document titled *Report of Explorations in the District Between Artillery Lake and Chesterfield Inlet.* In it he recommended that immediate measures be taken to protect the Barrens wildlife from human exploitation. The department took the suggestion seriously and passed it on to the Advisory Board on Wildlife Protection.

As a result, the government established a 15,000-square-mile sanctuary in the upper Thelon country. Today it is extended to 35,000 square miles and is one of the continent's largest protected wilderness areas. It is harder for a Canadian to cross that border than it is to travel to the United States. This great remote reserve has some of the toughest restrictive laws in the world, as I discovered myself when I managed, with difficulty, to get a permit to venture into the Thelon country by air.

Every desert has its oasis, and the Thelon sanctuary is no exception. Here, where the two rivers—Thelon and Hanbury—meet, are fat clumps of spruce with grassy meadows and green copses of willow growing on the bottom of an ancient lake, complete with sand dunes and beaches as white as Waikiki. Here the glossy muskoxen come to graze and grow fat at the edges of the round blue lakes. It was here that John Hornby wanted to spend his last days, far from the confusion of the civilized world. In effect he got his wish, although under tragic and unforeseen circumstances. But the great sanctuary remains his legacy, and he could not have wished for more.

Hornby in Northcote, Ontario, in 1925, looking very much the proper Englishman.

THREE

John Hornby returned to England in December 1925 in time to attend the funeral of his father, who had succumbed to a stroke. He felt awkward and ill at ease in the family home, Parkfield. The society in which he moved, with its public school accents and its emphasis on sport, was far removed from the frontier life for which he longed. "Here, no one is sincere," he wrote to his friend George Douglas, "and I feel like an absolute stranger. I am like a wild animal, caged."

This restlessness was exacerbated by his mother, who kept urging him to stay in England and give up his northern adventures. For Hornby that would be like giving up his right arm. He loved to talk about his hardships on the Barrens and his adventures on the lakes, but for that he needed an audience—someone who would listen wide-eyed to his tales, prod him with questions, and then enthusiastically demand more. His mother did not want to hear accounts of her son's moments of peril and privation. Only when he received an invitation from a cousin, Marguerite Christian, to visit her family at Bron Dirion in northern Wales did he find an attentive and enthusiastic listener in the person of his seventeen-year-old second cousin, Edgar. Just out of public school, Edgar gave him the adulation he craved.

There are few portraits of Edgar extant, but one tells us a great deal about this teenage hero-worshipper. Blue-eyed and blond, his child-like face unlined, young Edgar Christian is the picture of innocence— a guilelessness all the more heart-rending when we comprehend his ultimate tragedy.

The English had a special fondness for those adventurers who insisted on doing things the hard way, especially those who failed nobly. Hornby, with his tales of near starvation and his record of close calls, dovetailed neatly with the imperial credo, emphasizing "pluck" and "playing the game." Edgar peppered him with questions: had he really hiked hundreds of miles over the snowfields? Had he chopped a hole in the ice to catch a trout? It was the kind of wide-eyed adoration that spurred him on. Had he actually shot a bear? Had he seen herds of caribou?

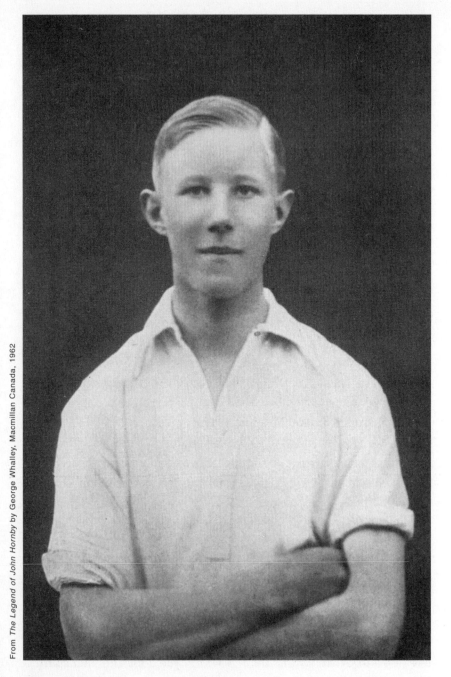

Edgar Christian's hero worship of Hornby later led to his own death by starvation.

Hornby responded gratefully and spun tales about *la foule* tramping through the forests and muskoxen loping across the Barrens.

He had no intention of staying in England in spite of or perhaps because of his mother's pleas. "She curiously thinks that money or an easy life are all that one can wish for," he wrote to Bullock. "Money, I admit, is all right but the latter does not appeal to me." But what would he do in Canada? Where would he go? He had already turned his back on Great Bear Lake. Any form of civilization appalled him. The Barren Ground beckoned him, but he needed an excuse to return to the tundra. He found that excuse in Edgar Christian's idolization. Christian, in turn, found in Hornby an acceptable excuse to leave home and seek adventure. Hornby would go to Canada as Christian's guide and mentor. Christian would fulfill Hornby's need for an appreciative one-man audience. Christian could set off with the assurance for his family that he was travelling under the guidance of the most experienced backwoodsman in Canada. What an opportunity! His aunt, his mother, and finally Colonel Christian all agreed, brushing aside his sister-in-law's objection. Why—it would make a man of him!

What were they thinking of? Here they were, dispatching a boy not old enough to vote and with little outdoor experience to accompany a man whose own plans for returning to the wilderness were vague and ephemeral. They do not appear to have made any searching inquiries in Canada about Hornby's abilities or qualifications. No doubt they, too, were impressed by Hornby's yarn spinning. There was an appealing quality about Hornby that charmed some, as it had once charmed Bullock. But there were enough old Northern hands available to dampen some of the enthusiasm that Hornby inspired. A less suitable companion for the Northern wilderness would have been hard to find. The family had no idea where he and Edgar were headed. Hornby probably didn't know himself. But Edgar had absolute faith in his fabulous cousin. "The more I get to know Jack, the nicer he seems to be," he wrote in the diary his father had urged him to keep. "His extraordinary knowledge on some subjects is really wonderful considering how long he has been living so far away from civilization."

They embarked for Halifax on April 19, 1926, and on arrival made their way to Ottawa where Guy Blanchet, the government surveyor, expressed concern about Hornby's plans, or lack of them. Christian, in a letter home, had written vaguely about trapping around Great Slave Lake or even prospecting near Fort Smith. In Toronto, Hornby made contact with George Douglas's wife, Kay, who was staying with friends and whose father, as George Douglas later recalled, "was full of forebodings as to what might happen to Edgar." Hornby talked vaguely about joining the gold rush to Red Lake in northwestern Ontario by way of Winnipeg. But when they reached Winnipeg there was no further talk about Red Lake. Hornby had apparently used that ploy only as an excuse to look up his old girlfriend, Olwen Newell, now living in Winnipeg. There, to her astonishment, he proposed marriage. She declined, using the excuse that she was returning to England as soon as she could afford the fare. Hornby, impulsive as ever, bought her a first-class ticket and told her he was redrafting his will to leave his entire fortune to her, a promise he never bothered to fulfill.

Olwen, who met and liked Edgar, also did her best to persuade Hornby not to take the boy farther north than Athabasca Landing, but now, with the prospect of a settled life with her fading, Hornby's resolve hardened. To see the real Canada—the uncivilized Canada beyond the trees—Edgar must experience the Barren Ground.

When they arrived in Edmonton, Hornby resumed his acquaintanceship with his cousins in Onoway and there ran into an old friend, twenty-seven-year-old Harold Adlard, behind the counter of the general store. Adlard reminded him of a vague promise he had made two years before. A veteran of the Royal Naval Air Service, Adlard had tried to join Hornby and Bullock on their earlier expedition, but Bullock had vetoed the idea. Hornby, feeling sorry for Adlard, had promised to take him on the next trip. Now he had a further reason to go back to the tundra; as Service had written, "a promise made is a debt unpaid and the North has its own stern code." There was also the safety factor to consider. Hornby and Bullock had concluded that three was the minimum number needed to take on any expedition into the Barren Ground. So three it would be, and the Barrens would be their ultimate goal.

Harold Adlard shown before the ill-fated trek to the Barrens that cost him his life.

223

The outfit that Hornby assembled for the venture was practical enough, indeed luxurious by his standards—a ton of supplies, excluding comestibles. It included a sheet-metal camp stove, a canvas tent and groundsheets, a Primus stove, a meat grinder, a felling axe, binoculars and a camera, three sheets of window glass, hammer, nails, files and drills, metal cutlery, and three rifles. Hornby undoubtedly had his critics in mind and also his responsibility to his two green companions; this outfit was a little out of keeping with his personal asceticism. There were deficiencies, however, in the provisions he assembled and these would have fatal consequences. Because of his unsupported conviction that anybody could live off the land, even in the Barrens, he did not take enough dried food. In spite of his experiences with the cold on his previous journey, he took only one caribou-hide parka for three people! Worst of all, he was leading his young greenhorns into a region where game birds were reasonably plentiful, yet he declined to bring along a shotgun. Hornby's eccentricities came to the fore when he refused to allow Christian to bring a Bible—a superfluous piece of weight—while at the same time he took along his formal dress suit, complete with gold cufflinks, in his own suitcase.

Again attempts were made by seasoned Northern veterans to talk Hornby out of this newest enterprise. At Fort Chipewyan they encountered Guy Blanchet, the government surveyor, who again did his best to talk Hornby out of wintering on the Thelon. Blanchet was reasonably sure that this was a summer breeding ground for the migrating caribou but not a winter one. No one really knew because no one had ever wintered in the verdant Thelon oasis, separated from the tree-line by miles of empty tundra. Hornby's stubborn response was that he had already made his plans and meant to keep his promise to Adlard as well as to Christian.

In Edgar Christian's eyes, Hornby could do no wrong. From Fort Smith he wrote an enthusiastic letter to his family with the reassuring words, "I am as safe as a house with Jack." Although the flies were bad, it was "a wonderful life and one could not wish for better. After going on this trip with Jack I shall never be in need of a Job if I want

224

one. I can be independent of any man because I can make my own headway in Lots of ways."

When they reached the site of old Fort Reliance, Edgar's enthusiasm had not waned. The Barrens lay just ahead, and he was eager to see the land that Hornby had boasted about. "Jack is going into a Country which has never been trapped by any one else before because it is too hard to get into with Supplies," he wrote to his family in a letter that suggests how thoroughly he had absorbed Hornby's offhand attitude to Arctic travel. ". . . & most men take Supplies and don't rely on the Country . . ." he told them.

It had taken three weeks to thread their way by canoe through the tangle of narrow lakes that led to Fort Reliance. The real back-breaking work, however, began when they took the portage route named for Warburton Pike to Artillery Lake. They were now forced to pack their ton of goods on their backs not once but at least eight times around rapids and waterfalls going from one small lake to another. By the time they left Artillery Lake they were beyond the treeline and into what the Indians called "the Stickless Land." The blackflies were almost unbearable, and hours were wasted seeking out brushwood to build smudges and cooking fires.

About August 12, at Sifton Lake near the headwaters of the Hanbury, Harold Adlard began a letter to his parents noting that it had been more than a month since they had seen another human being. "For a month now, I have lived on caribou and tea and like it," he wrote, explaining that they were heading for the oasis of woodland in the Thelon country. "About a dozen men all told have been through so far. . . . If you don't hear within three years make enquiries from the Royal Northwest Police." It was the first hint, and no more than a hint, that there might be trouble ahead.

By September they were canoeing down the broad and slow-moving Thelon below its junction with the Hanbury and making good time. In the heart of the wooded oasis they found, at last, a suitable camping spot overlooking the broad sweep of the river, and here they set about building a cabin.

This was not as easy a task as it would have been in wooded country. Setting aside the problem of getting logs, which was partially alleviated by the presence of a thicket of spruce trees, one must consider the problem of time: a shelter has to be complete before the harsh winter season advances. There is one other consideration. Three men jammed into a confined space and forced to wait out a storm or blizzard are often driven to that psychological condition, so familiar to Northerners, known as cabin fever. Hornby's original cabin at Fort Reliance was only six feet by eight. Opposed as he was to any kind of luxury in the wild, and with October fast approaching, he settled for a three-man domicile that was no more than fourteen feet square. The rear wall was a vertical bank of earth, revetted with spruce and brush and reindeer moss; the other three were composed of spruce logs between eight and eighteen inches in diameter, all felled with an axe because Hornby had balked at bringing along a crosscut saw. The roof was thatched with spruce branches, earth, and river shingle. What was left of the felled spruce was used to build a small adjoining storehouse. It was slow going: it took almost two months to complete the cabin while they shivered in a tent pitched against one side. They were short of tools, and besides, precious hours had to be used up in the continual search for food.

Had they missed the caribou, which, in the natives' famous phrase, "come like ghost, fill up the land, and vanish"? Hornby had been certain that *la foule* was a regular occurrence, always in late August or early September, when their meat was nutritious and edible. If the caribou were in prime condition, he reasoned, it would not be difficult to kill, freeze, and store the fifty carcasses the trio would need for the coming winter. He had selected this point on the curve of the Thelon believing that a considerable number would winter here. He based his forecast on his previous experience at Artillery Lake, but that was two hundred miles to the southwest.

All this was arrogant and wishful thinking on Hornby's part. It was obvious that they had missed any mass migration through this section of the Barrens if, indeed, there had been one. The evidence was flimsy since no one had ever wintered here. Moreover, as we learned in the Yukon, the migrating herds did not necessarily follow exactly the same routes season after season.

Equally serious was Hornby's decision not to take dogs—a view at odds with conventional wisdom. Without dogs to handle the loads it was not possible to travel any distance overland in the North. Hornby, who tended to believe he was a superman, and certainly wanted to give that impression, overruled the obvious.

He still clung to the unsubstantiated belief that small, isolated herds of caribou could be found near the woods that bordered the river. But what if he was wrong? What if it turned out that small breeding herds were farther away? It would not be possible to kill enough meat and transport the burden dozens of miles back to camp without dogs and sleds. What then? Bullock, after the fact, said he believed that Hornby, if driven to it, was prepared to kill muskoxen. They were a protected species but could be shot in the face of extreme destitution. If that was Hornby's fail-safe plan, it depended again on whether these elusive animals existed near the campsite.

Hornby had the only trapper's licence among the trio. Nonetheless it was Christian who kept an eye on the trapline whenever weather permitted. The results in the first three weeks were disappointing: three weasels, one marten, two whisky-jacks (Canada jays), some mice, a wolverine, and only one white fox, whose fur was to be the main harvest of the enterprise. That scarcely jibed with Hornby's earlier assertion that he was going "to make a fortune in fur for the boy."

The sparseness of the catch emphasized the other problem. The absence of a quantity of small fur-bearing animals suggested the absence as well of larger game, for the rodents habitually took advantage of leftovers from wolf and Indian kills of caribou.

Hornby had pooh-poohed Blanchet's belief that this was not a caribou winter range. He was still sure that caribou could be found somewhere in the area. In the absence of dogs, he suggested that a small cache be established some sixteen miles upstream where rations could be stored and where any killed meat could be held for later collection.

The cabin on the banks of the Thelon as a prospecting party found it a year after the tragedy. They missed Edgar Christian's diary, hidden in the stove.

229

This was done, but Christian's diary gives no details. It was written in spurts with gaps of days, even weeks, between. On November 21, after a silence of almost a month, he mentions being held up all day by a storm, "which meant 1 day's less hunting owing to lack of grub," an ominous note. The next morning he went out again but on return faced a strong, bitterly cold wind. "Could not keep hands and face warm at all." He had managed to travel the sixteen miles through the snow but with no useful result.

During one severe windstorm, all three were forced to huddle in the cabin for fear of frostbite. Wind chill is the curse of the Barrens, making it, in Clive Powell-Williams's description in *Cold Burial,* "the most inhospitable place in North America." Though exposed skin does not freeze until –50 degrees Fahrenheit, a twenty-five-mile-an-hour wind will have the same effect at –15 degrees. With only one parka among them, they could not even hunt for caribou when a strong wind was blowing. And, to what must have been Hornby's chagrin, they saw no muskoxen.

Now the food supply began to occupy them to the exclusion of all else. Edgar Christian's brief diary entries underline their growing concern:

25 November: Jack set net in Willow for ptarmigan . . . Harold looked at hook but no fish. . . .

26 November: All took it easy being cold all day and having no meat. Went with Jack to look at Ptarmigan net and disturbed about 20 from close by but none in the net, a stroke of bad luck.

27 November: A fine day but we are taking Life Easy to economize in grub. I went out to barrens and got 1 fox and reset trap. Jack dug up all the fish left, 60 in all, which will last just 2 weeks and then, if we have no meat we will be in a bad way.

On December 4 Hornby outlined their situation: no caribou and no muskox in any quantity; no wolves around and very few small mammals; with the river ice thickening, fishing was becoming difficult, and the ptarmigan nets didn't work. Christian wrote in his diary the following day that "we must throw up trapping and practically den up and get hold of any grub we can without creating big appetite by hunting in short cold days."

They had enough food for fourteen days at two fish a day and only one hundred pounds of flour until spring. He got one "damn thin" fox that day (December 6) and Harold Adlard got a wolverine, "so that's a good meal." By this time his diary was concerned entirely with food—a fish here, a fox there. Without a shotgun it was difficult to bring down a ptarmigan, nor did they know how to net one. The Inuit made a funnel out of willow sticks with a snare at the narrow end, but this technique was unknown to Hornby.

Cheerfulness in adversity—that was the code that every English schoolboy had soaked up with his breakfast porridge. But it was not an easy one to maintain in those close quarters when the spectre of starvation hovered over them. For Christmas they resurrected a caribou head, which they had saved for two and a half months. Christian told his diary that they "enjoyed the feast as much as any, although we had nothing in sight for tomorrow's breakfast. . . . I hope every one in England has enjoyed today, & at the same time hope to God we rustle enough grub for a month from now & not wish we had not feasted today." There is no sign here of the enthusiasm that marked the earlier entries.

A suspicion of approaching cabin fever appeared in early January when Adlard went for a walk after an altercation. "I think he said nothing all morning before going and never spoke for some time after coming in, which makes things so unpleasant for us." Powell-Williams suggests in *Cold Burial* that Hornby's "mindless boasting, yarning and theorizing" may have begun to get on Adlard's nerves and that having to watch Christian's passionate devotion to his cousin, he might have felt excluded.

January had arrived—the worst month of all on the Barrens. Hornby told his two charges that the weather was not likely to improve before the end of March, and the caribou could not be expected back before then. Spring would arrive about mid-May; could they hold out until then? On January 12, "all measured out grub today." They had enough fat for two months, enough flour for twenty days at the present rate, meat for one day and bones.

The heart-rending story of the eighteen weeks that followed comes almost entirely from Edgar Christian's diary, which he maintained faithfully if sporadically as he and his companions wasted away to shadows in their little cabin on the Thelon. We can see today that tragedy was foreordained from the moment that Hornby agreed to take Edgar Christian into his unrelenting realm. Hornby was a man incapable of planning for more than one day in advance—indeed, he made a fetish of his ineptness in this field. He should have learned from his own experience when he had come close to starvation at Fort Reliance. Luck had saved him that time, and he had always counted on it; but now his luck was running out and his young companions would bear the burden of his misplaced optimism. Here on the Barrens, as the thermometer dropped to –54 degrees Fahrenheit, there would be no second chance.

At the end of the month the weather relented, and Adlard, the best hunter of the three, shot five ptarmigan. On February 1, he spotted caribou crossing the river, shot one and wounded a second. Christian recorded his elation: "a great day of feasting. . . . Now we have grub on hand things are better and gives one a chance to have a damn good square meal even if we go shy a little later on."

Of course they did go shy in this land of feast and famine, and the ebullience Christian felt after his feast faded. "This game of going short of grub is hell," he wrote on February 16. A week later there was further tension in the cabin. Adlard had been laid up with frostbite while the other two, wrapped in blankets, checked the traplines. "A nice warm day & Harold thinking it warm declined to cut wood as Jack asked him to but suggested going for a walk in the afternoon. Not quite playing the game considering that we have been out on intense cold days all this month and cut wood on the cold days as well while he makes some excuse of his face freezing. Today I stayed in all the time feeling rotten. . . ."

The grumpiness ended when, two days later, Adlard shot a young bull caribou. Renewed by the fresh meat, Harold began to argue against Hornby's plan of clinging to their base camp. Christian noted that his cousin was beginning to flag after a long day, but he went along with Adlard's urging that they make one more hunting trip to their winter cache. They were in no condition for such an ordeal, but on March 5 Hornby and Adlard set off, leaving Christian resting in the cabin. The following day Hornby unexpectedly reappeared, explaining that they needed an extra rifle for hunting. Christian reluctantly agreed to go back with him, hoping that Adlard had managed to bring down a caribou or muskox in his absence. It was a hopeless venture. Gaunt, half starved, and exhausted, existing on rations of flour and pieces of caribou hide, they lost their way in a blizzard, stumbled across a large lake, and snowshoed over its surface hoping to find the river. That four-mile hike took three hours. They camped in a thicket of trees, and there Hornby and Adlard stayed awake to keep from freezing to death while Christian slept.

The following day, March 13, they gave up any attempt at hunting. They realized they must expend all their flagging energy in returning first to the cache and then to their cabin. They made it back to the cache in the late afternoon but were snowbound the next day with nothing to eat except a hide mat that had once done duty as tent flooring and was stored in the cache. On March 15 they gathered all the supplies the cache offered into their bulky packs and onto their sled and set off. They had no choice. They knew unless they made the full sixteen miles back to the shelter of their cabin that day they would die out on the Barrens. They trudged for ten hours through the soft snow long after darkness fell, "all feeling as weak & feeble as anything & intensely cold."

At eight that night they dumped all the dispensable food they had salvaged from the cache in order to lighten their loads. The exhausting journey had been useless. Two hours later they stumbled into their cabin. Hornby, in spite of suffering a bad fall on the trip, cut firewood, lit a fire, and made tea while the others slept. The next morning he was the first awake and shot a ptarmigan. But there is a note of alarm in Christian's diary. Hornby, who had exhausted himself more than the others because of his double trip back to the cabin for another rifle, "looks very poor and must feel it though he will keep agoing and doing most work and heavy packs." Now they made a heart-breaking discovery. While they had been exhausting themselves on a fruitless search for caribou, the caribou had come to them. The evidence was all around the cabin—hoof marks and wolverine tracks in the snow. Had they stayed put they could have bagged a caribou by simply thrusting a rifle through the window. With this revelation their morale probably reached a new low. The struggle back to the cache had sealed their fate, and they must have known it.

Hornby's mind now went back to February 1, when Adlard had shot a caribou. After butchering it they had left the paunch behind, and Hornby became obsessed with the idea of locating it. On April 2, he somehow managed to make the trip to that site and returned with some frozen blood but nothing else. Two days later, in spite of Christian's concern, he started out again, "all muffled up Looking as Cold as Charity and could hardly walk. . . ." After four hours spent creeping around the site he returned empty-handed. On April 6, he struggled out one final time looking for ptarmigan, and again with no result. Neither Adlard nor Christian was strong enough to fell any more trees and so were taking the small storehouse apart to keep the stove going.

They were all suffering from constipation, the result, they thought, of their diet of ground bones and wolverine hair. They improvised an enema-syringe from a glass test tube, but it didn't work for Hornby. For him the effort was too great.

By April 10, Hornby knew he was dying. On a torn page from his cousin's notebook he wrote out his will bequeathing everything to Christian. In the days that followed he wrote six short letters to relatives. "A farewell line," he scribbled to Colonel Christian. "Edgar is a perfect gem. Our hardships have been terrible & protracted."

He told the other two that he might live only two days and pointed out that since Harold, the better shot, could still walk, he should try to go after game and bring in the caribou paunch. Edgar should conserve his strength and wait, hopefully, for the arrival of spring and the coming of the caribou. Their only food at this point was five wolverine hides, but on April 15 Adlard shot a ptarmigan, the only fresh meat they had had since March 30. By this time, however, Hornby was too far gone to eat it. Yet he brightened up and was almost euphoric, a state that puzzled the others who did not understand that this was a final stage in death by starvation.

On the night of April 16, the hermit of the Barrens—"the finest man I have ever known"—died peacefully. Christian was knocked out by his passing and it was Adlard who comforted him. "He talked to me so wonderfully and Realized my Condition I am sure. . . . He kept fire during night and brought me tea and Aspirin to help along which was a relief as I was able to sleep." The following morning Adlard parcelled up the wasted body in a groundsheet, sewed it up to make a shroud, and dragged it toward the door.

Hornby's two young survivors were exhausted by starvation. They existed on whatever sustenance they could scrounge, and it was never enough: a few scraps here, then nothing, and later a few scraps more. Within a few days, Christian realized that his partner, too, was dying. What little energy he had was dissipated by the effort required for him to totter into the snow to salvage scraps of skin and guts and the occasional bit of raw meat that had been tossed away. Then he remembered the remains of a fox killed the previous December. He brought it back, kept the fire going by pulling down more of the storehouse for fuel, and gave himself an enema, which worked. Now he found that his appetite was "simply ravenous," which he put down to being bound up.

On April 27, Adlard's body went weak on his left side—a mild stroke, perhaps brought on as an effect of starvation. His condition worsened, but on May 3 he told Christian that he felt better and had shaken off the illness though he felt weak, a condition that jibes with Hornby's euphoria on the day of his death. Christian left the cabin to cut wood and get more water. When he returned Adlard told him that "he felt very queer and knew not what to do although not painful." He fell asleep that night never to awaken, leaving his younger partner alone in the cabin.

Christian closed the dead man's eyes, crossed his arms over his body, covered him with a blanket, and exhausted by these exertions, slept. The following day he rolled the corpse off the bunk, tied the blanket-shroud in place with packing twine, and dragged it to the door, head to toe with Hornby's remains. Harold Adlard died on May 3, 1927. Edgar Christian, younger by ten years, lived alone for the month that followed, his diary his only friend: "Having no one to talk to I must Relieve the desire by writing my thoughts." That diary, he knew, would be a monument to Hornby, whom he continued to worship, blind to the older man's shortcomings.

To say that he lived is an exaggeration. More accurately, he existed, eking out the days with discarded offal that he dug out of the snow with a small hand axe. By now his limbs and joints were those of a starving man. He awoke after one ten-hour sleep and noted to his surprise that he was "as thin as a rake about my Rump and my joints seemed to jerk in and out of position instead of smoothly." He could feel bone grinding on bone as he tried to stand and his body fat wasted away so that his joints lost their cushioning. His movements were more than sluggish; it took him two hours to write three hundred words in his diary.

Still, he kept at it, suffering both chills and a fever brought on by his wasted condition, shivering in the cabin, sweating in his blankets. "My shoulder blades and joints still seem to jerk in and out of place," he wrote on May 10, "and my nose gives way to bleeding." He was down to one meal a day—or what passed for a meal—and his appetite was failing, a sure sign of his condition. By this time he was tearing up the floorboards of the cabin and gathering wood chips from around the stumps of trees to feed the fire. On May 17: "If I cannot get grub tomorrow must make *preparations*." He didn't need to expand on that.

For the next ten days there were no entries in his diary. But when he took it up again he reported with some satisfaction that on May 22 he had "found lots of meat under snow and 4 good big meaty bones cov-

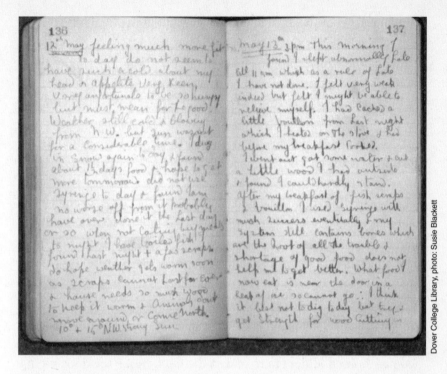

A passage from the journal kept by Edgar Christian a little more than a week before his death. He hid it in the stove to protect it from the damp.

ered in fat and Grease." That put him on his legs for three days. He had cut his last piece of wood to cook his food, and he was weaker than ever. "Have eaten all I can. Have food on hand but heart petering . . . Make *preparations* now." Two more lines followed later: "Got out too weak and all in now. Left Things Late."

He still had a few sheets of paper he had taken from the Windsor Hotel in Montreal, and on these he wrote brief letters to his parents. He crawled over to the unlit stove, shoved his diary in the ashes of the firebox, gathered a few more necessary papers together including the unfinished letter Harold Adlard had written to his parents, then shut and latched the stove door. That done, he managed to lay another blank sheet on top of the stove and write: "WHOEVER FINDS THIS LOOK INTO THE STOVE." His preparations complete, he managed to latch the cabin door, crawled to his bunk, pulled the red blanket over his face, closed his eyes and slept—for the last time.

Such is the isolation of the Thelon country that the cabin with its three corpses went undetected for some fourteen months. Then, on July 21, 1928, a prospecting party of four led by Harry S. Wilson, a mining engineer from Cobalt, ventured down the river in two canvas-covered boats. The police at Fort Smith had asked Wilson to keep a lookout for the Hornby party, and as he stepped ashore and saw the cabin he thought he had located their camp.

The dilapidated condition of the campsite—the window glass shattered, the roof sagging—gave him pause. The door was latched, but lying against the outside wall were two elongated bundles. One of the party attempted to make a hole in one with a clasp knife. He finally separated the edges with his fingers, and there staring at him were the sightless eye sockets of Harold Adlard. A rent in the second bundle revealed the skeleton of John Hornby.

They hammered on the door and shouted, but there was no response. Two put their shoulders to it, and as the latch broke the door swung open. Inside, the air was foul. A cooking pot containing the skull of an animal stood on a small box stove. On a rough table they found a half packet of tea, some ammunition, and two caribou skulls. Nearby were three leather suitcases, a tin trunk and a rattan cabin trunk, three home-made beds—two badly splintered—and one intact bed, in which lay the body of a man covered in a blanket. The body slid a little way down the bunk and the skull rolled sideways. Then an entire skeleton toppled over and dropped to the floor with a clatter.

The visitors left hurriedly, having missed the message underneath the cooking pot, a message half eaten away by damp and mould: WHO . . . LOOK . . . STOVE. On August 10, the four prospectors told their story to Staff Sergeant Joyce at Chesterfield Inlet. Four days later, the international press had the story, identifying Hornby and his two companions as the victims.

Another year went by before the RCMP investigation patrol reached the cabin. The date was July 25, 1929. Inspector Trundle found the contents in "deplorable condition," and now he unearthed Edgar Christian's diary (which would later be published under the title *Unflinching*) and other papers, all of which had been preserved against the damp by the ashes in the stove. The skeletons of the ill-fated trio were collected and buried under crosses on each of which their initials were carved. There was no epitaph, but Hornby's remarks to Denny LaNauze, when he said he wished he had been born an Indian, might have served as one:

> In civilization there is no peace. Here, in the North, in my country, there *is* peace. No past, no future, no regret, no anticipation: just doing. That is peace.

That, of course, was integral to the Hornby legend—a legend he himself had gone to some lengths to create. But it does not excuse him for the tragedy of which his own purposeless life was the root cause.

The graves of Christian, Hornby, and Adlard in the Thelon country.

CHAPTER 5
The Bard of the North

Robert Service on the porch of his Dawson City cabin, now a heritage site and tourist mecca. It was here that he wrote his first novel, The Trail of '98.

ONE

Robert W. Service is a hard man to define. Perhaps the best-known English-language poet of the twentieth century, and certainly the richest, he refused to call himself anything more than a rhymester. A shy man and a dreamer, he played a dozen roles in his lifetime, often with costumes to match, while plunging into each masquerade—a cowboy in Canada, an apache in the Paris underworld—with the intensity of a professional. A self-described vagabond, he soaked up the background for his hugely successful novels and poems wherever his wanderlust took him—Tahiti, Hungary, Soviet Russia—difficult corners of the globe where, to his delight, he was unrecognizable.

Service has been a presence in my life since childhood. My mother knew him when she was a young kindergarten teacher in Dawson City; he even asked her to a dance—the kind of social affair he usually avoided. His original log cabin stood directly across from my childhood home under the hill overlooking the town. Early in my television career I spent three days with him in Monte Carlo—the last interview he ever gave. Three decades ago I published a short character sketch about him in *My Country.* Yet I cannot say I really understand him—a poet who refused to call himself a poet, a hard worker who claimed to be the world's laziest man, a brilliant storyteller who invented himself in print.

I find it fascinating that he was able, thanks to his royalties, to purchase five thousand books for his library, yet scarcely any of them are books of poetry. "I'm not a poetry man," he once remarked, "though I've written a lot of verse." He made this clear in his autobiography, *Ploughman of the Moon.* "Verse, not poetry, is what I was after—something the man in the street would take notice of and the sweet old lady would paste in her album; something the schoolboy would spout and the fellow in the pub would quote. Yet I never wrote to please anyone but myself; it just happened that I belonged to simple folks whom I liked to please." He amplified these remarks in—what else?—a poem, which he called "A Verseman's Apology."

The classics! Well, most of them bore me
The Moderns I don't understand;
But I keep Burns, my kinsman, before me,
And Kipling, my friend, is at hand.
They taught me my trade as I know it,
Yet though at their feet I have sat,
For God-sake don't call me a poet,
For I've never been guilty of that.

By his own admission, the "Canadian Kipling," as he was universally dubbed, suffered all his life from an inferiority complex that made him keep his distance from many fellow writers of whom he stood in awe. In his comfortable years, when he retired to the Riviera, his neighbours included such luminaries as Somerset Maugham, Bernard Shaw, and Maxine Elliott. "Oh my, I'd be scared to meet Shaw," Service remarked to a friend. "Somerset Maugham was a neighbour of mine but I'm scared of these big fellows. I like eating in pubs and wearing old clothes. I love low life. I sit with all the riff raff in cafes and play the accordion for them."

Strangers encountering Service at the height of his fame were astonished to discover that he was not the rough, profane roustabout they had envisaged from his poetry. How could they identify this quiet, almost inconspicuous gentleman as the author of "The Shooting of Dan McGrew"? In Hollywood, the casting department of *The Spoilers,* in which the poet played himself, objected that he was "not the Service type." In Toronto, a reporter schooled in Service's best-selling ballads wrote that "his face is mild to the point of disbelief." Service agreed. "My face is much too mild," he said, "for one who has been a hobo, 'sourdough poet,' war correspondent, and soldier." He might have added ranch hand, ditch digger, and dishwasher in a brothel.

My mother, who arrived in Dawson in 1908, made a point of hurrying down to the Bank of Commerce as soon as Service was transferred there as a teller. She and a friend had thought of him "as a rip-roaring roisterer," she remembered, "but instead we found a shy

Service in Hollywood with Marlene Dietrich on the set of The Spoilers, *made up to look young. The casting department said he wasn't "the Service type."*

and nondescript man in his mid-thirties, with a fresh complexion, clear blue eyes, and a boyish figure that made him look younger. He had a soft, well-modulated voice and spoke with a slight drawl."

Robert Service could never escape the Yukon, no matter how much he tried. Of all the verses he wrote—and the number exceeded two thousand—the one he really loathed was the first one he published, which brought him the fortune he craved and the fame he despised. "The Shooting of Dan McGrew" owed as much to the American Wild West as it did to the Canadian North. Service in fact hadn't even reached the Klondike when the famous ballad first made its appearance in *Songs of a Sourdough.*

Now, almost a century later, it has become the best-known folk ballad of our time, shouted, whispered, roared out, and recited by half-inebriated monologists (including me) at a thousand parties and from a hundred stages—satirized, rewritten, set to music, parodied, praised, sneered at, and condemned. It is an abiding irony that so much of Service's work that excited interest at the time of publication has been forgotten, but "Dan McGrew" and its companion ballad "The Cremation of Sam McGee" have survived.

For the fifty years following his arrival in the Yukon, Service continued to churn out verse, much of it highly popular—his *Rhymes of a Red Cross Man* was on the *New York Times* best-seller list for almost two years—but it irked him that the first work he wrote at that time turned out to be the most enduring. "I loathe it," he told me toward the end of his life. "I was sick of it the moment I finished writing it." But for all of his long career he was asked to recite it, time and time again, and he did, almost to his dying day.

What might be called the Dan McGrew Industry began a decade or so after the ballad appeared in print. "Is there a Doughboy who has not heard 'The Shooting of Dan McGrew'?" Louis Untermeyer asked in *The Bookman* in 1922. Among the tens of thousands who committed it to memory were the Queen Mother, the Duke of Edinburgh, and former president Ronald Reagan. Bobby Clarke, the Broadway comedian, parodied it on the stage in *Star and Garter.* Miss Marple,

Hollywood made two movies based on "The Shooting of Dan McGrew." The first, shot in 1915, had a happy ending. The second (above) was faithful to the original.

Agatha Christie's fictional detective, quoted from it in one of the TV episodes that carried her name. Billy Bartlett, the British music-hall satirist, made a recording of it. So did Guy Lombardo, the bandleader. Tex Avery, the animation genius, spoofed it twice, in 1929 as Dangerous Dan McFoo and again in 1945 as Dangerous Dan McGoo, the title character being a cartoon dog. Hollywood turned the ballad into two silent films. The first, in 1915, was marred by a happy ending; the second, in 1924, starred Barbara Lamarr and Mae Busch, then the reigning queens of the silver screen.

"Dan McGrew" has been parodied again and again, often obscenely ("And there on the floor on top of a whore lay Vancouver Dan McGrew"). There is at least one gay version ("And there on the floor with his arse-hole tore . . .") that made the rounds of the mining camps in the Depression days and later. There is a hip version by Turk Murphy's Jazz Band. More recently, a new company, Pied Piper Productions, has been promoting its own version of the ballad with hand-carved puppets. The Royal Winnipeg Ballet's version, with music by *Hair*'s Galt McDermott, is still in the repertoire, the first-ever production of a ballet with a Canadian theme, while a recent novel by Robert Kroetsch, *The Man from the Creeks,* takes as its title a familiar line from the ballad.

Service was that curious mixture, a public figure who was always an intensely private man. When an article in *The Times* of London listed his name among the poets who had been killed in the Great War, he made no effort to correct it (the confusion arose because one of his brothers was killed at the Somme). "It rather pleased me that my efforts of self-obliteration had succeeded," he recalled. He was living in Nice at the time, where few of his neighbours knew who he was. "I enjoyed the irresponsibility of living in a foreign land where one is an onlooker, and cares nothing for the way things are run as long as one's comfort is assured."

His biographer James Mackay has called the poet's autobiography, *Ploughman of the Moon,* "a masterpiece of obfuscation." It contains not a single date and no proper names except those of his four elderly aunts. He does not tell us when or where he was born and raised, or who his spouse was; he simply refers to her as "the wife." The rest of the names in the book are entirely fictional. He refers scarcely at all to his mother and does not name any of his nine siblings. In spite of this, or perhaps because of it, *Ploughman* is a highly readable book, full of anecdotes, many of them exaggerated since Service was never one to let the truth get in the way of a good story. His second volume of memoirs, *Harper of Heaven,* is equally murky.

As a result, his biographers have been faced with the maddening task of trying to figure out who was who and where was where from Service's vague accounts of his career. The first two—Carl Klinck, 1976, and G. Wallace Lockhart, 1991—did their best but in the end gave up or got it wrong. One can only applaud the investigative work of Mackay, who managed to untangle the more baffling aspects of Service's literary career.

In spite of his soft accent, he was not born in Scotland, as so many of his fans have assumed, but in Lancashire, in January 1874. Four years later the family moved to Glasgow, but two of the Service boys, Robert and his younger brother, John, were off-loaded to live with their uncle, the postmaster of Kilwinning, an Ayrshire market town some twenty-four miles southwest of Glasgow. Apparently the burden of handling five boys and five girls was too much for Emily Service. In his autobiography Service makes no mention of John or indeed of any of his siblings. As a small boy he kept to himself and recorded in *Ploughman* hearing his grandfather remark, "Yon's a queer, wee callant. He's sooner play by himsel' than wi' the other lads." That was true, Service wrote. "Rather than join the boys in the street I would amuse myself alone in the garden, inventing imagination games. I would be a hunter in the jungle of the raspberry canes; I would be an explorer in the dark forest of the shrubbery; I would squat by my lonely campfire on the prairie, a little grass plot where the family washing was spread. I was absorbed in my games, speaking to myself or addressing imaginary companions." He looked forward, he remembered, to bedtime where he had "the most enchanting visions" of "shining processions of knights and fair ladies."

Here were the early clues to that wanderlust that would set Service off, always on his own, on voyages of exploration to distant climes, a solitary witness soaking up local colour or living vicariously through the lives of strange and, to him, exotic people. They also provide an insight into the role-playing that marked his adult life and his habit of choosing whatever costume he believed would allow him to merge with the background in those communities he sought out. When his royalty cheques raised him to the level of the wealthiest poet in Paris, he was not above depicting himself as a penniless scrivener in worn clothes, scarcely able to make ends meet. In that case his Scottish parsimony helped create the illusion.

"A ravenous reader" as a child, he gobbled up the works of every adventure writer from Captain Marryat to Jules Verne, not to mention Burns and Kipling, the only poets with whom he felt comfortable. There was more than a hint of the future rhymester when on his sixth birthday at a family feast he asked his grandfather if he might be allowed to say grace. Without waiting for an answer, he bowed his head and began:

> God bless the cakes and bless the jam;
> Bless the cheese and the cold boiled ham;
> Bless the scones Aunt Jeannie makes
> And save us all from bellyaches. Amen

In *Ploughman,* Service noted that this first poetic flutter "suggests tendencies in flights to come. First it had to do with the table, and much of my work has been inspired by food and drink. Second, it was concrete in character and I have always distrusted the abstract. Third, it had a tendency to be coarse, as witness the use of the word 'belly' when I might just as well have said 'stomach.' But I have always favoured an Anglo-Saxon word to a Latin one, and in my earthiness I have followed my kinsman, Burns. So, you see in that first bit of doggerel there were foreshadowed defects of my later verses."

Young Service did not see his father, a failed banker, for four years until the family was reunited in Glasgow, thanks to a legacy received by his mother. The balding figure with the mutton chop whiskers and "the reddest face I ever saw" failed to make an impression. "I cannot reproach him for his failings," Service was to write in a revealing passage, "for they were my own—laziness, day dreaming, a hatred of authority, and a quick temper. . . . I hated to work for others and freedom meant more to me than all else. I, too, was of the race of men who don't fit in."

Service was not popular at school. "I was too much of a lone dog and I disliked games." But these were some of his happiest youthful years. He wrote some poetry for small publications, dabbled in amateur theatrics, and for a time he had his future set on becoming a professional elocutionist, practising his craft, complete with gestures, in front of a mirror as so many of his avid readers would do when his own ballads appeared.

He left school in 1888 at the age of fourteen and took a job as apprentice in the local branch of the Commercial Bank of Scotland. "It was obvious," he remembered, "that I had no vocation for banking," but it suited what he always insisted was his "prejudice against hard work." It was an easy job and "I tried to make it still easier. I dawdled over my daily errands and dreamed over my ledger. I made rhymes as I cast up columns of figures." Was he really such a good-for-nothing as he makes out? James Mackay, examining such records as exist, suggests that he was well thought of by his superiors and was "a diligent, if unspectacular employee." Service's description of his banking career, such as it was, is another example of his lifelong practice of using self-deprecation to enhance his personal narrative.

It is this that makes him such a contradictory figure. Was he the solitary dreamer who drifts through his autobiographies? The lazy layabout doing his best to avoid hard work or, indeed, work of any kind? There is more than one suggestion that this was a pose to cover up what he constantly referred to as his inferiority complex or to assuage the guilt that nagged at him because he didn't think of himself as a real poet.

250

Service portrayed himself as a lonely wanderer, and that rings true. He thought nothing of deserting his family for weeks, even months, to travel to unlikely corners of the globe. The Yukon made him famous, but when he had the opportunity to return to his old Klondike haunts after the Second World War, he bowed out, sending his wife and daughter in his place. There is no evidence that he ever had a close or intimate friendship with anybody—no one to whom he could pour out his heart or relive old times. There are some hints of a schoolboy love in Glasgow and an affair, later, in Kamloops, B.C., but only hints. When Service came to write his memoirs he avoided such personal touches. He married, he tells us casually, because he needed a wife; fortunately he selected one who indulged his solitary inclinations. His parents and his siblings are all distant figures in his life; he barely recognized those he encountered in his later years. Who, then, was the real Robert Service? Who was that masked man? He was, I suggest, whomever you wanted him to be or what, at any moment, he decided to be. As a poet, his credo was to give the public what it wanted; as a human being, all he asked was to be left alone.

The book that changed Service's life was Morley Roberts's *The Western Avernus: Toil and Travel in Further North America*. Roberts, who had worked on the Canadian Pacific Railway in the construction period, seduced Service with his portrait of western Canada in the early 1880s. Service went to the Canadian immigration office and stocked up on pamphlets about the prairies—pamphlets that marked the beginning of the Liberal Party's immigration propaganda, which brought a million newcomers to the West. "Cattle ranching; that was the romantic side of farming, and it was romance that was luring me." Service's instinct told him that in quitting his bank job after seven years and making a clean break from the Old World he was doing the right thing. "I knew a joy that bordered on ecstasy as I thought: 'I too, will be a cowboy.'"

That was the first of his many roles. He bought a big knife with a spring blade, which he called a scalping knife, and also an air rifle so he could practise for hours being quick on the draw. His ambitions knew no horizons: "Henceforth I would be a fellow of brawn and thew. I would work in mines and sawmills, in lumber camps and railway gangs, on ships and ranches. I would run the gamut of toil. But before all I would be a cowboy."

He needed a costume—he would always need a costume—and he settled on a discarded Buffalo Bill outfit that his father had bought second-hand at an auction, together with a pair of high-heeled boots, a set of chaps, and a Mexican sombrero. He booked a steerage passage on a tramp steamer headed for Halifax, and there at the dockside, as his friends were bidding him farewell, his father appeared and handed him a small package. Service, who shunned displays of emotion, hurried aboard ship before opening his parting gift. It was a small Bible. He never bothered to read it but he kept it all his years, "the one possession that no one ever tried to steal."

He never saw his father again, although the old man wrote to him many times. In his final letter he begged his son to pay him one last visit. "Even if you cannot come just write and say you will." But Service never answered, and when his father died of a stroke, "I must confess I felt a sense of relief." The poet did not have much family feeling, then or later. He showed little curiosity about his ancestors, his immediate forebears, or his siblings, some of whom would give him up for dead in the years to come.

No sooner had he reached Canada than Service unpacked his Buffalo Bill costume and wore it constantly. The train that took him across Canada was crammed with immigrants like himself, all attired in such a variety of outlandish outfits that his own caused little comment. He had come to the new world to be a cowboy, but when he reached the end of his journey near Cowichan on Vancouver Island, his first jobs were disappointingly mundane—picking up acres of stones for a future farm and weeding endless rows of turnips.

It was monotonous, back-breaking work. Service endured it because he found the surrounding scenery so magnificent. He revelled in "the blue purity of the sky, the mountains that rose to meet it, the unexplored bush that came right down to the clearing . . . a dream world worthy of a dreamer." Later he moved north to a farm near Duncan, a three-mile tramp through the woods. He lived in a shack, the most remote in the Cowichan Valley, where his chores were minimal and his isolation gratifying. Primed by a newly discovered hate for hard labour, he "energetically cultivated laziness," or so he says in his self-belittling memoir.

That fall of 1896 he moved again, milking a herd of Holsteins for a dairy farm; but in November, when the frost-caked mud was knee-deep in the yard, he decided to head south toward California. "I was pleased to see how I had risen to the occasion. I could earn my bread by the sweat of my brow. . . . I was not a little proud, and ready for the next phase in the adventure of living."

For the next year Service drifted about the American southwest, living like a hobo, taking odd jobs, and dreaming away the weeks and months without any firm plan. Within a month in Seattle his grubstake of one hundred dollars had dwindled to half. Thanks to a rate war he got himself a narrow steerage bunk for a dollar on the ss *Mariposa* bound for San Francisco. Service found himself jammed into the hold with a dozen others; "the air was so thick you felt you could slice it like Camembert." Everybody aboard that wallowing craft was deathly ill, including Service, who was so exhausted that when the man on the bunk above him vomited on his upturned face, he did not have the energy to turn his head away. It was not an auspicious introduction to the sunny south.

In San Francisco he found a room at the base of Telegraph Hill for fifty cents a day. He haunted the sleazier dives of Chinatown where he could buy a beer and watch a stage show for ten cents. After a month and close to destitution, he was overcome with a "first feeling of fear." The misery he saw, the derelicts and down-and-outers with whom he rubbed shoulders filled him with disgust. "Frankly, I was scared."

He answered an ad on a blackboard offering two dollars a day for labourers. He took it without knowing what it entailed and found himself shipped by train to a contractor who put him into a gang driving a half-mile tunnel through the wall of San Gabriel Canyon to the Sacramento Valley. In the dank and murky bowels of the earth he toiled ten hours a day until, happily, he was transferred to another dawn-to-dusk job shovelling gravel. When at last he quit he was given a pay-cheque for twenty dollars, which he found he could not cash. He discounted it to a stage driver for half its value and slept that night in a chicken house.

In Los Angeles he secured a room for a dollar a week and managed to keep alive on fifteen cents a day. On First Street, he found he could get a five-course meal for ten cents. The portions were small but included four grey slices of bread. Service would select a spot opposite a cus-tomer who was just finishing his meal, and if there was any bread left he would ask for it. Each evening he would hang around the fruit mar-ket looking for an apple or orange that had fallen into the gutter. After seven, the agnostic poet would head for the Pacific Coast Gospel Saloon, where, to obtain a piece of dry bread and coffee, he would join in prayers for an hour. "The bread was cut in fair-sized chunks," he remembered, "and some of us grabbed two. I was a 'twofer.'" Later he offered to wash the coffee cups and was given an extra piece of bread for the task.

Surprisingly, in spite of such vicissitudes, these were days of seren-ity for Service. "I knew now that brute toil was not for such as I," he wrote. "Was I not free and without responsibilities? No duties, no grind-ing toil, no authority over me." Occasionally, in an introspective moment, he would ask himself if he was fitted for anything. "I had moments in which I saw disaster in front of me; but for the most part I was buoyant and enchanted with my surroundings. . . . If I was head-ing for disaster, I was doing it very cheerfully."

In the public library, "that sanctuary of books," he felt at peace with all mankind. San Francisco had made him want to write stories, "but this city made me want to make poetry . . . newspaper poetry, the kind that simple folks clip out and paste in scrap books." He sent some sam-ples to a local paper, which promptly published them. One, called "The Hobo's Lullaby," carried the line: "My belly's got a bulge with Christmas cheer"—"typical," Service remembered "of my tendency to the coarse and the concrete." In this way, he discovered that he "would rather win the approval of a barman than the praise of a professor."

254

The library provided food for the soul, but in his straitened circumstances not enough for the body. He thought constantly of food and was often light-headed because of the lack of it. He would lurk for hours before restaurant doors just to imbibe the smells of cooking, and then he would return to his room to munch on stale bread and imagine it was roast beef. Once, "I actually found myself scraping with my teeth on a banana skin a man threw on the sidewalk. He turned and caught me at it, but I pretended I had picked it up to prevent someone slipping on it. He looked hard at me and tendered me a dime, which I proudly refused."

He could not bring himself to write home for help: "I would have died rather than confess my humiliating plight." At the age of twenty-four he saw nothing but hard work and poverty in his future. There were times when he suffered a sense of panic as the prospect of starvation stared him in the face. When an acquaintance told him the season for orange picking was just beginning, he went to work for a Mexican contractor scrubbing the fruit clean in a tub and later—a promotion!—actually picking it from the trees. For Service that was heaven itself. "As I plucked the golden fruit, often I paused to look around with something like rapture. About me, the grove billowed like a green sea, while above me was a blue sky of perfect serenity. I was so happy up there in my leafy world, I hated to descend." He sang gaily as he worked. This was a job for a poet! "How I wished it would last forever." But, of course, it didn't. As a last resort, Service decided to take out a classified ad in a local paper:

> Stone-broke in a strange city. Young man, University non-graduate, desires employment of any kind. Understands Latin, and Greek. Speaks French, German, and Chinook. Knowledge of book-keeping and shorthand; also of Art and Literature. Accept any job, but secretarial work preferred.

To this published plea he received but one reply, from a shabby man in a shabby room in a suspiciously shabby building. His job, he was told, would be to tutor three young girls in San Diego "who want to

learn how to talk about books and art stuff." Service took the job, bar-
gained the agent down to a two-dollar fee, and bought a train ticket for
another six, leaving himself with three dollars. He proceeded, as
directed, to a San Diego suburb. There he located the remote Villa Lilla,
with a cupola from which dangled a red lantern. He was greeted by a
Madame Ambrose, "a capacious lady draped in a Spanish shawl," who
told him he was the seventh sucker the commission agent had sent
down on an errand. "He'll get hisself into trouble one of these days,"
she said, darkly.

The villa was, of course, a high-class bordello, a truth that slowly
dawned on the naive poet only after several days. The Madame and
her three "daughters" liked him, especially when he sang and accom-
panied himself on a guitar that they lent him. Madame Ambrose gave
him a job as a handyman, and in return Service showed them respect
and "a humble desire to please."

He was shy and diffident, for it was some time since he had spoken
to a woman. When he finally made his farewells they all insisted on
kissing him on both cheeks, to his embarrassment, and presenting him
with the guitar. As he walked off down the path they waved to him
cheerfully from the porch. "In that Mission setting," he remarked, "they
might have been a Mother Superior and three Sisters."

Service now decided to walk to Mexico "because it would be a pity
not to visit that romantic land." He travelled gypsy-fashion, sleeping
on the mesa or on a beach, for he "had the arrogance of wide spaces
and the disdain for folks who sleep in beds." In ten days of wandering
he found he had only spent a dollar. "I was in rare walking fettle and
could reel off my thirty miles between dawn and dusk." Only one thing
bothered him: he could not afford to buy a new pair of shoes and did
his best to save leather by taking them off and trudging along the highway barefoot.

He slept one night in a dry ditch on the outskirts of Santa Ana. The
following day he suddenly felt forlorn. He hadn't shaved for days, his
trousers and jumper were stained and torn, and people were staring at
him "as they would at a half-crazy man." Even the guitar failed to bring

him solace. "When one is gloomy one does not make gay music." He returned to Los Angeles early one morning "like a whipped dog," rented a small cubicle in a Salvation Army hostel, "the headquarters of the hobo fraternity," and the next day sat in a public square trying to figure out his future. He managed to get a job burrowing into a hill to make a tramway tunnel until two of his fellow workers were injured. He quit, went back to the derelicts in the square, and wrote some verses called "The Wage Slave," which he says he never submitted to any newspaper. However, years later he saw them included in an anthology by Upton Sinclair.

He took a job as a dishwasher but was no good at that. Back on a park bench, he saw a newspaper with a headline about a ton of gold arriving from the frozen North. "It did not interest me a bit. *The Klondike?* Bah! Let others seek their fortune in that icy land. Give me the sunshine and the South." He would hit the gypsy trail again: Colorado, Nevada, Arizona, Texas, "magic names that appealed to the imagination." While others struggled up the frozen passes, Service sauntered idly through the American southwest.

"Among my cherished souvenirs," he wrote many years later, "is a worn dime. I think I must have tendered it a hundred times with a hollow smile, saying: 'Excuse me, Ma'am, but I'm so hungry I'm willing to give my last ten cents for a bit of dry bread and a glass of water. I'm not a bum, ma'am. Please let me pay.'" They never did, but in the majority of cases Service got a free meal.

As the result of a narrow escape from a locomotive while crossing a wooden trestle, Service lost his zest for wandering. He returned to Los Angeles, briefly toyed with the idea of joining Teddy Roosevelt's Rough Riders in the Spanish-American War, but instead decided to return to the Cowichan Valley. His days there as a cowboy came to an end when a big Holstein bull knocked him over, cracking two ribs. Fate then intervened when the local storekeeper departed and Service replaced him, exchanging the bunkhouse for a bedroom.

"I have had great moments in my life," Service was to write, "when it seemed the gates of Heaven opened wide and I stepped through them from the depths of hell." Now, suddenly, he was transformed into a middle-class storekeeper with a starched collar and a blue serge suit, a welcome guest at his employer's dinner table.

His euphoria did not last and his job began to pall. "I hated the buying and selling, and I loathed the arid forms of the Post Office." He began to imagine himself as a pedagogue. "I saw myself in a frock coat with a gold Albert across a rounded waistcoat." Why not? He would go to college and become a Master of Arts. No sooner had he reached that decision than he stopped reading novels and concentrated on textbooks. But it was hard to keep his mind on his studies. "Often I wanted to throw the hated things out of the window and write mad sonnets to the moon." Algebra had defeated him.

When he was writing *Ploughman of the Moon,* Service was always conscious of the title; the work is studded with references to the moon and moonlight. Now, he says, at this point in his career, the moon came to his aid: "Its serene light seemed to solace me. It said, 'Don't worry. All will come out right, but you're on the wrong track. It's writing you should be, not bothering your brain with bloodless abstractions.'" According to Service, "the moon whispered a poem in my ear." He sent it to *Munsey's Magazine.* Two months later it was printed and he received a cheque for five dollars. He had already quit his job in Cowichan and moved into a friend's shack to cram for his exams. Having saved two hundred dollars, he thought he had enough to carry him through his college term. There were problems: he passed his exams in Victoria with high marks except for algebra and French. That meant supplementary exams; to keep up with his well-dressed and younger classmates he would need a new suit and accessories. The clothes cost one hundred dollars and by the time he paid for his textbooks, he was down to sixty. It just wasn't enough. "I was indeed a failure. I had tried to storm the citadel of decent society, and been thrown into the ditch. . . . To what shabby fate was I drifting?"

What else could he do? During his long nocturnal walks he tried to figure out a future for himself. Ragtime kid in a honky-tonk? Parisian apache? Rose gardener? Herring fisherman? He was at the end of his tether. "Where now was that guardian angel who always interposed to save me in my extremities?"

No angel appeared. But on Service's wall there reposed a dog-eared scrap of paper that, magically, would be the means by which he changed his life. It was a testimonial that he had obtained from his Scottish bank manager seven years before. It was this that got him a job with the Canadian Bank of Commerce, even though he was older than most applicants. The bank took him on trial for fifty dollars a month. To Service that figure was so astonishing that he actually tried to bargain the bank down to half the amount. "I'm Scotch," he told the inspector. "I could get along on that." He was finally persuaded to accept the offer and went to work in the winter of 1903–4 at the Victoria branch at the corner of Government and Fort streets.

This marked a major turning point in Service's peripatetic career. Now he could afford to rent a piano and a ready-made dinner jacket. In July 1904, he was transferred to the bank's branch in Kamloops where he immediately bought a pony and tried to take up polo. He hated the game but loved the costume and had himself photographed in it to send to his family. He bought himself a banjo and strummed away at it happily during his leisure hours.

At this time literature ceased to exist for Service. He scarcely bothered to read a book. "My sense of poetry, so strong in my poverty and my desert wanderings, now seemed to have deserted me. My whole ambition was to get on in the bank, and I was prepared to give it my lifelong loyalty. I knew I was not suited for the job, yet I had no hope in any other direction, and I was intensely grateful for the safety and social standing it offered."

He was well settled when the bank told him they were transferring him to the Yukon and presented him with a two-hundred-dollar cheque to buy a coonskin coat. He bought the coat for one hundred dollars, pocketed the profit, and left for the North where, unlike the stampeders of 1898, he had no intention of making his fortune. But he did so in a manner putting the Kings of Eldorado to shame.

TWO

Service was given his first introduction to the Yukon from a passenger coach on the White Pass and Yukon Railway during its one-day transit through the Coastal Mountains from Skagway to Whitehorse. Weaving along beside the track was a worn pathway still bearing the visible marks of thousands of boots—the famous Trail of '98. Bursting from a dark tunnel and onto a dizzy trestle, the train passed over the notorious Dead Horse Gulch where three thousand pack animals had perished during the great stampede. On the far side of the summit, the train rattled past the green headwater lakes—sinuous glacial fingers that led to the Yukon River. After that came the gloomy gorge of Miles Canyon and the frothing waters of the Whitehorse Rapids. At the end of the line Service could see a huddle of frame buildings, log cabins, and wooden sidewalks, nestling beneath the low hills on the banks of the mighty Yukon.

This was Whitehorse, the gateway to the North, but hardly the rough-and-tumble community of legend. Here Service would find himself passing the plate in the Anglican Church. "Though I may not believe in religion," he was to write, "I believe in churches. They give me a sense of social stability."

When the hectic summer came to an end and the tourists as well as prospectors and traders had departed, the bank's business dropped off. Those who were left behind made their own fun, and the winter season was marked by a round of dances, concerts, at-homes, receptions, and other community events. In those days, long before radio and television, when the movies were silent, the art of elocution flourished.

When Service recalled those days, he remarked with his usual diffidence, "My only claim to social consideration at this time was as an entertainer, and a pretty punk one at that. I could sing a song and vamp an accompaniment, but mainly I was a prize specimen of that ingenuous ass, the amateur reciter." His repertoire included those old stand-bys "Casey at the Bat," "Gunga Din," and "The Face on the Bar Room Floor." These soon became stale from repetition, and Service was at a loss until the town's leading journalist, Stroller White, suggested he recite something of his own. After all, he recalled, Service had once submitted a poem to the *Whitehorse Star* during his days in Victoria.

The suggestion intrigued the would-be rhymester. He knew he wanted a dramatic ballad suitable for recitation. But what? He needed a theme. What about revenge, he asked himself. "Then you have to have a story to embody your theme. What about the old triangle—the faithless wife, the betrayed husband? . . . . Give it a setting in a Yukon saloon and make the two guys shoot it out."

But that was too banal. Service realized he needed a new twist to an outworn theme. It struck him then to "tell the story by musical suggestion." It was a brilliant concept and one that would help transform the one-time hobo into a wealthy celebrity.

On a Saturday night, returning from one of his many nocturnal walks, he passed an open bar. The sound of revelry gave him his opening line: "A bunch of the boys were whooping it up . . ." Excited by this idea, and not wanting to disturb Leonard De Gex, the bank manager, and his wife, he crept down the stairs from his room above the bank, entered the teller's cage, and started to complete the ballad. Unfortunately, Service wrote in *Ploughman of the Moon*, he had not reckoned with the ledger keeper stationed in the guardroom, who, on hearing a noise near the safe, thought it was being burgled. He levelled his revolver and "closing his eyes pointed it at the skulking shade." Luckily, Service wrote, "he was a poor shot or 'The Shooting of Dan McGrew' might never have been written."

The story is pure hokum. When, in 1958, I challenged him on it, Service cheerfully admitted to making it up. "I'd *like* to say he fired a shot at me," he said. "And I'd say it too but there are men still living who were there and I can't get away with it, you see." But of course he did get away with it. The story of the scene in the teller's cage went unchallenged for years.

Service finished his ballad but could not recite it at the church social; it was too raw and, its author remarked to me, it contained "too many cuss words." Then, one evening, he encountered a big mining man from Dawson, portly and important, who removed his cigar long enough to remark, "I'll tell you a story Jack London never got," and spun a yarn about a man who cremated his pal. A light bulb flashed in Service's mind: "I had a feeling that here was a decisive moment of destiny." He left and went for a long, solitary walk. On that moonlit evening, his mind "seething with excitement and a strange ecstasy," the opening lines of "The Cremation of Sam McGee" burst upon him, and soon "verse after verse developed with scarce a check." After six hours, the entire ballad was in his head, and on the following day "with scarcely any effort of memory" he put the words down on paper.

It makes an appealing and romantic story, this sudden inspiration on "one of those nights of brilliant moonlight that almost goad me to madness" and it certainly jibes with the title of his memoirs. Service liked to suggest that it was all play and no work for him, that he never needed to correct his first drafts, but the facts, certainly in the case of "Sam McGee," are at variance. Here is the first stanza that Service claimed poured out of him intact on that moonlit evening:

> There are strange things done in the Midnight sun
> By the men who moil for gold;
> The Arctic trails have their secret tales
> That would make your blood run cold;
> The Northern Lights have seen queer sights,
> But the queerest they ever did see
> Was that night on the marge of Lake Lebarge
> I cremated Sam McGee.

Grubbing through the Yukon Archives, James Mackay came upon the original draft of the ballad, which shows how carefully Service would polish and refine his work:

> There are strange things done after half past one
> By the men who search for gold;
> The arctic histories have their eerie mysteries
> That would make your feet go cold

The Aurora Borealis has seen where Montreal is
But the queerest it ever did spot
Was the night on the periphery of Lake McKiflery
I cremated Sam McKlot.

In this early version of the ballad, we can see Service struggling to develop the galloping rhythm that gave his work such an appeal to platform performers. Here he introduced the inner rhyming that is not present in "McGrew" but marks so many of his later ballads. Each of his lines is seven beats long, divided into two sections; the first four beats contain the inner rhyme: "The Arctic trails have their secret tales" while the next three beats repeat, amplify, or expand the original statement, "that would make your blood run cold."

Service's audiences were used to this pattern through the nursery rhymes of childhood ("Jack and Jill," "Old King Cole," for example) and school-book standbys such as "The Wreck of the Hesperus." Service himself was brought up with this metre, and in his ballads he rarely departed from it. But it must have galled him in later years to realize that these twin efforts, which he tossed aside in a drawer with his shirts, should be the ones that would enshrine his reputation. He wrote some two thousand verses and published at least a thousand, but these two ballads, along with "The Spell of the Yukon"—a phrase he put into the language—are the only ones that are still remembered, and all from that first collection. Of the three, the one he loathed, "The Shooting of Dan McGrew," is still the most often quoted.

The two ballads are quite different. "McGrew" preserves the theatrical unities; it takes place on a single set, the Malamute Saloon, and in "real" time: the entire action occupies not much more than ten minutes. "The Cremation of Sam McGee," by contrast, is acted out like a wide-screen movie. It moves through time and space along the Dawson Trail to Lake Laberge, and it depends entirely on its Yukon environment ("And the heavens scowled and the huskies howled and the wind began to blow"). "McGrew," by contrast, is that old standby, the Western shoot-'em-up, or it seems to be.

Service's personal lexicon was crowded with short, blunt words that fitted his subjects. In "McGee," for instance, there is scarcely a word longer than two syllables, and the exception "cre-ma-tor-ium" is spelled out thus for bizarre and comic effect. Service changed "search for gold" to "moil for gold" and made that unexpected verb his own. It is so intrinsically connected to the ballad that I doubt any writer would dare use it for fear of being called a copycat. (Curiously, one Service scholar, Edward Hirsch, managed to get it wrong when he quoted the line as "men who toil for gold.") Occasionally, when Service couldn't find an offbeat word to suit his purpose, he made one up. Thus, in "McGrew," the stranger's eyes "went rubbering round the room." It's not in the Oxford dictionary as a verb, but it certainly fits.

The author of "McGee" was not above adding a bizarre and mystic note to his work—as when he flings the frozen corpse into the roaring furnace of a derelict steamboat, the *Alice May,* which lies rotting on Lake Laberge (or Lebarge, as he spells it), to pin down the rhyme. There was indeed a derelict steamer, *Olive May,* rotting away at the southern tip of the lake not far from Whitehorse, which Service would have encountered on one of his lonely walks. As a youth he had been fascinated and horrified by the stories of martyrs burned at the stake in Foxe's *Book of Martyrs,* and that surely was in his mind when he revised the ballad, with McGee thawing out gratefully "in the heart of the furnace roar" and providing Service with a tag line that always brought a laugh from his audience: "it's the first time I've been warm!"

Some critics believe that "McGee" is the better of the two ballads; certainly it has received as much applause. There is little doubt, however, that it has been outdistanced by "McGrew," and I believe a case can be made that of the pair "McGrew" is a superior work.

What is it that gives this piece of verse so much staying power? Service saw it as a drama in three acts. In the first, he sets the scene, introduces the characters, and supplied the tension. A solo game is in progress (solo, which resembles pinochle, is rarely played today), and here we meet the villain, Dan McGrew, and his girlfriend, the faithless

Lou. The door is flung open and a stranger, "dog dirty and loaded for bear," stumbles into the bar, flings down a poke of gold, and stands everybody a drink. We don't know who he is, but he gets our respect when he staggers over to the ragtime piano.

Now the second act opens, and it is here that the tale is lifted above the standard Western ballad. Service's decision to tell the tale of McGrew's villainy and Lou's betrayal gives the story its power. He himself was a musician, self-taught on the piano, the banjo, the ukulele, the guitar, and the accordion. We can hear the piano in our minds as the ballad progresses. The man arrived from the creeks turns out to be a gifted musician ("My God How That Man Could Play!"). The music sets the scene in what Service calls the Great Alone: the ice-sheathed mountains, reflecting the soft blaze of the Aurora, tell the story of one man's loneliness, a man driven by his own hunger for gold to the exclusion of all that is natural. The music brings back the memory of a home dominated by a woman's love, a woman "true as heaven is true" and superimposed on those features is the ghastly rouged face of the strumpet clinging to McGrew. The music modulates to a softer tone followed by an intense feeling of rage and despair, and then, as McGrew coolly continues to play his hand, rises to a crescendo as the audience hears the cry for revenge hidden in the chords that crash to a climax.

The third act follows. The stranger whirls about on his piano stool, his eyes "blind with blood," points to McGrew as a "hound of hell," and the inevitable gun battle follows as the lights go out momentarily and a woman screams through the blackness. The two antagonists lie crumpled on the floor as Lou flings herself upon the body of the dying stranger, clutches him to her breast, and plants kisses on his brow.

Service, of course, has no intention of continuing with such a melodramatic and saccharine ending. That was never his style. He has a sardonic surprise: Lou's embrace is simply a cover for her avarice. As the man from the creeks is breathing his last, she has been searching for the same poke he tilted on the bar a short time before. Service has the final line: "The woman that kissed him and pinched his poke was the lady that's known as Lou."

The twist ending was a Service trademark, more suited to his ballads than to his lyric poetry, which he continued to compose without any thought of publication while he went for long tramps in the woods with a book of poetry in his pocket, usually Kipling. One day, he was standing on the heights above Miles Canyon when a new verse popped into his mind. He called it "The Spell of the Yukon." In the month that followed he wrote something every day during those lonely walks. "I bubbled verse like an artesian well," he remembered. Then, suddenly, all inspiration ceased.

He did not realize that hidden away in his bureau drawer lay the seeds of future triumphs. He came upon his "miserable manuscript" one day and decided to show it to Mrs. De Gex, his landlady. She thought his rhymes were "not so dusty" and suggested he combine them into a pamphlet to send to his friends at Christmas: "it would be such a nice souvenir of the Yukon." Of course, she remarked, he'd have to leave out the rougher poems—"McGrew" and "McGee"—and also such efforts as "My Madonna" and "The Harpy," which reflected Service's fascination with fallen women and the seamier side of life.

Since the bank had given him a hundred-dollar Christmas bonus, he decided to follow her suggestion and have a hundred copies printed to give to his friends as "my final gesture of literary impotence . . . my farewell to literature, a monument on the grave of my misguided Muse." He was finished with poetry for good; he would study finance and become "a stuffy little banker."

He could not foresee that this slim volume would be his epiphany: the mild bank clerk would be transformed, phoenix-like, into a figure of towering reputation for what was, in truth, a mere grab bag of verses old and new, some previously published, others resurrected and revised. In spite of the title, *Songs of a Sourdough*, half of the poems in the collection had nothing to do with the Yukon. Several, indeed, dealt with the Boer War. None of that seemed to matter to the three million readers who eventually bought the book as edition after edition rolled off the presses. More than half a century later the critic Arthur Phelps noted of Service that "no anthology of Canadian verse dare leave him out.

No academic critic knows what to do with him. He has become an event in the working annals of Canada on his own terms."

Service kept the "coarse" poems in the collection—the ones that Mrs. De Gex wanted him to leave out. He retained "The Harpy," in which he wrote sympathetically about a prostitute from her own point of view, and "My Madonna," where a painting of a woman from the streets ends up in a church being worshipped as the Virgin Mary. He was not an ardent feminist, but he did treat women with understanding. To him, the Yukon itself was feminine. In the opening line of "The Law of the Yukon" the land is "she." Service sees her as a celibate earth mother longing for men who are "grit to the core" ("Them will I take to my bosom, them will I call my sons").

Service's Scottish heritage cautioned him to hedge his bet by laying off a half-interest in the book for fifty dollars to a fellow Scot who occasionally offered him a loan at 10 percent a month. The "village Shylock," as Service called him, turned the offer down. "Who buys poetry in this blasted burg? . . . Ye can jist stick yer poetry up yer bonnie wee behind." When later he learned what a fifty-dollar investment in *Songs of a Sourdough* might have brought him, Service joked, "I think it broke his heart. . . . I know," he added, "it would have broken mine if I had been obliged to give half the dough that book brought me in royalties."

Service typed out his selection of rhymes and sent it and a cheque to his father, now in Toronto, who peddled it to William Briggs's Methodist Book and Publishing House, which did vanity work on the side. The poet almost immediately regretted this rash action. His inferiority complex convinced him that people would laugh at him when the book came out. "It would be the joke of the town." He had wasted one hundred dollars.

He didn't even bother to read the letter the publisher eventually sent. When he finally opened it, a cheque fell out; the firm was returning his money. Only when he read the letter did it dawn on him that he was being offered a contract to publish his work with a royalty of 10 percent on the list price. He could hardly believe it. "The words danced before my eyes . . . my whole being seemed lit up with rapture." Service was sure that he must have a guardian angel overseeing his career. That guardian angel finally appeared in the guise of Robert Bond, a twenty-three-year-old salesman for the publisher who had been about to leave on his annual sales trip to the West when the firm's literary editor handed him a set of proofs. "We're bringing out a book of poetry for a man who lives in the Yukon. You're going to the west coast; you may be able to sell some to the trade out there. It's the author's publication and we're printing it for him. Try to sell some for him, if you can."

Bond, who was already packed and leaving for the station, stuffed the proofs into his pocket and forgot about them until that night. Sitting in the diner with nothing else to read, he dipped into "The Cremation of Sam McGee." He was so entertained that he forgot his meal and burst out laughing when he reached the final line. Across the aisle, a commercial traveller asked what he was laughing at.

"It's poetry," Bond told him, and the man's face fell. "It's unusual," he explained, "and it's Canadian and it might even sell." He began to read the ballad aloud and as he read, his fellow passenger began to squirm in his chair and then, at the last line, howled with laughter. "He coughed till he choked," Bond recounted later, "and had to leave the dining-car."

In the smoking car after dinner, a crowd had gathered and pressed Bond to read the ballad. "When I finished," he recalled, "bedlam broke loose—and everybody spoke at once. Some of the men even quoted lines that stuck in their memory." Others, who had come in late, asked Bond to read the poem again. He did it several times before the night was over, so that by the time they reached Fort William he knew it by heart. He began to walk into bookstores to recite it. Whenever he was able to do that, the store ordered books.

When the first copies of *Songs* reached Bond in Revelstoke, he was appalled. "How I swore! It was a poor-looking thin book, bound in green cloth." The company, disturbed by the frankness of some of the poems, had tried to shuck off responsibility by marking it "Author's Edition." To Bond the cover price of seventy-five cents was an insult;

he had been quoting it to retailers at a dollar. With the first edition already on the verge of selling out, Bond urged his firm to buy the rights and sell it on a royalty basis. When the first royalty cheque arrived, Service thought there must be some mistake and wrote to ask how long the royalties might continue. Fifty years later, Bond told an interviewer, "I have no doubt he is still wondering, for certainly no Canadian poet, or possibly any poet has received as much as Mr. Service has received."

Service near the end of his life would remark that he had made a million dollars out of *Songs*. He soon managed to increase the royalty rate from 10 percent to 15 and the publisher at once raised the cover price to one dollar, suggesting a future profit to Service of $450,000. But of course the cover price increased over the years, so that Service's own estimate of a cool million is probably an understatement.

Only a minority of Service's readers outside the Yukon realized that he had written the poems without ever having seen the Klondike. Most believed he had actually taken part in the great stampede, as a study of memoirs of that time makes clear. One respected author and jurist, the Honourable James Wickersham, wrote in *Old Yukon* that in Skagway in 1901, "in one of the banks, a gentlemanly clerk named Bob Service was introduced [to me]." Thames Williamson in *Far North Country* declared that "Service was in the Klondike during the fevered days of the gold rush." Glenn Chesney Quiett made the same error in his *Pay Dirt*. In February 1934, Philip Gershel, aged seventy-one, claimed he was the original Rag Time Kid of Service's best-known ballad. "I knew Dan McGrew and all the others," he declared and went on to describe the Lady That's Known as Lou as "a big blonde, tough but big-hearted." Gershel said the shooting took place in the Monte Carlo Saloon; Mike Mahoney claimed it happened in the Dominion. "I was right there when it happened," he insisted to an interviewer in 1936. He claimed that Lou was still alive and living in Dawson City. (James Mackay claimed that she was a cabaret performer who drowned when the *Princess Sophia* sank off Alaska—in 1918.) Mahoney, the hero of Merrill Denison's book *Klondike Mike,* recited "Dan McGrew" so often he came to believe in it. When he was challenged at a Sourdough Convention in Seattle by Monte Snow, who had been in Dawson for all of the gold-rush period and knew that Mahoney's story was fictitious, the assembly of old-timers gave Klondike Mike the greatest ovation of his life. They did not want to hear the truth.

Service himself felt that he ought to have been in the stampede and considered himself a bit of a charlatan because he was writing about events in which he had not taken part. In the fall of 1907, having spent three years with the bank, he was due for a three-month leave. He did not relish the idea because he knew it could lead to a reassignment that might take him away from the North. "That would be a catastrophe; I realized how much I loved the Yukon, and how something in my nature linked me to it. I would be heart-broken if I could not return. Besides, I wanted to write more about it, to interpret it. I felt I had another book in me, and would be desperate if I did not get a chance to do it."

Fortunately, his guardian angel, this time in the form of the bank inspector, was on hand after Service took his holiday. "You'll be sorry to hear you're going back to the North. I have decided to send you to Dawson as teller."

Service was more than relieved. "I was keen to get on the job. I wanted to write the story of the Yukon . . . and the essential story of the Yukon was that of the Klondike. . . . Here was my land. . . . I would be its interpreter because I was one with it. And this feeling has never left me . . . of all my life the eight years I spent there are the ones I would most like to live over."

Dawson in 1908 had five times the population of Whitehorse but was on the way to becoming a ghost town. In the evenings, Service wandered abandoned streets, trying "to summon up the ghosts of the argonauts," gathering material for another book, *Ballads of a Cheechako*. He was just far enough removed from the manic days of the stampede to stand back and see the romance, the tragedy, the adventure, and the folly. His verses sprang out of incidents that were common occurrences in the Dawson of that time: Clancy, the policeman, mushing into the north to bring back a crazed prospector; the Man from Eldorado hitting town, flinging his money away, and ending up in the gutter; Hard Luck Henry, who gets a message in an egg and tracks down the sender, only to find that she has been married for months (Dawson-bound eggs unfortunately were ripe with age). These themes were not fiction, as "McGrew" was. As a boy in Dawson, I watched Sergeant Cronkhite of the Mounted Police, his parka sugared with frost, mush into town with a crazy man in a straitjacket lashed to his sledge. As a teenager, working on the creeks, I saw a prospector on a binge light his cigar with a ten-dollar bill, fling all his loose change into the gutter, and lose his year's take in a blackjack game. The eggs we ate, like Hard Luck Henry's, came in over the ice packed in water glass, strong as cheese, orange as the setting sun.

My mother, then a kindergarten teacher, remembered Service strolling curiously about in the spring sunshine, peering at the boarded-up gaming houses and the shuttered dance halls. "He was a good mixer among men and spent a lot of time with sourdoughs, but we could never get him to any of our parties. 'I'm not a party man,' he would say. 'Ask me sometime when you're by yourselves.'"

He seldom attended any of the receptions or Government House affairs, and soon people got out of the habit of inviting him. When a distinguished visitor arrived in town, Service would have to be hunted down at the last moment, for they always insisted; and the poet, if pressed, dutifully made an appearance. My mother remembered how Earl Grey, the governor general, on a visit electrified Dawson by asking why Service hadn't been on the guest list for a reception. "We had all forgotten how important the poet was."

Service, who felt he had to undergo every type of experience, wangled permission to attend a hanging that fall. He stayed at the foot of the gibbet until the black flag went up and then, visibly unnerved, moved with uncertain step to the bank mess hall and downed a tumbler of whisky. It was decades before he could bring himself to compose a ballad based on that experience.

In one of his rare visits to the cottage where the kindergarten teachers lived, he discussed some of the new poems he was writing. "In his soft voice well modulated but strangely vibrant and emotional when

271

he talked of the Yukon," he read my mother parts of "The Ballad of Blasphemous Bill." "I cannot say I was greatly impressed," she remembered, "for it seemed to me a near duplicate of the Sam McGee story, and I said so.

"I mean it's the same style—one man's body stuffed in a fiery furnace—the other's a frozen corpse sewn up and jammed in a coffin," she told him.

"Exactly!" Service exclaimed. "That's what I tried for. That's the stuff the public wants. That's what they pay for. And I mean to give it to them."

Service's thoughts, at this period, were always on his work. He danced with my mother once during one of his rare appearances at the Arctic Brotherhood Hall. In those days each dance number—waltz, two-step, fox trot, and medley—was followed by a long promenade around the floor. When the music stopped for such an interlude the absent-minded poet, deep in creation, forgot to remove his arm from my mother's waist. As she recalled in *I Married the Klondike,* "We meandered, thus entwined, around the entire floor, and in those days a man's arm around a lady's waist meant a great deal more than it does now. The whole assembly noticed it and grinned and whispered until Service came out of his brown study."

Working from midnight to three each morning, Service was able to finish the new book in four months. It consisted largely of ballads in the metre of "Dan McGrew" and "Sam McGee." Service's love of alliteration can be seen in the names of the leading characters: Pious Pete, Gum-Boot Ben, Hard Luck Henry. For his several character sketches of Klondike stereotypes—the Black Sheep, the Wood Cutter, the Prospector, and the Telegraph Operator—he chose a different rhythm:

> I will not wash my face;
> I will not brush my hair;
> I "pig" around the place
> There's nobody to care.
> Nothing but rock and tree;

Nothing but wood and stone;
Oh God! it's hell to be
Alone, alone, alone.

I recall such a character when, at the age of six, I drifted with my family down the Yukon River from Whitehorse to Dawson. Above us on the bank stood a lonely cabin, and from it emerged its sole occupant, the telegraph operator. He called to us and insisted we stay for lunch—porcupine stew. When we took our leave and made our way down the bank to our poling boat, he followed. "Don't go yet. Stay! Stay for dinner. Stay all night. Stay a week!" Every time I pick up *Ballads of a Cheechako* I think of him.

The Dawson of Service's day was still crowded with men who had climbed the passes to reach their goal. No man caught the obsession or the fury of that moment in history better than Service had in his novel *The Trail of '98*—a phrase he embedded in the language. Here he used his words like drumbeats that seem to echo the steady tramp of those who plodded upward toward the summit—in a measured tread that came to be dubbed the Chilkoot Lockstep.

Never was seen such an army, pitiful, futile, unfit;
Never was seen such a spirit, manifold courage and grit;
Never has been such a cohort under one banner enrolled,
As surged to the ragged-edged Arctic, urged by the
    arch-tempter—Gold!

It is easy to see why so many of Service's readers were convinced that the poet had been in the forefront of that army. As he himself put it, "It was written on the spot and reeking with reality." He sent the manuscript to his publisher who promptly returned it, complaining of "the coarseness of the language and my lack of morality." A brief struggle followed by telegraph, which Service won by threatening to offer the book to a rival publisher. Once published, the book became another best-seller.

Dawson City's Front Street with its false-fronted buildings a few years before Service arrived. The literary gold he panned was better than any prospector's.

Service's poems, alas, did not impress the parents of a pretty young stenographer with whom he kept company. They did not marry. As my mother has recorded, "The report we had was that her family did not approve of Service. His wild verses upset them and, because of his themes, they were convinced that he drank."

This attitude to Service's work gives an insight into the publishing practices and taboos of the time. Lorne Pierce, one of the editors at the Methodist (later Ryerson) Press at the time and eventually his publisher, harboured "an aesthetic dislike for Service's work" according to a paper given before the Bibliographical Society of Canada in 1996. As a book editor, Pierce dedicated himself and his company to publishing a Canadian literature cultivating "a sympathetic atmosphere in which the sublimest beauty, the sweetest music, the loftiest justice and the divine truth might be expected to take hold and flourish."

That, of course, ran counter to everything that Service was producing, but what could his publisher do? To put it crudely, publishers needed the income and the international kudos. By the time his next royalty cheque arrived, Service had achieved his original plan of saving five thousand dollars. He immediately launched into a second plan. "Ten thousand would put me in a spot where I could thumb my nose at the world . . . having written two books I could now sit down and do nothing for the rest of my life."

For the next two years he did just that. In the winter, Dawson vibrated with self-made entertainment: skating parties, bob-sledding, snowshoe treks, formal dinners, and two dances a week, "a glorious time—not much work, lots of fun, money flowing in." But for Service it all began to pall. In his memoirs he portrays himself as a man too lazy to work, but it is clear that by late 1909 something was gnawing at him. On one of his jaunts up the Klondike Valley it came to him. Why not a novel about the gold rush? The idea, percolating in his mind, began to excite him. He would "recreate a past that otherwise would be lost forever."

When the time came to start writing, however, he found he couldn't do it. "My words came with difficulty. My imagination lagged. Something was wrong." What he needed, he knew, was seclusion, but he could not find it in the bank. About this time he was offered a handsome promotion to become manager of the Whitehorse branch. Service recoiled. "It would worry me to death. I am a meek soul. I cannot give orders to others." And he could not leave the Klondike with a novel germinating in his brain. On the spur of the moment, he told the bank manager that he would be leaving his job after the requisite three months' notice.

His boss gave him a long look and asked how much he was making. About six thousand dollars a year from his books and one thousand from the bank, Service told him. There was a gasp: "Why, it's more than I'm making myself." And that was that.

Service needed a cabin in which to work and found one on Eighth Avenue overlooking the town. In later years it became a shrine, and I can still remember standing on the kitchen porch of our house across the street, watching Chappie Chapman's big orange bus disgorge its newest load of Service fans. They had come down the river on the stern-wheeler *Casca* to squeeze into the little room where he wrote his verse using a carpenter's pencil on huge rolls of brown paper hung from the walls. It has since become an official heritage site, and each summer, in the front yard, an actor on contract to the Klondike Visitors Association recites the bard's poems.

It was in this cabin that Service wrote his first novel, *The Trail of '98.* Its main character is patterned on himself. "I made him a romantic

Courtesy Anne Longépé

In this cabin on Eighth Avenue in Dawson, Service wrote some of his best-known work, using a carpenter's pencil and sheets of brown paper tacked to the walls.

dreamer . . . at odds with his environment . . . in short, like myself, he was destined to be a failure; but while I escaped by a fluke I took it out on my poor devil of a hero and gave him the works." The name of his heroine, Berna, was taken from the label of a can of condensed milk. As Service described her, she "was purely imaginary and unimaginably pure." (Briggs, his Methodist publisher, had urged him to make her "an inspiration to virtue.") The novel itself, a best-seller in its time, is virtually unreadable today, the love scenes so saccharine as to cause nausea, the melodrama over the top, the dialogue unreal:

> From under his bristling brows he glared at us. As he swayed there he minded me of an evil beast, a savage creature, a mad, desperate thing. He reeled in the doorway, and to steady himself put out his gloved hand. Then with a malignant laugh, the sneering laugh of a fiend, he stepped into the room.
>
> "So! Seems as if I'd lighted on a pretty nest of lovebirds. Ho! Ho! My sweet! You're not satisfied with one lover, you must have two . . ."

What worked for Service in rhyme sadly failed him in prose. Nevertheless, Hollywood bought the novel and made it into a film, starring Dolores del Rio as Berna.

Service, who never stopped counting his profits, finished the novel in April 1910, and terrified of losing his work in the mails decided to take it personally to his American publisher, Dodd, Mead, in New York. On the train east—the first time he had ever been in a Pullman—he was so rattled by the unaccustomed luxury that he left his wallet on his seat and found it gone with all his money. He wired New York to send fifty dollars to him in Chicago and lived out the intervening days on sixty-five cents—an apple here, a couple of doughnuts there. When he reached New York, his publisher was surprised that he looked so commonplace. "We expected you to arrive in mukluks and a parka driving a dog team down Fifth Avenue," said one of the staff. "Why didn't you? It would have been a great ad."

After three months in New York, seeing the sights from Broadway to Chinatown and growing fat in the process, Service decided to get back in shape by taking to the road, as in the old days—a little stroll to New Orleans, staying in cheap hotels en route. The stormy weather put him off, and after three days he completed the trip to New Orleans by train. Then, on an impulse, he took a boat to Cuba where he put up at a chic hotel and lived a life of ease for three weeks.

There was no escape from the furnace-like heat and Service began to long "for the snow and tonic air of the North." Lingering on the Prado one day, as he idly turned over the pages of an American magazine his eyes fell on an article titled "I Had a Good Mother." Service, who paid so little attention to his blood relatives, suddenly thought, "I too had a perfectly good mother." He realized that he hadn't seen her for fifteen years, his father was dead, and the family had moved briefly to Toronto from Scotland and then to Vegreville, Alberta. Service—being Service— devised a sudden and dramatic storybook plan for a reunion. He would go straight to the family's homestead unannounced and would walk in as if he'd never been separated from them. By evening he had the open- ing lines of greeting worked out: "How about a spot of tea? By the way, in case you don't remember, I'm your first-born."

He reached Vegreville in the late autumn with the snow already cov- ering the ground, knocked on the frosted door of a frame farmhouse, and was greeted by a pretty girl. His sister? He had no way of know- ing. He said he was an encyclopaedia salesman and she ushered him into a cozy but primitive kitchen. A little elderly woman who was wash- ing dishes at the sink came forward, drying her hands. "Why, if it isn't our Willie," she said. As Service noted, "We Scotch are economical in our emotions. We exchanged the same conventional kiss we had indulged in when I left fifteen years before. My sisters were introduced and I pecked at their cheeks." Then, following his own script, he asked, "What about a cup of tea, Ma? I could do with a spot."

He spent the winter of 1910–11 roaming the prairie trails, usually walking twenty miles a day and bunking nightly with accommodating neighbours. By the time spring came he was again in superb physical

278

condition. "I wanted to keep going till I reached the Land of the Midnight Sun," he thought, so he went back to the homestead and told his family—the two youngest boys and three sisters—that he was returning to Dawson. "Are you crazy?" they asked. He could go anywhere: India, China, the South Seas and "you're going back to a ghost town where you'll be as lonely as hell." Which, of course, is exactly what he longed for—"peace and quiet, to be far from the world."

Having made up his mind, Service decided to go back the hard way—not by Pullman car, luxury liner, or paddlewheel steamer—but by the so-called Edmonton Trail, the 2,000-mile route that some of the gold seekers had opted for in '98 to their eventual regret. The route followed the Mackenzie River almost to the rim of the Arctic Ocean and then curved west in a huge semicircle across the divide that separates the Mackenzie country from the Yukon, eventually reaching Dawson by the back door. The back-breaking effort in hauling boats and barges up and over the Mackenzie Mountains made the Chilkoot Pass seem like a pleasant outing. More men died, drowned, starved, or froze to death using this much vaunted "All-Canadian Route" than on any of the other trails to the Klondike. Not long before Service decided upon the venture, four Mounted Policemen on patrol near Fort McPherson had starved to death trying to reach Dawson. Service's superb physical condition and his own guardian angel—luck—got him through.

Why did he put himself through it? No doubt because he was trying to prove himself. People thought he had toughed it out on the gold-rush trails. He still felt like a fraud among the genuine sourdoughs. This was his way of joining that exclusive fraternity. He was also hoping to soak up new material for another book of verse. More, he wanted to get as far from civilization as he could. In that he was certainly successful. In those days, this far-off corner of Canada was virtually unknown to anyone save the traders, the natives, and a handful of missionaries and Mounted Police. Service was equipping himself to pan untrammelled ground.

In late May 1911, he took the stagecoach from Edmonton to Athabasca Landing, hoping to get on the Hudson's Bay Company's flotilla travelling north. When he discovered the barges had left, he set out in pursuit by birchbark canoe. It took him three days to catch up. The flotilla took him to Fort McMurray, where they were welcomed with enthusiasm. The barge fleet was the first contact the residents had had with the outside world for a year. The festive air was dampened for Service by the local Indian agent, an ex-parson, who, on learning the poet's destination was Dawson, shook his head solemnly and declared, "Young man, you're going to your doom."

A week later Service boarded the river steamer *Grahame* and almost confirmed the agent's doom-saying when against the advice of an old-timer he dived into the swirling Athabasca River, was caught in the undertow, and was swept a mile downstream. He only saved himself by seizing an overhanging branch.

At Fort Smith, following a twenty-mile portage around a series of rapids, he took another steamer across Great Slave Lake to Fort Simpson, where he bought "the finest birch bark canoe in the North" from a veteran canoe maker. He christened her *Coquette*. The trip down the Mackenzie from Fort Simpson was marred by the discovery of the corpses of two trappers in a cabin, both dead of gunshot wounds—one a murder, the other a suicide, both the victims of cabin fever. To Service, the Mackenzie was a far more murderous river than the Yukon. "Its law was harder, its tribute higher. It killed most of those that I knew." At Fort McPherson, he bought some flour and bacon, and here, at the mouth of the Peel River, an old man with a patriarchal white beard warned him against continuing his mad project. "Don't! Don't go on," he said. "Go back the way you came like a good little boy." The Mounted Police sergeant on duty had the same advice. "Don't you do it. Just think of the Lost Patrol." As Service put it, "I think he expected me to reconstruct the tragedy in verse; but I never like to write about realities, so *The Ballad of the Lost Patrol* was left 'unperpetrated.'"

Faced with these warnings, Service worried about his planned trip up the Peel River and over the divide. In a few days, the sternwheeler that had brought him from Fort Simpson would leave on her return journey, and everybody was urging him to board it. He was tempted to follow that advice but could not bring himself to quit. "If you do it," he told himself, "you'll never respect yourself again."

He faced a journey of one hundred miles over a trail that was all but impassable. It was doubtful if his frail canoe could handle the trip, nor would any of the natives at Fort McPherson agree to carry it to the headwaters. It seemed to Service that he was up a blind alley. "I was planning to spend the next nine months in the Arctic when an unbelievable bit of luck happened to me." Two men and a woman arrived in a scow, the *Ophelia*. Her captain, a free trader whom Service called McTosh, announced that he was planning to be the first to take a scow over the mountains and invited Service to sign on as crew member. The poet enthusiastically accepted, and off they went up the Peel, the captain, his wife, and the first mate in *Ophelia* with Service paddling in *Coquette*. The river wound its way through the stark tundra, but when they reached the tributary Rat River, Service knew his days of paddling were over. The canoe was hoisted aboard the half-ton barge, and all four toiled to force their way against the increasingly stiff current. It was the hardest work that Service, the self-professed layabout, had done in his life. "It was grotesque, incredible. I had imagined I would use my canoe for most of the trip, and here I was roped in to do a job that would have made a Volga boatman look like a slacker."

For twelve hours a day he was harnessed to a tow line that was attached to a rope laid out along the bank. Most of that time he was slogging, sometimes knee-deep, in the water. One day they entered a canyon with the river waist-deep. Suddenly the first mate (whom Service called Jake Skilly) lost control of the barge and it swung back downstream. Service, at the end of the line, was jerked off his feet and dragged behind it, his back bumping over the boulders. Fortunately, the scow struck a rock at the end of the canyon and was held up until Jake could bring it under control. McTosh fished Service out, hauled him to a gravel bar, and worked over him. "My back felt broken, my bones too, but a slug of brandy brought me round. 'What a great headline in the papers you've gone and spoiled: "YUKON BARD MEETS WATERY DOOM." '" McTosh's levity, Service thought, was ill-timed.

Service in his canoe Coquette *when he had decided to return to Dawson the hard way, over the Edmonton Trail. At the end of the trip he felt like a true sourdough.*

Day after day they struggled up the Rat. McTosh's wife lashed herself to the rope, pulling like a man. Some days it took a dozen hours to make half a mile. At times, all of them would have to get under the big scow and haul her, foot by heartbreaking foot, over the rocky stream bed. The mountain peaks closed in about them as the river narrowed to a single channel. Suddenly they realized they were no longer climbing: they had reached the height of the divide. In the distance they could see a small lake, "shining like a jewel under the cold blue sky." They knew they were on the right track, for beyond the lake was the pass, "wild and savage, the stark mountains looking as if they were cast of iron."

They unloaded the scow, and using the mast and their four poles as rails and skis, they pushed her forward, a foot at a time. It took them ten hours to reach the lake. They then had to retrace their steps, often up to their waists in mud, and shuttle the supplies, including Service's canoe, down to the limpid water.

At the far end of the lake, hidden in a deep gully fringed with willows, they found the gushing headwaters of the river that would take them down to the Yukon. Once again they got under the scow, hefted her up, and tried to let her down by rope. Service did not hang on very hard, and "it was with vicious joy I saw her break away and crash through embattled willows to the foaming water."

His descent by canoe through a series of rapids and cascades was "a bit of hell." The water seemed to seize *Coquette* with a giant hand and "shake her like a terrier does a rat." Waist-deep in foam, he had to haul his frail craft downstream. At times he thought she would be smashed like an eggshell. At others she would be gripped by fang-like boulders and held clear out of the water. He was alone and knew what it would mean if he lost the flour and bacon he had bought in Fort McPherson.

He joined *Ophelia* and her crew on a sandbar on the Bell River. The scow's boards had been sprung and she was half full of water. "I felt no desire to give them a hand. McTosh loved her like a father but I hated her with the venom of the bitter days I had spent heaving her over the Summit." He bade them all goodbye and launched his canoe on the placid surface of the Bell, moving from turbulence into tranquility.

284

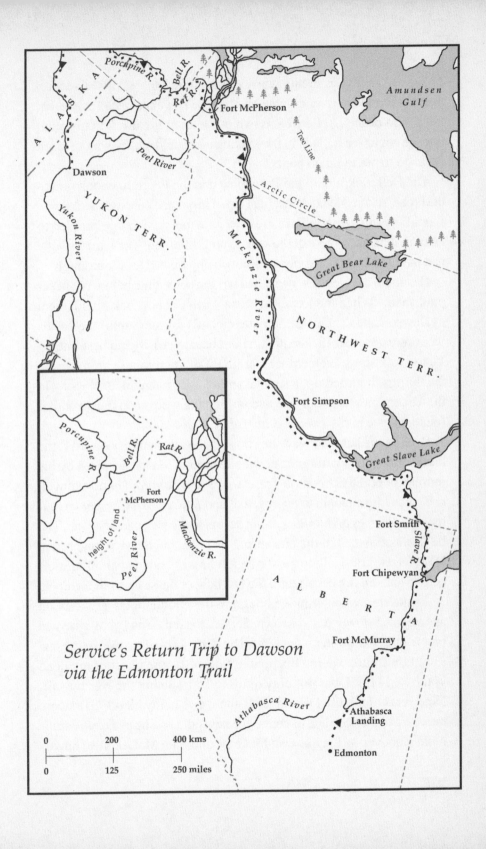

Service's Return Trip to Dawson
via the Edmonton Trail

This was "an idyllic stream worthy of Arcadia," the woods alive with ptarmigan and the river crowded with more fish than he had ever seen. "In placid peace . . . I drifted down my river of dreams." In his mind now he could see ballads in the making and could hardly wait to reach Dawson to put them on paper.

The Bell took him to the Porcupine and the Porcupine took him to the broad Yukon. He made the final lap of his journey aboard the *Tanana,* a small sternwheeler whose crew were astonished and impressed to learn that he had come all the way from Edmonton. The hard struggle had paid off; Robert Service was now being treated as a sourdough.

He taught the crew a song he had written some time before but never published, "When the Iceworms Nest Again." They took it with them to Dawson and sang it on their steamboat's journeys until the verses were spread across the territory, and it became easily the best-known Yukon folk song. I remember learning it in my mining-camp days in the thirties. It turned up in several anthologies uncredited. Nobody in the Yukon knew that Service had written the words and music until it found a place in his *Twenty Bath-Tub Ballads.*

Back in his beloved Dawson cabin in the late summer of 1911, the bard commenced work on a new collection of verses, inspired by his journey over the Edmonton Trail. *Songs of a Sourdough,* he claimed, had taken him a month to put together and *Ballads of a Cheechako* four months. *Rhymes of a Rolling Stone* occupied the best part of a year. The book was finished in the late spring of 1912, but Service lingered in Dawson. He was loath to go, for he felt he was leaving part of himself behind and did not depart until the last boat of the season left the dock.

As the sternwheeler moved out into the middle of the grey Yukon and steamed slowly past the town, Service looked up and his eyes rested on the little log cabin on the hill. "The door seemed to open and I saw a solitary figure waving his pipe in farewell—the ghost of my dead youth. . . . I felt I was not only quitting Dawson but the North itself. Nine years of my life I had given it and it was in my blood." He swore he would come back but, of course, he never did. Yet he could not escape it, then or ever, as long as Dan McGrew and Sam McGee lived on.

—THREE—

Service's plan was to take a long trip to the South Seas and laze under the sheltering palms. Captivated by the prospect of never having to work again, thanks to his mounting royalties, he dreamed of "starry-eyed sirens strumming ukuleles on coral strands." He postponed that idyll when the *Toronto Star* offered to send him to Europe to cover the first Balkan War, which had begun in October 1912 when Bulgaria, Serbia, Greece, and Montenegro opened hostilities against Turkey. Service could not resist the challenge. By mid-November he was in Istanbul, dressed for his newest role in khaki breeches and tunic, lounging on a café terrace, "a fez cocked over one eye, a gilt-tipped cigarette between my lips and a gorgeous concoction called a *Susanna* at my elbow—marvelously happy and delightfully lit up."

He joined the Turkish Red Crescent to get nearer the action and was sent to the cholera camp at San Stefano, west of Istanbul, where one of his jobs was to carry out the corpses of the victims. With the war over in December, he donned civilian clothes and began six months of wandering through Europe. That included a month living in a nondescript hotel in Budapest. In all that time, he tells us with considerable satisfaction, he did not speak to a single soul except for a few words to satisfy his needs. "How I enjoyed my silence! I glutted my hunger for obscurity. . . ."

After this lengthy walkabout he ended in Paris on a lovely spring morning. "I felt as if I were coming home and my heart sang. Here, I thought, is where I fit in." He decided to stay for at least two months; he remained for fifteen years before moving to Nice.

In Paris, Service met a Canadian couple both of whom were painters. Through them he met other artists and at once plunged into a new role. Now he was an art student, dressed in a broad-brimmed hat and a velveteen jacket with a butterfly tie. He took sketching lessons and life classes, watched a model undress—the first time, he claimed, he'd ever seen a nude female. (In Lousetown, Dawson's red-light district, you

Service in uniform. He served in both the Red Crescent and the Red Cross during the Balkan and Great Wars.

288

paid extra if your partner removed all her clothes.) "I dramatized myself in my new role," he wrote, "for, like an actor, I was never happy unless I was playing a part. Most people play one character in their lives; I enacted a dozen, and always with my whole heart."

He now found himself on the fringes of the artistic and literary community, basking in the light of the famous, including the noted poet and critic Edmund Gosse. At a dinner party for Gosse, Service went so far as to wear evening clothes and to present a book of his verse to his new hero. "Rather a pretty binding," Gosse remarked patronizingly, but he did not open the book and totally ignored its author. "In those days," Service recalled, "I took contumely meekly. . . . I was inclined to agree with the dispraise of the mandarins of letters."

In the second volume of his autobiography, *Harper of Heaven,* he writes that he became fed up with Paris and so set off to tour Normandy and Brittany. He had written a series of articles for the *Toronto Star* titled "Zig-Zags of a Vagabond," and the paper wanted more. During his ramblings he spotted "a little red-roofed house that stood on a sea-jutting rock." Was it for sale? He asked his hotel landlord, who told him that it belonged to the local mayor and "is the apple of his eye . . . he is a hard man and wants too much—twenty-five thousand francs. . . ."

"Would he not come down a bit?" Service asked.

"Not if you begged him with your derriere sticking out of your pants," was the answer. "He will never take a franc less."

Service had fallen in love with this house on the Channel coast; he called it his Dream Haven. He immediately adopted the role of a poverty-stricken traveller. He went to his hotel, dressed himself in stained pants, a ragged shirt, and a broken straw hat and returned to offer the mayor seventeen thousand francs. "My poor monsieur, you mock me," the owner replied, whereupon Service jumped in. "Wait a moment. I do not know if I will be able to pay you even that sum." He offered a down payment of seven thousand and, with the owner's agreement, said he'd try to beg, borrow, or steal the rest. If he failed, he promised he would forfeit the money. He returned next day with the ten thousand, togged out in flannels crafted by a Paris tailor. He would never forget, Service wrote, the look of disgust on the owner's face.

He needed a wife, he decided, and found one when he rescued two sisters from a jostling crowd that had gathered to view a passing military parade. This led to an invitation to tea and further visits. "I visioned the younger sister in the frame of Dream Haven, and thought I could not do better." After a brief friendship, he said to her, "Let's get hitched. I'm only a poet and, as you know, poets don't make money but I guess we can manage to rub along."

She accepted, and they were married in June 1913—a happy and content partnership that lasted forty-four years until his death (she lived to be 101). They moved into a tiny two-room apartment on the Boulevard Montparnasse, and there he plunged into his second novel, *The Pretender,* based on his experiences in the Latin Quarter of Paris. Once the book was finished he took his wife to London on a belated honeymoon, followed by a bicycle tour through France.

On the way, Service claims, they arrived at the little Breton fishing village, Lancieux, where he had bought Dream Haven. When he suggested they go over and have a look at the place, his new wife, Germaine, protested. "The owner might not like it if we go in. Perhaps they might set a dog on us." Service persisted, tried the door handle, found it wasn't locked, and beckoned her inside. She was nervous, fearing they might be taken for burglars; he replied that they could pretend they wanted to buy the house. "We haven't any money," she said, trembling.

At that moment she gave a scream as a smiling peasant woman greeted them. "Welcome, Monsieur," she said. "I've been expecting you." At that, Service wrote, knowing that the jig was up, he turned to his bride and confessed, "I'm a miserable deceiver."

Service was in his mid-seventies when he wrote *Harper of Heaven,* and much of the confusion in that romantic tale can be laid to his memory of events that had taken place some thirty-five years before. One cannot discount, however, his long practice of mingling fact with fiction in the interest of getting a better story. His account of dealing with

Germaine, the young woman Service picked out of a crowd during a parade in Paris. He decided she was the wife he "needed." She lived to be 101 years old.

291

the mayor of Lancieux for his Dream Haven is pure invention. He did not buy the house until some time after his marriage, and he bought it with the help of his wife, who was accompanying him on a boat trip. They spotted it by examining the houses on the heights above the shoreline. The actual negotiations were carried out through a real estate agent.

Germaine certainly knew her husband could afford the purchase. During their courtship he did not tell her that he was an impoverished poet but that he was a journalist in the pay of a Toronto newspaper, which was true enough. Later, a girlfriend revealed to Germaine's mother that he was a famous poet who had written about the *incineration* of Sam McGee. Service even got the details of his honeymoon wrong. It did not take place weeks or months after his marriage but the very next day. In telling the story of Dream Haven, Service was doing what he always did: giving the public what it wanted.

The Services spent a romantic summer at Dream Haven in 1914, the year his novel *The Pretender* was published. He thought it his best work to date but was disappointed when it did not achieve the success of his earlier books. The Great War ended their idyll in August. Service tried to enlist but was rejected because of varicose veins in his legs. He was probably more valuable to the Allied cause as a war correspondent, but the implacable Canadian censor, Lieutenant Colonel Ernest J. Chambers, didn't see it that way. Service, who had volunteered for the Red Cross in order to get closer to the action, was dispatching on-the-spot reports to the *Ottawa Journal,* the *Toronto Star,* and other papers, which irked Chambers.

"I cannot turn the car in that narrow road with the wounded lying under my wheels," Service wrote in 1916 from France. "Two mangled heaps are lifted in. One has been wounded by a bursting gun. There seems to be no part of him that is not burned. . . . The skin of his breast is of a bluish colour and cracked open in ridges—I'm sorry I saw him."

That would never do. The authorities were doing their best to present the war as a kind of manly picnic, an adventure for young men who wanted to prove their mettle in combat. Horrified by Service's plain speaking, Chambers forced the *Journal*'s editor, P. D. Ross, to

292

The home in the little Breton fishing village that Service called his "dream haven."

pledge that the poet's material would be expurgated or at the very least sanitized. "The more I see of Robert Service's matter from the front," Chambers wrote, "the more impressed I become that it is of a character to seriously interfere with recruiting in Canada."

A severe attack of boils put Service out of business as an ambulance driver but gave him time to produce another volume of verse during his convalescence. *Rhymes of a Red Cross Man* was a smashing success. It was, as a writer in *The New Yorker* later noted, "by far the most popular book of poetry published in this country." In 1917 and 1918 it headed the non-fiction lists. In *The Dial,* Service was praised as "a poetic phenomenon. More or less ignored by the critics," Whitter Brynner declared, "he has won a vast following. And it seems to me time for a fellow craftsman to protest that in this case the public is right. . . . We have been inquiring for the poetry of war. In my judgment, here it is. . . ."

Service's war poems differ radically from those of such English war poets as Siegfried Sassoon and Robert Graves. He was not interested

293

in tactics or strategy or the philosophy of war. There are no officers in *Rhymes*; the ordinary soldier holds the spotlight.

> Jim as lies there in the dug-out wiv 'is blanket round 'is 'ead,
> To keep his brains from mixin' wiv the mud;
> And 'is face as white as putty, and his overcoat all red,
> Like 'e's spilt a bloomin' paint-pot—but it's blood.

After the book was translated into Norwegian, Carl J. Hambro, a literary critic who was to become president of the League of Nations, took issue with a colleague who had translated a collection of war poems but had not included any by Service: "This in spite of the fact that the note is one of the most unusual and the voice one of the most masculine in the entire orchestra of war." In one literary quarterly, the *Texas Review*, an academic made clear his belief that the Canadian Kipling was a genius in his own right. "Kipling failed utterly to contribute anything of poetic value to the literary output of the Great War," he pointed out.

After the United States entered the war, the ambulance corps was disbanded. In February 1918 Service's life lost its radiance. Germaine had given birth to twin girls, Doris and Iris, the previous year. Now, while the little family was visiting the Riviera, Doris, aged thirteen months, died of scarlet fever. It was a blow to the poet, who marked the tragedy with a tender poem, a cry of anguish that was never published.

> My little girl, whose smile so right
> I'll see while sight endures
> This life of mine I'd give tonight
> Could I but ransom yours.

Five months later, as he confessed to a friend, he could not think of her without bursting into tears.

The Canadian government, meanwhile, offered him a dream job: to tour the war front, reporting on the Canadian Expeditionary Force. He travelled about with a Cadillac, a driver, and an officer guide with freedom to go anywhere he wished, inspecting field kitchens, forestry camps, airfields and hospitals. Back in Paris, with the war winding down, he embarked on a new book that he planned to call "War Winners," all about unsung heroes. He was pounding away on his Remington one morning when he heard the clanging of hundreds of church bells and realized the war was over. That night he took the manuscript and tore it into tatters. "No more war. Not in my lifetime. Curse the memory of it. Now I will rest and forget. Now will I enjoy the peace and sweetness of Dream Haven."

Paris was suffering from a housing shortage, but Service managed to secure a two-story, five-bedroom flat on the Place de Pantheon by bribing the concierge. He equipped the large upper studio as a library to contain the one thousand books he had purchased on his most recent trip to London. Now the man who had once walked barefoot down the highways of California to save shoe leather took on the persona of a "plutocratic poet," complete with tailored suit and monocle. "People in Paris accepted it without derision and I made an effort to live up to it. Behind it I concealed my inferiority complex. Screwing it in my eye I looked superciliously at the world."

With the stock market rising, he realized he was "in danger of becoming a millionaire, a fate I would not have wished on my worst enemy." He felt a sense of shame: it wasn't fair to make so much money. Since he could do nothing about it, he launched into a new book, *Ballads of a Bohemian,* the most autobiographical of his works in verse and the least successful. The manuscript was completed by Christmas 1919, but his publishers did not print it until 1921. Meanwhile bank stocks plummeted and Service, who had considered taking a flyer in real estate, instead bought life annuities, which would keep him secure for the rest of his life.

At about the same time, a movie studio bought the film rights to "The Shooting of Dan McGrew" for five thousand dollars, and the normally canny poet decided, on an impulse, to blow the money on a family trip to Hollywood. There, his mother, whom he had not seen for a decade, joined the family from Alberta, and Service determined to fulfill his ambition to visit the South Seas. He set off all by himself to Tahiti and spent the next two months lazing and wandering about the islands, gathering background for a novel that eventually became *The Roughneck.*

His introduction to the film world had persuaded him that he should write more novels, hoping that they would become successful motion pictures, which in turn would provide a larger audience for his books. Service may not have been the first novelist to understand the value of this literary cross-pollination, but he was certainly a pioneer in that field. *The Poisoned Paradise,* published in 1922, was a minor critical success, and the newly formed MGM turned it into a motion picture starring Clara Bow.

The Services were back in Paris by the fall of 1922. *The Roughneck, A Tale of Tahiti* was published the following year. Service immediately started another novel, *The Master of the Microbe,* and followed it with *The House of Fear.* Both books were thrillers, urged on him by his mother, who had a penchant for detective novels. Long out of print, they are barely remembered today. He launched the bulk of his prose writing just as the age of Hemingway began. His prose now seems dated and to many young readers may have seemed dated then, as this passage from *The Poisoned Paradise* suggests:

> "I've had enough," he cried, and his eyes flashed in his white face. He wrenched the bottle from the man's hand. "You swine, you! Where I come from there are men who would give their heart's blood for a mouthful of that wine you're wasting like filthy water."

Service had no illusions about his detective novels, which were very successful at the time. "I was fed up with this form of imaginative debauch," he wrote. "These four thrillers had purged me of my passion for pulpwood fiction."

He spent night after night in the slums of Paris, soaking up local colour for his fiction. As usual, he disguised himself in old clothes and wore a stained beret on his head, a costume that astonished an old friend from the United States who came upon him by accident as he explored the alleyways. "Why, Rubbert," he exclaimed, "what part are you playing now?"

"I'm an *apaché*," Service told him. " You don't want to be seen with me. As a matter of fact I'm documenting myself on the underworld. Dressed as I am, I go to places you would never dare to enter." That's how he tells it in *Harper of Heaven*. Years later when I met him in the poisoned paradise of Monte Carlo, he told me the police had taken him around the area in a squad car.

In Hollywood and the South Seas, Service had gained twenty-five pounds. To regain his waistline he threw himself into a rigid regime of dieting, vigorous exercise involving much weight lifting, and two hours daily of gymnasium workouts. Each afternoon he took a brisk three-hour hike and in the evening indulged in amateur boxing. In January 1924 he turned fifty and, because he planned to enter a boxing tournament, decided to undergo a medical checkup. His doctor was shocked. In developing his muscles, Service had injured his heart. He had entered the doctor's office playing one role—that of a superbly muscled athlete with bulging biceps and a washboard stomach. He slunk out in a different guise: "I walked wearily with what I thought was a look of pathetic resignation. I even imagined that passersby were regarding me with pity."

On the doctor's advice he spent three seasons at a health resort, changed his diet and his lifestyle, and, of course, produced a book about it entitled *Why Not Grow Young? Keeping Fit at Fifty*. He gave up alcohol, tobacco, chocolate, red meat, and coffee until "he hummed like a top with health." He chewed every mouthful of food thirty times, brushed his teeth three times a day, and he claims began eating an astonishing number of potatoes—twenty-two thousand a year or an average of sixty a day—as well as quantities of cabbage and onions. "The potato is my standby," he wrote; "I love the candour of the cabbage and the exquisite irony of the onion." *Why Not Grow Young?* is the only one of Service's works that he names in his two autobiographies. Today it would take its place on the shelves with the rising tide of self-help books that have made fortunes for their authors. But in 1928 it was a failure and caused a break with Service's English publisher, Fisher Unwin, who refused it. If Service's novels were behind the times, his book on health was certainly ahead of them.

Service published no new verse between 1921 and 1939, which helps explain why so many of his readers were convinced he was long dead. The "fresh fields of endeavour" that he hoped would add to his stature were abandoned when he was faced with a libel suit so flimsy that, as one biographer has noted, any current lawyer would dismiss it out of hand. A peer of the realm was suing him because he believed he was the Lord Strathbogie mentioned briefly in *The House of Fear.* The word "sanctimonious" attached to the fictional character was enough to cause the ninth Baron Strabolgi to threaten suit.

According to Service's autobiography, the libel threat derailed him as a writer for five years. H. G. Wells, who was an admirer and an acquaintance, urged him to call the noble earl's bluff and defend the suit. Service declined. "With my inferiority complex I would cut a pitiable figure. Though as innocent as a lamb I would give the impression of a sinister criminal." The whole affair, which cost him ten thousand pounds, left him "with a feeling of disgust. . . . If authorship, I thought, exposes one to such injustice, then to hell with it." During the thirties, after the family moved to the Riviera, Service gave no thought to writing. When the press reported him as dead, confusing him with a younger brother who had been killed at the Somme, he felt no concern. "I never bothered to deny it for I savoured a kind word, even if I had to pass on to win it," he wrote.

He was content to remain anonymous. "Here, in a slum of Nice, no one had ever heard of me. I cultivated obscurity as assiduously as others strive for publicity. Very few of my neighbours knew that I wrote. I was just one of them, content to go on like that to the end. . . . I enjoyed the irresponsibility of living in a foreign land where one is an onlooker and cares nothing for the way things are run as long as one's comfort is assured." During this period, two volumes of his collected verse were published, but since his rhymes defied translation into French, his anonymity was assured.

At the end of the thirties he published *Twenty Bath-Tub Ballads,* both words and music, which he described as "a colossal flop." But even as the book appeared, he began to consider another. In 1938 he booked passage, alone as usual, to the Soviet Union. He wanted to see for himself whether it was the paradise it claimed to be. In his two months in Russia, Service saw everything his Intourist guide permitted—from the Winter Palace in Saint Petersburg to the corpse of Lenin, waxen in its tomb. He greatly admired the stoicism of the Russian people but came to despise the political system. When he returned to his family, he had the urge to begin writing again and started on a manuscript to be titled "Four Blind Mice," an escape novel with a Russian setting. By the time he had written ten thousand words, however, he realized he didn't know enough about the country to write a hundred thousand. Once again through Intourist, he went back, signed up for a cruise down the Volga, and continued on to Rostov-on-Don and then the Black Sea.

He had chosen a difficult and dangerous period to investigate the Soviet Union. On the very day he arrived at Odessa, August 23, 1939, Germany and Russia signed the notorious non-aggression pact and the spectre of war hung over the city. Odessa was blacked out; searchlight beams stabbed at the night sky. The next day, as part of his Intourist program, Service took the train to Kiev, determined to flee the country. There was a train leaving that night, but the Intourist girl was unable to find his passport among the pile in front of her. To Service, Kiev seemed like a prison. He could not sleep and began to experience a sense of panic. When the passport finally turned up the next day, he was able to take the noon train for Warsaw on the way to Berlin and Paris, only to find the German border closed. A Polish officer climbed aboard shouting, "We are now in armed conflict with the Reich. It is war, war, WAR!"

In Warsaw, Service was warned by the British consul to leave Poland at once. The sound of Luftwaffe bombs hammering the district of Praga

Service at the typewriter. For almost twenty years he wrote not a word of verse.

301

assailed his ears and aroused his sense of drama. "Here was a book, a big book for my making—one of the documents of the war." But as a British subject, he could not stay. He found himself crammed with half-drunken soldiers into a third-class compartment headed for Wilno. From there he went on to Latvia and then Estonia. A steamer eventually took him to Stockholm where he spent three anxious days, mostly in the office of a reluctant consul, trying to get a visa for Norway. Eventually he sat up all night in a third-class carriage to Oslo where he had to struggle to board another train to Bergen on the coast. There he faced an agonizing wait in the shipping office, trying to get passage on the Bergen–Newcastle run. It was, alas, fully booked. A young CPR ticket agent helped him out by persuading the captain and engineer to give up their cabins to Service and another Canadian whom he called Mrs. Moosejaw in his memoirs. Since the vessel ran on a ten-day schedule and the first whistle was already blowing, they were forced to make a dash for the wharf minutes before the ss *Venus* pulled away.

Now, after a hectic and nerve-racking two weeks, Service was at last able to relax, or so he thought. He took the train from Newcastle to London and hurried to the French consulate, only to learn that all visas had been suspended. "Despair! After all my tribulations I was stranded in London." There was nothing he could do but queue up with hundreds of others, day after day, often in a chilly rain. After three weeks, with his passport at last restored and stamped, he was able to leave.

Back in Nice, he spent the winter "strutting around in Savile Row suits" and giving birth to another verse book, *Bar-Room Ballads,* his first in nineteen years, conceived during his many walks and reveries. Published in 1940 during the first year of the war it was, he wrote offhandedly, "neither better nor worse than any of my previous volumes and was received with the same gentle tolerance."

"These poems will go over big in this dark hour when a bit of levity is needed to cheer a man," the *Globe and Mail*'s critic wrote. Service himself was convinced that the collection would be his last literary effort. "I was growing tired of myself in the role of Rhyme-smith," he wrote. Nor would he write any more novels of the "authentic type."

302

With the fall of France in mid-June 1940, Service realized the time had come to leave the country. In spite of his self-confessed laziness, much of which was a pose, he acted in this instance with dispatch and decision. He reconnoitred the Breton coast town of St. Malo, discovered four tramp steamers evacuating wounded British troops, and learned shortly before sailing time that there just might be space for him and his family. Hurrying back to nearby Dream Haven at Lancieux, he ran into Germaine and Iris on a road jammed with refugees. "We're going," he told them. "There's to be no sniveling. You must keep control of your nerves. You can only take one suitcase each and I give you half an hour to pack."

They managed to board the *Hull Trader,* a coal carrier loaded with wounded, just half an hour before she sailed. Germaine and Iris were sent to the captain's cabin and Service to a bunk forward, which he gave up to a soldier so seriously wounded that he died during the voyage. The poet made his way back to the captain's cabin and found it jammed with female refugees and five babies squalling on his berth. He escaped to a deck strewn with wounded and crawled into the hold, where he lay down on a box of high explosives with more wounded men all about him. "Oh, what a gorgeous target we were!" wrote Service. "There were U-boats and mines to fret about. That water was just staked with disaster, and every moment of that night I lay awaiting the shock of being hurled to eternity." But the trip was made without mishap, and the Services rented a flat in Chelsea as the first bombs in the prelude to the Battle of Britain began to fall on southern England.

In late July the Services sailed to Canada. The Canadian edition of *Bar-Room Ballads* had just been published, and its author was involved in the usual interviews, book signings, and receptions. Sitting in the lobby of the Windsor Hotel in Montreal, he watched a youngish man approach him cautiously. "He was good looking and well built with an air of professional prosperity," Service recalled.

"Do you know who I am?" he said.

"No, I'm afraid I don't," Service replied.

"I'm your brother, Stanley," the stranger announced, and, as Service wrote, "he told me so persuasively that I was forced to believe him. Twenty years do make a difference."

In Vancouver, he was accosted by a good-looking woman who said, "Do you know who I am?" Service had no idea until she told him "I'm your sister, Agnes."

"It took me quite a while before I got used to folks coming up to me and saying: 'Hullo Bob, why I thought you were dead.' Indeed, so many seemed to think that I had passed on I began to feel like a veritable ghost."

In Vancouver, Service was reunited with a second brother, Peter, proprietor of the Sourdough Bookshop where Service's two volumes of *Selected Verse* were much in demand. The bard himself would be much in demand in his five years of exile, especially in Hollywood, where the family spent the winter months. In the first four years the poet did not write a single line but was constantly called on to recite "The Shooting of Dan McGrew." When it was learned that he would be present at the Sourdough Convention in Seattle in 1942 the demand for tickets was so great that two separate banquet halls in two hotels had to be reserved to handle the overflow crowds. When in the spring of 1945 he attended the premiere of *The Belle of the Yukon*, seated with the two stars of the movie, Dinah Shore and Gypsy Rose Lee, he stole the show by again reciting "Dan McGrew." He was by this time something of a movie star himself, appearing in a cameo role in *The Spoilers,* starring John Wayne and Randolph Scott. Frank Lloyd, who had directed the movie version of *The Pretender,* talked him into appearing in a scene with the film's co-star, Marlene Dietrich. Service was made up to look much younger than his sixty-seven years by the same makeup artist who had turned Boris Karloff into Frankenstein's monster. The film was set in Nome, Alaska, not Dawson City. Service appeared as himself, scribbling away at a table when Dietrich as Cherry Malote, the gambling queen, approaches:

"Ah, I see you are writing a new poem, Mr. Service. About me?"

"No, not this time, Cherry. I'm writing about a Lady known as Lou."

"Is there a man in the story?"

"Yes, a fellow named Dan McGrew. He's a bad actor. He gets shot."

"Ah, The Shooting of Dan McGrew, eh?"

Service spoke his lines more than a dozen times until finally the dramatic director was brought in to coach him. According to Service, when the scene was complete, Lloyd gave it his final assessment: "It's lousy but we'll let it go."

Though Service continued to protest that he hated the poem and only took the movie job because his finances were low, he cheerfully recited "Dan McGrew" on the scores of occasions when he was asked to perform. Once again, he was playing a role, at least in his autobiography, as the Impoverished Poet. When he was given a cheque for $225 for his cameo in *The Spoilers*, he turned it over to the Canadian Red Cross, which was launching a nine-million-dollar fund-raising drive. "As play acting is not my regular line," Service wrote, kicking off the campaign, "I do not wish to earn money in this way." Some months after Pearl Harbor, he embarked on a five-month tour of army camps for the USO reciting "McGrew" and "McGee" to crowds of cheering soldiers.

By then, according to Service, "there was scarcely a day I could call my own. . . . I was becoming a busy man and I hated it." The solution was to embark on a project that would give him an excuse to get out of business meetings, autographings, lunches, and lectures. That project was to write his autobiography—*Ploughman of the Moon*. It took a year, and because he had by then reached only the year 1912 in his narrative, he began a second volume, *Harper of Heaven*.

The North American version of *Ploughman* was published in September 1945 and the English edition a year later. The book became a best-seller, widely quoted in the popular press as usual, but treated with reservations by the literary elite. Stanley Walker, in the *New York Herald,* hit the nail on the head when he wrote, "Despite his frequent protestations it is clear that he regards himself as a highly romantic figure." It was, in Walker's view, "not a very good book." But in spite of the overwriting and the clichés, "there is no getting away from it—he hit on something that somehow struck a response among millions of rhyme lovers, and thus became the singer of the Common Man."

Harper of Heaven was published in 1948 after the Service family returned to France and eventually exchanged Nice for Monte Carlo. (In Brittany, their winter residence, Dream Haven, had to undergo extensive repairs as a result of the German occupation.) Service's second volume of autobiography is a rambling piece of work, as much a travelogue as a memoir. Subtitled *A Record of Radiant Living,* it covers his career following the Yukon period. But by the time it appeared, "the old codger," as he called himself, was approaching seventy-five and giving some thought to the hereafter, as the quatrain on the book's title page suggests:

> Although my sum of years may be
> Nigh seventy and seven,
> With eyes of ecstasy I see
> And hear the Harps of Heaven

With worldwide reviews that ranged from "a tough, violent book" (*London Daily Herald*) to "this gem of a book" (*Seattle Post-Intelligencer*), one might have expected Service, with sixteen bestsellers to his credit, to take life easy after a long and successful career and spend his declining years lazing about as he always insisted he wished to do. On the contrary, he plunged into a veritable orgy of creation. Between 1949 and 1958 he published nine original books of verse with the alliterative titles that had become his trademark, such as *Songs of a Sun-Lover, Rhymes of a Roughneck, Lyrics of a Lowbrow, Carols of an Old Codger*. He also published *More Collected Verse* and *Later Collected Verse* and a new edition of *Why Not Grow Young*.

For all that period, Service wrote a verse a day while still indulging in his three-hour walks every afternoon. He didn't need to write for money. The royalties kept coming. It was as if Service had taken a new

306

The poet in his final years surrounded by family and friends.

lease of life and was writing as much for himself as for his dwindling audience. "The writing racket is not what it used to be," he remarked at the time, "but this old codger still sells." James Mackay has noted, ". . . it is ironic, that much of his best work, truly sublime poetry, should come at a time when Robert was no longer fashionable."

When I interviewed him in Monte Carlo in 1958 he was well past his eightieth year, having published at least one thousand poems with perhaps as many unpublished. I was appearing on the Canadian Broadcasting Corporation's Sunday night flagship program *Close-Up* at the time and was assigned to visit him in Monaco to prepare a half-hour television interview. There was some difficulty in clearing the assignment since several members of the corporation's upper echelon kept insisting that Service was dead. However, a letter from the poet himself cleared that up: "For me this will probably be a unique television show as I am now crowding eighty-five and the ancient carcass will soon cease to function. For that reason I hope you will bring it off successfully. My home here makes a nice setting for an interview, which if well planned could be quite attractive."

Patrick Watson, my producer, and I arrived with a television crew in May. The poet met us at the door of his Villa Aurore, overlooking the warm Mediterranean, and introduced us to his wife, Germaine. He was casually dressed in a sleeveless sweater and slacks—a small, birdlike man with brightly veined cheeks, a sharp nose, and a mild, Scottish accent. We had started to discuss the interview when Service held up his hand.

"It's all arranged," he said. "I spent the week working it up. Here's your script. I'm afraid you've got the smaller part because, you see, this is *my* show!" He handed me two sheets of paper, stapled and folded. "It's in two parts," he said. "We can do the first after lunch. Now you boys go back to your hotel and you [to me] learn your lines. I already know mine, letter perfect. Come back this afternoon and we'll do it."

I looked at Watson. This is not the way spontaneous television interviews are conducted. He gave a kind of helpless shrug and we left.

"What do we do now?" I asked.

"I guess we'd better read what he's written," Watson said.

What Service had written, it turned out, was pretty good—lively, witty, self-effacing, romantic: "I'm eighty-five now and I guess this will be my last show on the screen. Oh, I'm feeling fine though I'm a bit of a cardiac. In middle age I strained my heart trying to walk on my hands. After sixty a man shouldn't try to be an athlete. Only yesterday I was talking politics to a chap on the street. I'm 'Right' and he was 'Left' so we got to shouting, when suddenly I felt the old ticker conk on me, and I had to go home in a taxi, chewing white pills. Say, wouldn't it be a sensation if I croaked in the middle of this interview?"

When we returned, Service was easily persuaded to submit to an unscripted interview. But whenever one of my questions coincided with one in the script, he gave me a word-perfect answer, and that included the line about croaking on television. Service, the old actor, even managed to make that sound spontaneous.

In between set-ups, the poet and I talked about the Yukon. He remembered my mother very well and talked about Lousetown, the tenderloin district across the Klondike River. "We used to go down the line every Saturday night," he said, employing a euphemistic colloquialism that was still part of the jargon in my mining-camp days.

In the interview that was spread over three days we went over some of the highlights of his career, including the intervention of the bank inspector who had first sent him to the Yukon and so changed his life. "He was the God in my machine," said Service. "I often wished I had thanked him before he died." We talked about his various adventures such as his days with the Turkish Red Crescent, when he worked in the cholera camp at San Stefano. "I couldn't stick it any longer. I deserted, really," Service admitted. He told of his time in the Paris slums. "I went with the police gang and they took me all through every part of Paris that was disreputable," he said, thus disputing the stories in his own autobiography. "I got to know that side, the seamy side of Paris, better than any writer of the time knew it," he said, a little proudly.

And we talked about "The Shooting of Dan McGrew," which he insisted he loathed. "It's not exactly what I would call tripe, but there's no poetry—no real poetry to it to my mind," he said, and added, "I

The author interviewing Service at his Monaco home in the spring of 1958 for the CBC's flagship program, Close-up. *The poet died three months later.*

don't write poetry anyway so there's no use talking like that. Here I am—crucified on the cross of Dan McGrew. There you are."

Yet when the time came to recite for television his best-known work, he showed an eagerness that belied his own critique. "I'm looking forward to it," he said when we arrived on the third morning to get his verse and his voice on film. He was in great fettle and his eyes were bright as he began, "A bunch of the boys were whooping it up . . ."

When the filming was complete, Service with great ceremony opened a bottle of champagne that he had put aside for the occasion. All during the filming he had been an enthusiastic interview subject, lively and ebullient.

"It's made me young again," he said. "I'm just living it." Now, as we toasted him, he seemed cast down.

"Is it really over?" he said. "Haven't you got any more questions? I could go on, you know." But the crew was already packing up the equipment.

"Oh, I do wish we could go on," said Service. "I wish it didn't have to stop." He stood in his dressing gown in the doorway of his villa, and the wind catching the silver of his hair and blowing it over his face gave him an oddly dishevelled look.

"I wish it could go on forever," said Robert Service, and I caught, briefly, the memory of the telegraph operator, running along the river-bank, pleading with us to stay just a little longer.

The interview was shown in June and was a great success. The scene that caught everyone's fancy was Service's "spontaneous" remark about croaking in front of the cameras. It was indeed his last performance. That September in his Dream Haven in Brittany, his heart finally did give out, and the bard of the Yukon was buried under the sun he loved so well and far, far from that lovely but chilly domain that in capturing him would give him fame and fortune.

Afterword

The five disparate characters who make up this chronicle—a builder, an explorer, a titled lady, an eccentric, and a poet—are unique. At first glance they seem to have had little in common save for their links with the North. On closer inspection, however, we can see that they shared certain traits that made them exceptional. They were all rugged individualists—impatient of authority, restless, energetic, and ambitious. They were secure within themselves—and driven by a romantic wanderlust that freed them from the run-of-the-mill existence on which they so often turned their backs.

They belong to an era when the going was tough and travel was a challenge and sometimes a hardship. Joe Boyle, arriving at Carmack's Post on the Yukon and finding himself among a group of stranded tenderfeet, goaded these incompetents by threatening and cajoling to work their way on foot with him through the mountains in the worst possible weather to the nearest seaport. They gave him a gold watch for that.

Vilhjalmur Stefansson spent his Arctic career trotting for thousands of miles behind a dog team, rarely taking his ease on the sledge.

Lady Franklin never encountered a mountain she didn't want to climb and thought nothing of crossing Van Diemen's Land on foot on a journey that had killed those who came before.

John Hornby made a fetish of his ruggedness, doing everything the hard way, trudging for fifty miles through a Barrens blizzard and boasting about it.

Robert Service, who survived the Rat River trail, made a habit of working out every afternoon until his doctors slowed him down.

They lived by their own rules, these five—flouting authority, contemptuous of regulations, confident of their own instincts and abilities. Boyle played catch-me-if-you-can with the military and political authorities who tried vainly to hem him in. Stefansson resisted all efforts to pull him out of the Arctic and instead of going south, as ordered, headed farther into the North. Jane Franklin had her own ideas about her husband's fate and when these were ignored took on the job of searching for him herself. Hornby was a wild card who exulted in his role and died tragically, rejecting sensible advice, while Service shunned the dictates of society and went his own way, a loner to the end.

They were all loners. Did any of them have the kind of intimate friend to whom one can pour out one's heart? There is little evidence of that in their varied sagas. In all too brief moments Boyle enjoyed a relationship of sorts with Queen Marie, and also, perhaps, was at ease with his old friend Teddy Bredenberg in his dying months, but there is little indication of any traditional understanding. Like the others, he was not a family man. He was quite prepared to run off to sea with scarcely a word to his kin, nor was either of the marriages into which he plunged successful. The two offspring he did not abandon were in awe of him, but their relationship cannot be described as close.

Stefansson enjoyed several lengthy affairs, but he scarcely mentioned the novelist Fannie Hurst, who was his mistress for seventeen years. He refused to recognize his son, Alex, the product of his liaison with the capable Inuit widow Pannigabluk. His four-year romance with Betty Brainerd faded after he ignored her letters to him. It is clear that he put his work and his ambitions first; his various relationships came close to being afterthoughts. Only after he had done with exploring did he take the time and trouble to marry. He rejected outward intimacies. They were, as his friend Richard Finnie remarked, out of keeping with his image as a rough, independent explorer. He would have recoiled had he heard his wife remark publicly, as she did after his death, that she had enjoyed the best sex of her life with him.

Jane Franklin in her youth had many aspirants after her heart but only one companion in her later years, her fanatically loyal niece, Sophy Cracroft, who, one suspects, was more of a nurse than an intimate. Her personal relations with the husband whose memory was to dominate her life for nearly thirty years seemed casual, marked as they were by long separations, especially when she was exploring the Mediterranean, which occupied a full year after he was recalled to England, before coming home to him.

It is impossible to think of John Hornby as having an intimate relationship of any kind. Critchell-Bullock does not fit the bill; he could never inveigle his partner into any kind of serious conversation. The ribald stories that male friends often exchange were anathema to Hornby. Olwen Newell was prepared to marry him, but he put her off, explaining that he was not the marrying kind. When, years later, he finally made a stab at proposing, she found an excuse to reject him.

Service was a loner all his life. In later years he had difficulty recognizing his own siblings. He went off to Canada on a whim, rejecting his father's attempt at farewell at the dockside, and on another whim turned up unexpectedly on the doorstep of his mother's Alberta home, to be greeted after a dozen years' absence no more emotionally than with a peck on the cheek. In his memoirs he suggests that he married because he "needed" a wife. He made a good choice because she indulged him when he wanted to be left alone. He went off to exotic and little-known corners of the globe such as Tahiti and Soviet Russia, but he did not take her with him. During the Second World War, when he was exiled to Canada, he did not bother to travel back to the Yukon, which was the basis for his fortune. His wife and daughter went off in his stead.

Restless, rugged, independent loners—this is the culture shared by these prisoners of the north. There is one other quality: all, in their own ways, were driven by an ambition that they achieved during their lifetime, or thought they had. In the end that ambition turned out to be a chimera.

Boyle wanted to build the largest gold dredges in history, and he succeeded, over the skepticism of others, only to find his empire taken over by others. His relationship outside the Yukon with the romantic Romanian queen contributed to that loss, and the bitter truth was that the true love for which he yearned could never be more than an unfulfilled longing.

Stefansson was determined to be the greatest of all Arctic explorers. He came close, but he tried too hard; his theories about the "blond Eskimos," his loss of the *Karluk,* his attempts to colonize a small island off the Siberian coast still continue to sully his reputation.

Lady Franklin moved heaven and earth to achieve her ambition—to enshrine her husband as the true discoverer of the Northwest Passage. When the appropriate plaque went up in Westminster Abbey shortly after her death, she seemed to have succeeded. But in recent years, the revisionists have downgraded Franklin's achievements and bestowed the accolade on Robert McClure.

John Hornby in his day was seen as a legendary, albeit tragic, figure hailed while being mourned as the epitome of the romantic Englishman, facing hardships and surviving trials in unknown country. But over the ensuing years that legend has been torn to shreds.

Of these five, Service is to me the most interesting and baffling. In his lifetime he overcame the put-downs of his critics and emerged as the people's poet. If that was his ambition, he succeeded only partially. It surely must have galled him to realize, at the end, that the only lasting works he produced were his first two published poems, "Dan McGrew" and "Sam McGee." All the others, including his much-praised wartime poems, have lost much of their lustre. When one reads Service's memoirs, a Shakespearean sort of phrase pops into the mind: Methinks the poet doth protest too much. He tells us again and again that he's a rhymester, not a "real" poet. Does that mask an unstated desire to be something more? He pretends that he is lazy, that he is shy, that he suffers from an inferiority complex. He constantly plays down his work as mere rhymes, ballads, and songs. "I'm afraid of these big fellows," he says in reference to "real" poets. That can be seen as his way of saying that he is afraid to take a chance, to attempt any other style than the one that made his reputation. In my view, Service had nothing to be ashamed of, yet one suspects that there may have been moments when he could have wished to be likened to Wordsworth or Shelley and seen by his snootier critics as something more than a profiteer from his Northern ballads.

For all of his career, Service considered himself a Northerner. His poems identified him as a true sourdough, and his struggle over the Edmonton Trail confirmed it to himself. That was true in various ways

316

of the others as well: Boyle in his trademark uniform, garnished with gold nuggets; Stefansson creating his miniature iglu on the Dartmouth campus; Jane Franklin soaking up every available scrap of Arctic lore; Hornby appropriating the Barrens as his own domain.

They belonged to a vanishing era, these five—one that was fading fast. There can never be another Klondike-style stampede. Today the Chilkoot Pass is for sightseers who go on to Dawson by bus or automobile. The thrill of discovery that once lured explorers has been replaced by the thrill of stranger discoveries in outer space. The bush plane, the snowmobile, and the radio have made another Franklin-style search unnecessary while at the same time diminishing the hazards of the Barrens.

There are still men and women among us who are captivated by the North, but not in the way these five were: willing prisoners who for a time gave themselves to it heart and soul, driven by the kind of passion that bespeaks a love-hate relationship. The North, in its turn, gave them something they might hope for but did not expect—a measure of immortality. It was, I think, a fair exchange.

Acknowledgements

I want to express my gratitude to the dedicated team of associates who have worked with me on most of my books of narrative history: Elsa Franklin, producer and organizer; Barbara Sears, research assistant; Janet Berton, editorial backstop; Janice Tyrwhitt, editor; Janet Craig, copy editor. Without this meticulous and dedicated quintet, I could not have brought these works to fruition. To it, I must also gratefully add the name of Amy Black, Doubleday's associate editor, who oversaw the manuscript on its journey to the printed page.

318

Index